D0352146

HELPING FAMILIES WITH TROUBLED CHILDREN

A Preventive Approach

Carole Sutton PhD

Faculty of Health and Community Studies, De Montfort University, Leicester, UK

JOHN WILEY & SONS

Chichester · New York · Weinheim · Brisbane · Singapore · Toronto

Copyright © 1999 by John Wiley & Sons Ltd,
Baffins Lane, Chichester,
West Sussex PO19 1UD, England

National   01243 779777
International   (+44) 1243 779777
e-mail (for orders and customer service enquiries):
cs-book@wiley.co.uk
Visit our Home Page on http://www.wiley.co.uk
or http://www.wiley.com

All Rights Reserved. No part of this publication may be reproduced, stored in a
retrieval system, or transmitted, in any form or by any means, electronic, mechanical,
photocopying, recording, scanning or otherwise, except under the terms of the Copyright,
Designs and Patents Act 1988 or under the terms of a licence issued by the Copyright
Licensing Agency, 90 Tottenham Court Road, London, W1P 9HE, UK, without the
permission in writing of the Publisher.

Other Wiley Editorial Offices

John Wiley & Sons, Inc., 605 Third Avenue,
New York, NY 10158-0012, USA

WILEY-VCH Verlag GmbH, Pappelallee 3,
D-69469 Weinheim, Germany

Jacaranda Wiley Ltd, 33 Park Road, Milton,
Queensland 4064, Australia

John Wiley & Sons (Asia) Pte Ltd, 2 Clementi Loop #02-01,
Jin Xing Distripark, Singapore 129809

John Wiley & Sons (Canada) Ltd, 22 Worcester Road,
Rexdale, Ontario M9W 1L1, Canada

Library of Congress Cataloging-in-Publication Data

Sutton, Carole.
    Helping families with troubled children : a preventive approach /
by Carole Sutton.
        p.   cm.
    Includes bibliographical references and index.
    ISBN 0-471-97551-6. — ISBN 0-471-98299-7
    1. Social work with children.   2. Behavior disorders in children.
3. Problem children.   4. Family social work.   I. Title.
HV713.S9   1999
362.74—dc21   98-38575
                                                        CIP

British Library Cataloguing in Publication Data

A catalogue record for this book is available from the British Library

ISBN 0-471-97551-6 (hb)   0-471-98299-7 (pb)

Typeset in 11pt Palatino by Dorwyn Ltd, Rowlands Castle, Hants.
Printed and bound in Great Britain by Biddles Ltd, Guildford and King's Lynn.
This book is printed on acid-free paper responsibly manufactured from sustainable
forestry, in which at least two trees are planted for each one used for paper production.

To all those practitioners, health visitors, social workers, nursery staff, teachers and so many others who work with such commitment to help troubled children

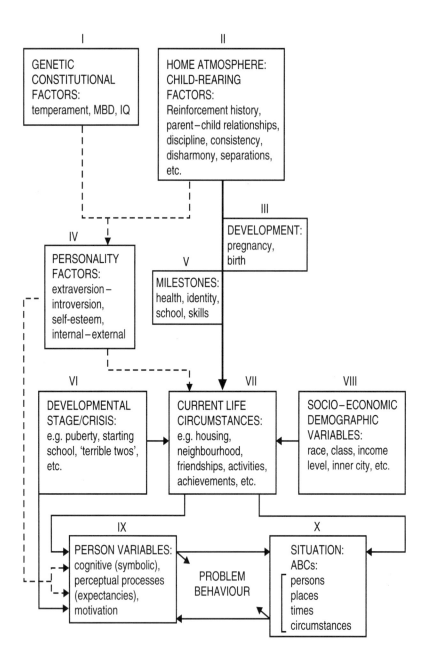

FRONTISPIECE   The ten-factor clinical formation (Herbert, 1981, adapted from Clark, 1977) This can be seen as a 'systems' formulation.
The dotted line represents indirect pre-disposing contributory factors.

CONTENTS

ABOUT THE AUTHOR

Carole Sutton is a Principal Lecturer in Psychology at De Montfort University and has worked as a social worker in the fields of health, mental health and children and families. Her professional work and her experiences as a parent led to a concern for preventive work to support young families. She undertook a doctorate in parent education working with Professor Martin Herbert. She is a Chartered Psychologist. This book has grown out of her subsequent experiences in teaching and training professional workers, health visitors, social workers in field and residential settings, psychologists, family therapists, teachers and doctors in supporting parents in helping their troubled children.

ACKNOWLEDGEMENTS

I should like to thank the staff of the library of De Montfort University for their unfailing helpfulness, good humour and efficiency in dealing with my enquiries.

Certain diagrams and charts used in the text are derived from material developed in my teaching and writing within De Montfort University or modified from versions in my earlier publications.

I should also like to give special thanks to Dr Jean Macqueen for carrying out the indexing of the text so swiftly and fully.

INTRODUCTION

There is deep public concern about the numbers of children who, themselves clearly unhappy, are causing heartache to their families and exasperation to their teachers. Newspaper headlines convey this concern: 'Fourfold rise in expulsion of under-12s' (*The Times*, 28 May 1996); 'Rise in primary exclusions' (*Times Educational Supplement*, 1 November 1996). 'Violence in schools not being tackled' (*The Guardian*, 1 September 1997). Data from the Department of Health (1995) concerning 10 year-old children indicate that, according to the location studied, between 6% and 10% display aggressive, disruptive and destructive conduct, while between 4% and 9.9% show emotional disorders: anxiety, phobias and depression.

When these children first come to the attention of helping agencies they are often at an age when patterns of behaviour are already deeply established and hard to change. Many not only come from disadvantaged backgrounds in respect of poverty and poor housing but also experience much adversity as a result of disrupted relationships with parents or other important people in their lives. *To offer services when behaviours are entrenched is too late*. It is in the earliest years of life when children are at their most vulnerable; we should be focusing upon supporting families with young children and providing preventive services in these earliest years. As Bowlby (1979) insisted:

> The key point of my thesis is that there is a strong causal relationship between an individual's experiences with his [sic] parents and his later capacity to make affectional bonds.

If children's capacities to make these bonds are damaged by their experiences, then when they become parents their capacities to build bonds with *their* children are already impaired; the vicious cycle may continue generation after generation.

What happens in these first seven or eight years—the age when the foundations of children's future health and mental health are being laid down? How do they develop so quickly from being delightful babies and toddlers into deeply unhappy, troubled children, often rejected by other children, disliked by their teachers and even by their parents?

It is known that a substantial proportion of the children will have been neglected or abused, physically, sexually or emotionally; some children have experienced several forms of abuse. Box I.1 shows the numbers and percentages of children and young people on English registers at 31 March 1997, by various categories. A disproportionate number have had disturbing experiences while in the care of local authorities.

Box I.1: Children and young people on child protection registers at 31 March 1997: figures rounded (Department of Health, 1998)

Category of abuse	Numbers	(%)
Neglect	12 200	34
Physical injury	10 900	30
Sexual abuse	7 400	20
Emotional abuse	5 000	14
Other	600	2

Warren (1997), writing in *Children UK,* the influential publication of the National Children's Bureau, reported:

> A Barnardo's study of 145 children in seven projects in Scotland . . . found that they averaged 3.7 moves each while being looked after by local authorities. Thirty-one of them had experienced more than five moves and one primary school-aged child had already moved 40 times.

How could any children be expected to cope with such disruption? Of course they cannot. All too many of them emerge harmed from the experience of being in care.

There are, however, also hundreds of children who are not in care but at home in situations which are becoming increasingly difficult both for themselves and for the families who care for them. In my own work, one parent said to me, 'They get you to a pitch where you could really harm them . . .'; another said, 'If I don't get away from him, I'm going to kill him . . .' and 'There were times when I could have killed him . . . There were times when I was suicidal—when I was on the point of ringing Social Services and saying, "Take him . . ." '. Now, these were not sadistic, rejecting parents, anxious to get rid of their children. Far from it: they were ordinary mothers and fathers, driven frantic by the aggressiveness and disruptiveness of their children, both to themselves and to people outside the family. Moreover, they were asking, sometimes begging, for help but it was not readily forthcoming. This was not because no-one had tried to help: they had doctors, social workers and health visitors, but in many instances they had used common sense as the basis of their advice and common sense had let them down. What is needed to help these families is *refined common sense*, that is, help based on principles which are not contrary to common sense but which are informed by extensive research in many parts of the world. So this book attempts not only to explore how some children's difficulties develop but also to suggest practical strategies, grounded in research, which parents can use to improve their young children's behaviour. Throughout, the emphasis is upon *prevention and evidence-based practice*.

THE GROUNDS FOR CONCERN ARE SERIOUS

Many of the problems of troubled children are attributable to changing economic circumstances, to acute poverty among the most needy sections of society and to structural factors beyond the scope of this book. As we shall see, however, despite these difficulties parents are still prepared to seek help; they still want to love their children and to have their children love them. They do not, typically, blame stress as the reason for their difficulties in coping with their children; they are much more likely to blame the children themselves. The services established to help families with

troubled children and young people are overwhelmed with demand; the *preventive* approach which I advocate should begin at
the earliest possible age; probably at about two years or even eigh-
teen months. Indeed, some health visitors with whom I am working are seeking to identify vulnerable parents at ante-natal clinics.

SOME COMMON THEMES EMERGING FROM THE RESEARCH

A number of themes emerge from the research literature:

1. The importance of a multi-factorial model of causation.
2. The contribution of structural variables to children's difficulties.
3. The inescapability of subjective perception and personal meanings.
4. The importance of social learning/cognitive-behavioural approaches to helping children.

A Multi-factorial Model of Causation

As the quality of research has improved, so it has become apparent
that a veritable tapestry of variables contributes to the development of distress on the part of a given child. It is no longer a matter
of debate as to whether 'nature' or 'nurture' contributes more to
the aetiologies of children's difficulties; the interactions are shown
to be of extraordinary complexity. Our interventions have to be
sensitive to that complexity. This tapestry of interacting variables
can only be accommodated by a multi-factorial model; thus, the
frontispiece to this book is 'The 10-factor clinical formulation' developed by Herbert (1981). This shows the interplay of influences
which may eventually lead to the occurrence of an instance of
problem behaviour, such as a child assaulting a teacher.

The Contribution of Structural Variables to Children's Difficulties

The evidence continues to accumulate that structural variables,
those associated with a child's socio-economic status, housing and

the poverty and/or unemployment of their parents all contribute substantially to the probability of children becoming troubled. The early studies by Rutter and colleagues (1975a, b) showed that children in a typical Inner London borough showed a level of disturbance twice that of children in the Isle of Wight, and that this increased level was associated essentially with socio-economic factors such as large family size and unemployment: these findings have been confirmed by studies in other countries. This evidence will be considered further in Chapter 1.

This book, however, is written for practitioners who are relatively powerless to influence some of the variables included here; we cannot change, except marginally, people's income levels, their employment circumstances or their housing; we cannot change events which have happened in the past—although we can help people talk about these events and their continuing impact upon them. We can, however, support families and help those who care for distressed and troubled children in ways which, as the research shows, may relieve something of that distress.

The Inescapability of Personal Perception and Subjectivity

There is no escaping personal, idiosyncratic perception and no means of arriving at total objectivity in the world of human interaction. People really do see the same situation differently. They notice different things, they interpret them differently and they respond to them differently; they also attribute different things to the same stimulus or group of stimuli. Kelly (1955), in developing 'personal construct theory', has shown that each of us carries about with us a set of personal meanings as a framework into which we fit perceptions and events—all the while oblivious that these meanings are highly subjective or that other people have totally different sets of meanings. The nearest analogy I can suggest is that perceiving and interpreting a scene is akin to 'seeing pictures in the fire'; the same scene is presented to everyone, but each person interprets it differently. As we shall see in Chapter 10, aggressive boys perceive neutral events as far more threatening than do non-aggressive boys and are ready to react to them with aggression far more swiftly. This evidence underpins the concepts shown in panels IX and X in the frontispiece.

The Usefulness of Cognitive-Behavioural Approaches in Helping Troubled Children

This body of theoretical concepts, which initially were sometimes called 'social learning theory', has been shown in repeated studies to be of great help in supporting families with troubled children. Box I.2 shows just some of the areas of research where there is firm evidence of their usefulness. Many of these areas will be addressed in this book.

Box I.2:   Areas of research in which cognitive-behavioural theory has been found helpful

Emotional disorders in children	Harrington (1994)
Eating difficulties	Hampton (1996)
Sleeping difficulties	Ferber (1986)
Interventions in emotional abuse and neglect	Iwaniec (1995)
Conduct disorders in children	Herbert (1987), Earls (1994)
Attention deficit hyperactivity disorder	Barkley (1995)
Enuresis	Shaffer (1994)
Soiling	Hersov (1994)

This trend is set to continue: cognitive-behavioural theory is here to stay, established by painstaking research in many countries and grounded upon methods of working which respect a family's or person's dignity, culture and traditions and seek to empower its members. A detailed assessment of each child's circumstances is of course essential: organic explanations for a child's difficulties must be explored; 'life events' in the child's past and present must be addressed; but in addition we have at last a body of theory on the basis of which it is possible to help many, many children on a day-by-day basis and to undertake preventive work with their parents.

UNDERTAKING PREVENTIVE WORK

Dr Stephen Scott of the Institute of Psychiatry in London reported the costs of *not* taking steps to prevent children's difficulties. On the BBC programme *Panorama*, shown on 23 September 1996, he described how, if a young child shows serious misbehaviour and the family receives no help with this, he or she is likely to require the intervention first of school nurses or school counsellors, then of education officers if he or she is excluded from school and then of social workers if he or she is received into care. If then, as sometimes happens, such children become petty offenders and then more serious offenders, they will be involved with further social workers or probation officers. If any such child continues a career of offending and is imprisoned, the overall cost to society by the time he or she is a young adult is of the order of *£one million*. How can this situation be allowed to continue?

A coordinated strategy for preventive work with young children is urgently required. The existing services are woefully inadequate. The main professional group with duties of supporting families with pre-school children in the United Kingdom are health visitors, but they typically have responsibilities for screening children for medical and related difficulties: they are not routinely trained to guide parents in the management of aggressive and disruptive behaviour or anxiety-related disorders. I have the highest regard for health visitors and know of their commitment to distressed families, but without specific training they cannot undertake more than a fraction of the necessary preventive work. The other major professional group with responsibility to support children are field social workers, but they, for the most part, are stretched to breaking point with child protection work and have few resources for preventive work. Voluntary organisations, such as Family Services and specific resources like Child and Family Guidance Services, typically have long waiting lists and can work only with the most seriously troubled children.

Many children thus slip through these nets. If no-one is able to help them in the pre-school years, many, especially those displaying aggressive and disruptive behaviours, are likely to take their difficulties into the primary schools. Here school nurses may, in some local authorities, be involved in attempting to support families but they too are not specifically trained to work using evidence-based approaches. Certainly, they can offer a listening ear and general support to troubled children and their distressed families but the skills of helping family members to live together and to develop positive and constructive family relationships cannot be based solely on common sense: they require a thorough grasp of and extensive experience in using a body of theoretical ideas, cognitive-behavioural theory, which can provide a positive framework for practice.

If children are not helped in primary schools, they are likely to take their difficulties into the even more demanding environments of secondary education, where they may contribute to the numbers of exclusions and expulsions of children seen by governing bodies as unmanageable; once excluded, few children are able to return to school without difficulty. Educational psychologists and social workers do their best to support them and their families, but by now children are becoming entrenched in patterns of misbehaviour and of disaffection from school; they are unlikely to respond positively to subsequent attempts to engage them in learning for the worlds of work and adulthood. *It is just common sense to do all that we can to prevent these difficulties from occurring in the first place.*

There is an inevitable shortage of trained personnel. The relevant body of theoretical ideas has only recently been confirmed by the distillation from huge research endeavours by meta-analysis—a process in which the data from hundreds of research studies are brought together and trends which might be indistinguishable in individual studies become apparent. For example, the research by Lipsey and colleagues in the field of juvenile offending, which showed the central usefulness of cognitive-behavioural approaches, was only published in 1992 and the dissemination of training skills based upon that body of concepts is still in its initial stages.

However, recognition of this evidence *is* becoming disseminated, as witness the Report of the Committee of the House of Commons upon Child and Adolescent Mental Health Services (House of Commons Health Committee, 1997) which includes the following passage:

> We were impressed with what we heard of Parent Management Training, and recommend that the DoH should support this and

similar techniques, while at the same time ensuring that they receive systematic evaluation and monitoring as to their effectiveness and cost-effectiveness (p. xxiv).

To critics who point out the stresses under which parents of poverty and disadvantage coping with children are living, I acknowledge their case, but would point out two things. First, most parents seek to do their best for their children and want to continue to care for their children themselves; they do not want them to be removed by social workers because they are being neglected or maltreated. The body of ideas which I am proposing gives families skills for managing their children in ways which make them easier to handle and easier to love. One mother, whom I have never met, but whom I was able to teach how to manage her very active two year old twins by telephone, said 'I used to hate those two, but now I love them'. Second, teaching parents these skills of child management is not in conflict with the provision of better services: social workers and health visitors can work towards setting up more crèches, more day nurseries, more family support services, *as well as* teaching caregivers how to manage their children's sleeping and behaviour difficulties effectively. The two strategies should together be among a range of tools in the practitioner's repertoire: it is a matter not of 'either/or' but of 'both/and'.

DISSEMINATION OF THE NECESSARY SKILLS

I am glad to be able to report that a number of professional bodies have been persuaded by the evidence which I and other researchers have been able to offer and I am already engaged in disseminating the skills arising from this body of knowledge among health visitors and social workers in several parts of the country. Now they, in turn, are running sleep clinics and behaviour management groups for parents and caregivers and are reporting the same sorts of success as I myself have had. My hope is that this book will persuade others, both individuals and agencies, to listen to the evidence emerging from the research and seek training to help families to help their troubled children.

I

SOME GENERAL PRINCIPLES FOR HELPING FAMILIES

RESEARCH CONCERNING TROUBLED CHILDREN

The recognition that many of the difficulties experienced by young people and adults have their origins in childhood has led to huge research undertakings within psychology, psychiatry and related disciplines. This research may be divided into five main fields:

1. The needs of children.
2. The nature and prevalence of young children's difficulties.
3. Continuities of difficulty from early to later childhood and into adolescence.
4. How some children become troubled; what causes or contributes to their difficulties.
5. The effectiveness of interventions to help them.

Each will be considered below.

THE NEEDS OF CHILDREN

There have been extensive investigations of children's needs, since, by definition, troubled children are those whose needs have not been met. One of the clearest is that of Cooper (1985), whose conclusions are summarised in Box 1.1.

Box 1.1:   The needs of children (reproduced with permission from Cooper, 1985)

- *Basic physical care*, which includes warmth, shelter, adequate food and rest, grooming (hygiene) and protection from danger.

- *Affection*, which includes physical contact, holding, stroking, cuddling and kissing, comforting, admiration, delight, tenderness, patience, time, making allowances for annoying behaviour, general companionship and approval.

- *Security*, which involves continuity of care, the expectation of continuing in the stable family unit, a predictable environment, consistent patterns of care and daily routine, simple rules and consistent controls, and a harmonious family group.

- *Stimulation of innate potential* by praise, by encouraging curiosity and exploratory behaviour, by developing skills through responsiveness to questions and to play, and by promoting educational opportunities.

- *Guidance and control* to teach adequate social behaviour, which includes discipline within the child's understanding and capacity, and which requires patience and a model for the child to copy, for example in honesty and concern and kindness for others.

- *Responsibility* for small things at first, such as self-care, tidying playthings, or taking dishes to the kitchen, and gradually elaborating the decision-making the child has to learn in order to function adequately; gaining experience through mistakes as well as successes, and receiving praise and encouragement to strive and do better.

- *Independence* to make their own decisions, first about small things but increasingly about the various aspects of life within the confines of the family and society's codes. Parents use fine judgement in encouraging independence, and in letting the child see and feel the outcome of his or her own poor judgement and mistakes, but within the compass of the child's capacity. Protection is needed, but over-protection is as bad as too early responsibility and independence.

THE NATURE AND PREVALENCE OF CHILDREN'S DIFFICULTIES

What is Meant by 'Troubled Children'

The expression 'troubled children' means those who have psychological difficulties which interfere with their day-to-day lives but which may or may not show themselves in overt patterns of behaviour. It refers to children whose difficulties are persisting, not those who show transient upsets and unhappiness. It is known that certain difficulties are more common at certain developmental stages than at others and this must of course be taken into account.

Box 1.2 shows a table devised by Rutter (1987) from data drawn from studies of the World Health Organization, which spans research endeavours across the world, upon the main broad categories of children's emotional and behavioural difficulties. Indicators concerning associated conditions and the probable response to intervention are also given. It will be noted that boys outnumber girls in all areas of difficulty excepting emotional difficulties where the proportions of boys and girls are the same. For example, in respect of this category of emotional difficulties, onset may occur at any time, there is no particular association with reading difficulties

Box 1.2: Variables differentiating diagnostic categories (reproduced with permission from Rutter, 1975)

Diagnostic group	Age of onset (years)	Sex	Reading difficulties	Family discord	Response to treatment
Emotional disorder (anxieties, phobias, obsessions, depression)	Any	=	−	−	++++
Conduct disorder (aggressiveness, disruptiveness, tantrums)	Any	M	++	++	+
Hyperactivity (AD/HD)	< 5	M	+++	+	+
Autism	< 2.5	M	+++	−	+
Developmental delay	Infancy	M	+++	−	++

Table 1.1: Prevalence of specific child and adolescent mental health disorders (reproduced with permission from Department of Health, 1995)

Emotional disorders with onset in childhood	4.5–9.9% of 10 year-olds 25–33% among clinic attenders
Major depression	0.5–2.5% among children 2–8% among adolescents
Conduct disorders	6.2–10.8% among 10 year-olds 33–50% among clinic attenders
Tic disorders	1–13% of boys and 1–11% of girls
Obsessive-compulsive disorder	1.9% of adolescents
Hyperkinetic disorder	1.7% of primary school boys 1 in 200 in the whole population suffer severe hyperkinetic disorders. Up to 17% suffer at least some hyperkinetic disorders
Encopresis (faecal soiling)	2.3% of boys and 0.7% of girls aged 7–8 years 1.3% of boys and 0.3% of girls aged 11–12 years
Anorexia nervosa	0.5–1% of 12–19 year-olds 8–11 times more common in girls
Bulimia nervosa	1% of adolescent girls and young women
Attempted suicide	2–4% of adolescents
Suicide	7.6 per 100 000 15–19 year-olds
Substance misuse: Alcohol	79% of 13 year-olds have drunk alcohol, with 29% usually drinking once a week
Solvents and illegal drugs	16% of 16 year-olds involved in regular use
Minor tranquillisers	Very few involved in regular consumption
Cannabis	3–5% of 11–16 year-olds have used it; 17% in older teenagers
Heroin and cocaine	Less than 1%
Hallucinogens	Increase reported

or with family distress, and there is a very positive prognosis—that is, help given to children with emotional difficulties is likely to be effective and the children are very likely to become less troubled.

Prevalence of Children's Difficulties

Table 1.1 gives details of data drawn from hundreds of studies concerning the prevalence of a number of specific child and adolescent disorders. Where two figures are given, for example 4.5–9.9% of 10 year-olds with emotional disorder, this reflects evidence found in different studies, perhaps in different parts of the country, such as a comparison between a rural and an urban setting.

Let us look in more detail at some of these studies:

1. *Pre-school children.* There have been several studies of the prevalence of behaviour difficulties among young children. In a typical early study in the UK, Richman, Stevenson and Graham (1982) met with over 700 parents in a one in four sample of pre-school children in a London borough and found that approximately 7% of the children had a moderate to severe behaviour problem, while a further 15% had a mild behaviour problem. Richman (1985) reported:

   > The most common clinical picture was of a child who was restless, attention-seeking and difficult to manage; relatively few of the children were described as anxious or unhappy (p. 337).

   Families of children with difficulties were more likely than families of children without such difficulties to have suffered stressful circumstances over the previous year. The same questionnaire used in an American rural community found that about a quarter of the three year-old children showed difficult or disturbed behaviour (Earls, 1982). This range, 22–25% of pre-school children in the UK and in the USA displaying unhappiness or disturbance, seems worryingly high.

2. *Infant school children.* A more recent study of children aged four to seven in inner London infant schools gave further grounds for concern. The teachers of these children considered that 16% had definite behaviour problems and a further 17%

had mild behaviour problems. These figures were confirmed by independent assessors in the classrooms (Tizard et al, 1988).

3. *Primary school age children.* The National Child Development Study followed the progress of some 17 000 children born in one week in March 1958. There was an inevitable loss of participants, but some 11 000 were still available for study when the children were in primary school. Assessment of the children's behaviour by teachers indicated that 22% were seen as showing some signs of 'maladjustment', while of these, 14% were seen as presenting serious behaviour problems (Davie, Butler and Goldstein, 1972).

4. *Older primary school children.* Rutter and colleagues (1975a, b) examined over 1000 10 year-old children in an inner London borough and a comparable number in the Isle of Wight. The researchers sought the views of both parents and teachers about the children and estimated that there was a prevalence rate for 'psychiatric' difficulties, that is, serious emotional and behavioural disorders, of approximately 6% on the Island, while that in the London borough was about double that figure.

The discrepancies between figures require comment. It is very difficult to arrive at an accepted criterion of a behaviour disorder and although assessment schedules are improving, there are inevitably differences of perception among parents and others who care for a child. Further, as stated, studies are purposely undertaken in differnt places in order to try to determine the impact upon children of different environments. In these circumstances, the figures in Table 1.1 may be the most reliable guide.

There are also major issues concerning cultural expectations of acceptable behaviour and substantial evidence that behaviour which is adapted to one social or cultural context may be seen as 'maladjusted' in another (Woodhead, 1995). While acknowledging these reservations, there is increasing concern about the number of children who are not only unhappy themselves but cause much unhappiness to others, for example by bullying and by placing additional stress upon family relationships. In view of the evidence to be considered further below, that many of the unacceptable behaviours displayed by adolescents and adults had their origins in the early years of children's lives, it is imperative that we take all possible steps not only to identify children showing early signs of unhappiness and troubled behaviour but also to offer help to them and their parents. If we do not, these same children take their difficulties into adult life, affecting *their* children and those about them in turn.

CONTINUITIES OF CHILDREN'S BEHAVIOUR DIFFICULTIES

Pre-school to First School

There seems to be a body of opinion among the general public that children 'grow out of' many of their difficult patterns of behaviour but, as Box 1.2 shows, there is clinical evidence to support the view that only children with emotional disorders can usually be fairly reliably helped. The prognosis for conduct disorders, and to some extent for hyperactivity, is generally less favourable.

Turning to specific studies of persistence from early to later behaviour, Richman, Stevenson and Graham (1982) examined continuities between pre-school and school behaviour in nearly 100 three year-olds and found that 63% of those with behaviour problems at age three were still considered to be difficult at age four and 62% had problems at age eight: by contrast, of children in a control group matched for age and class but without behaviour problems at age three, only 11% had difficulties at age four and 22% had difficulties at age eight. Of the former group, 38% had made contact with Child Guidance services, while only 16% of the latter had done so.

Other studies have reported similar findings. In the USA, Spivack, Marcus and Swift (1986) found that seriously difficult behaviour in a child at age three and four predicted later contact with the police, while in New Zealand, White and colleagues (1990) found that early disruptive behaviour and being difficult to manage predicted anti-social behaviour at age 11.

Basic to Secondary Education

There are more studies of continuities in the difficulties of children at early and later school age. An extremely important American study is that of Robins (1966), who managed to follow up in adulthood 436 of 524 children seen in a St Louis Child Guidance clinic in the 1920s; 80% of the children had appeared before a juvenile court and 50% had been sent to correctional institutions. Herbert (1991) has drawn attention to Robins's finding that there were particular dangers when the anti-social behaviour in childhood was frequent and varied and when it occurred outside the family and the child's immediate circle.

The longitudinal study by West and Farrington (1973) monitored the progress of 411 London boys aged 8–17 years and beyond and, using information from the boys themselves, their parents and teachers, sought to distinguish variables associated with boys who became delinquent from those who did not. Analyses were conducted to determine the effect of each variable, holding others constant. These showed that *early* troublesome behaviour was a distinguishing factor between the groups.

This same worrying pattern was also found in the study by Mitchell and Rosa (1981), who used longitudinal data from a large sample of boys in Buckinghamshire, UK. Outcomes for boys whose behaviour was seen as deviating from that typical of other boys of school age were compared with outcomes for a control group who displayed 'normal' behaviour. The authors reported that over a 15-year period, those in the 'deviator' group were significantly more likely both to become offenders and to become recidivists. They noted the important finding that parental reports of anti-social behaviour, such as stealing, lying and destructiveness, carried the worst prognosis for subsequent convictions, especially where teachers' reports confirmed those of parents. Similarly, Tremblay and colleagues (1988) in Montreal showed that ratings of a child's aggressiveness by teachers and peers when the child was aged six predicted self-reported delinquency at age 14–15.

Farrington (1995b) summarised the extensive work available and identified four major associated factors in patterns of anti-social behaviour arising in childhood and continuing in adulthood:

1. Economic deprivation, as seen in low family income, poor housing and low social class.
2. Family criminality, as seen in convicted parents and delinquent siblings.

3. Parental mishandling, as seen in poor supervision and poor parental child-rearing behaviour.
4. School failure, as seen in low vocabulary, low IQ and truancy.

The best single predictor of delinquency was teachers' and peers' rating of the boys' troublesomeness at age eight.

Stability over Time of Male Aggressive Reaction Patterns

Olweus (1979) reviewed 16 studies concerning continuity of aggressive patterns in males. The studies included early ones over short intervals, involving both small and large numbers of children (from 36 to 200), and others which spanned intervals as long as 20 years. Olweus concluded that the degree of stability in the area of aggression was substantial and, of particular importance, he found that 'marked individual differences in habitual aggression level manifest themselves early in life, certainly by the age of three'. Olweus made two main points: first, that the degree of consistency in aggressive behaviour is much greater than that suggested by those who hold the view that behaviour is primarily 'situation specific', and second, that important variables linked with this consistency can be distinguished early in life. As we have seen above, early indicators can be gathered from the teachers and peers of children aged six to eight.

On the other hand, it looks at first sight as if the major longitudinal study of the National Children's Bureau, concerned with over 17 000 children born in the week 3–9 March 1958 in England, Scotland and Wales, provided evidence conflicting with the indications of continuity between childhood and subsequent difficult behaviour. Data were gathered upon many aspects of the children's development, including separate ratings of behaviour at home and at school, at ages 7, 11 and 16. Fogelman (1983) summarised findings upon many aspects of the children's progress. In respect of behaviour rated at home and at school, the 13% of children with the highest ratings of disorder were considered as showing 'deviant' behaviour (Fogelman acknowledged that the figure of 13% was an arbitrary one). The researchers concluded that only small numbers of children, around 2.2%, remained in the 'deviant' group at all three ages, 7, 11 and 16. Fogelman (1983) commented:

> What can be said with assurance from these results is that, in inter-preting research studies, they give considerable warning against assuming a static and pathological stage for children identified as deviant.

If we look more closely at this statement, however, it seems to give false grounds for reassurance: if 2.2% of the children 're-mained in the "deviant" group at all three ages', this represents, of the 11 000 or so children available for follow-up, no less than 242 of the children born in one week who were 'deviant' for the greater part of their childhood. This gives an annual figure of 12 584 con-tinuously 'deviant' children—a most conservative estimate, since it is based upon only 11 000 of the original 17 000 children in the sample. Surely there is no room for complacent reassurance in such a situation!

THE ORIGINS OF SOME OF THE DIFFICULTIES: SOME WAYS IN WHICH CHILDREN BECOME TROUBLED

There is little evidence that large numbers of children are *born* troubled, although some seem to be born with predispositions to restlessness and impulsiveness (Barkley, 1995). Of course, a sub-stantial number of children are born with disabilities, but these do not of themselves lead to depression or difficult behaviour: rather, it is the response to the disability of the child and of the family which influence whether the child will become troubled or not. Having considered the fundamental needs of children which, if met, enable them to develop into stable and confident human beings (see Box 1.1), we shall now consider in a more detailed fashion the factors which jeopardise the development of that sta-bility and which may lead to emotional and behavioural diffi-culties. The frontispiece to this book (Herbert, 1981) illustrates the tapestry of interacting variables and their effects upon children. It is to this that we now turn. Reference will be made to the groups of variables shown in the boxes.

Table 1.2: Childhood temperament: patterns among young children which tend to persist beyond infancy (after Thomas and Chess, 1977)

The 'easy' child	These young children are adaptable and easy to manage. They move early in life into regular patterns of sleeping and waking, and seem contented and flexible
The 'difficult' child	These young children are less adaptable. It is more difficult to get them into a routine of sleeping and feeding regularly, and they seem more tense and irritable in their responses to new situations or people
The 'slow to warm up' child	These children fall between the two patterns shown above, but it takes considerable time to settle them into a routine. Having made that adjustment, however, they are fairly easy to manage

Genetic and Constitutional Variables

Many studies have shown marked and persisting differences in temperament among children born of the same parents. The best known of these were carried out by Thomas and Chess (1977) who, in a longitudinal study of babies through childhood and adolescence, found that 65% of them fell into three main categories, showing temperamental characteristics in infancy which tended to persist into childhood and beyond (see Table 1.2).

This research suggests that there is a genetic *contribution* to personality. However, there is broad agreement among researchers that it is the impact of experience and of the environment, of parenting styles, of life events and of stressors such as poverty or isolation, which contribute the greater part of the influences which lead to children becoming troubled. There is thus a continuous interaction between innate and environmental factors.

Child-rearing Factors

Since this book will consider many of these variables, they will not be explored in detail here; suffice it to draw attention to the

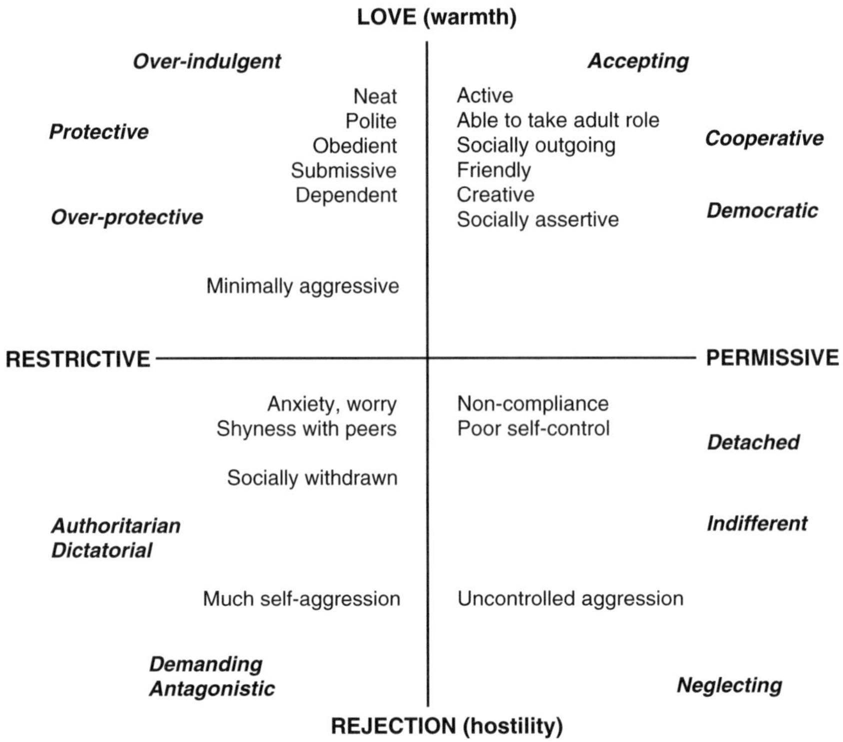

LOVE (warmth)

Over-indulgent			*Accepting*
Protective	Neat Polite Obedient Submissive Dependent	Active Able to take adult role Socially outgoing Friendly Creative Socially assertive	*Cooperative*
Over-protective			*Democratic*

Minimally aggressive

RESTRICTIVE ———————————————————— **PERMISSIVE**

	Anxiety, worry Shyness with peers	Non-compliance Poor self-control	*Detached*
	Socially withdrawn		
Authoritarian *Dictatorial*			*Indifferent*
	Much self-aggression	Uncontrolled aggression	
Demanding *Antagonistic*			*Neglecting*

REJECTION (hostility)

Figure 1.1:   Patterns of parenting and of children's behaviour responses
                  (after Maccoby and Martin, 1983)

research upon the impact of different 'parenting styles'. Baumrind
(1971), for example, has shown that certain styles tend to lead to
different patterns of responses in children, and the details devised
by Maccoby and Martin (1983) (Figure 1.1) illustrate some of the
relationships which have been teased out.

Developmental Factors in Very Early Life

Some children have a stressful and even dangerous start in life.
They may be born with physical or learning disabilities, with
inherited vulnerabilities or with damage associated with difficult
birth processes. Some may be premature and it has been

documented by Drillien (1964) that such babies are likely to experience greater challenges and difficulties than babies born at full term. Describing her work, Herbert (1991) writes:

> Drillien (1964) studied (longitudinally) the sequelae of premature births in over 1000 mothers. Using the British Social Adjustment Guide, she tested the school-going children at ages six and seven. She found that the proportion of children considered maladjusted or unsettled increased as birth weight decreased. Obstetric difficulties—severe complications of pregnancy or birth—were associated with increased risk of disturbed behaviour in the offspring.

Drillien's conclusions have received recent support from the study by Sykes and colleagues (1997), who followed up a cohort of 243 prematurely born, very low birth weight (less than 1501 grams) babies, together with a control group of babies whose birth weight was within the normal range. The researchers reported that the 'findings indicate that the children born pre-term (both male and female) were rated by their teachers as expressing more behaviour problems than their controls, and were less well adjusted to the school environment'. The researchers found no differences across social class and they speculated that 'the problem behaviours reflect a failure in self-regulatory functions'.

Some babies get off to a difficult start in respect of patterns of feeding and sleeping. Many have feeding problems, which mean that feeds are a source of tension, and these are so common that a chapter upon both feeding and sleeping has been included in this book. Moreover all babies cry some of the time, but some—reported by Bee (1992, p. 114) to be between 15% and 20%—experience spells of the acute, piercing pain known as colic, often in the late afternoon or evening. This can be deeply stressful to parents, especially inexperienced ones, and can lead to children getting off to a poor start. As children develop, the birth of a new sibling may be a time of acute stress and distress to young children and Bee again reported substantial evidence that many show major disturbances, such as more frequent crying, increased demands for maternal attention as well as reversion to patterns of behaviour typical of younger children.

Personality Factors

As children mature they begin to develop a sense of self and of confidence in themselves and those who care for them. Cooley (1902), an early theorist, hypothesised that we build up our sense of self from the reactions of others to us and how we believe they view us. There is now considerable evidence that this sense of confidence and self-worth is *learned*, so that young children take into themselves the messages about themselves which they hear from parents and those about them. If toddlers experience acceptance, hear loving endearments and have clear boundaries set for their behaviour, they grow up as secure and confident children and adults, having internalised these views of themselves. As I have written earlier (Sutton, 1979):

> The well-beloved child, wanted by his parents and welcomed into the world, is told from infancy by his mother's and father's actions and words that he is 'a beautiful baby', 'a wonderful boy' . . . the effect of their love and care is to establish his worth in his own eyes.
>
> By contrast, the child born fifth in line to a harassed mother, coping perhaps on her own or in terrible housing conditions, may receive only a minimum of time and attention because of so many other pressing demands on the mother . . . So the child may only learn that he is 'nothing but a nuisance', 'a little pest', and 'always clumsy and careless' before he even gets to school.
>
> This process goes on throughout life; the fortunate children, whose view of themselves is positive when they go to school, are likely to have this view of themselves strengthened by teachers and neighbours: the unfortunate ones, whose view is predominantly negative, are likely to have this view strengthened too.

Milestones: Life Experiences for Children

These include the many life events which children experience and which affect their sense of security and confidence. These include of course their health, their sense of identity as a person valued or under-valued by others, their experiences of 'success' or 'failure', whether in school or in some other non-academic field, their friendliness or friendlessness, their experience of being bullied or discriminated against, and all the myriad of small events which make a child feel safe in and able to affect the world or, alternatively, powerless and helpless in the face of adversity. Since responses to these life circumstances and life events are so idiosyncratic, one way of teasing these out for a given child may be the study of Horowitz, Wilner and Alvarez (1979), who explored the impacts of events upon children of this age. Readers are referred to the work of these researchers.

Developmental Stage

Here we may consider the many variables to take into account when considering whether a given pattern of behaviour is a transient one, characteristic of the maturational stage of many children and thus likely to follow a predictable course, or whether it is uncharacteristic and unpredictable. Examples are the increased independence of children aged two to three; Woodhead (1995) cites the work of Jenkins et al (1984):

> They interviewed parents and doctors of children at seven intervals between six weeks and four years six months. During the early years, the incidence of problems was relatively low, at most affecting 13% of the children as judged by parents, or 10% as judged by doctors. But at three years of age these rates rose dramatically (to 23% and 27% respectively). However, by four years six months they had already started to decline again.

Another recognised pattern which occurs with maturation is the increase in fears and anxieties and depression in children in early adolescence. Children aged 10–11, for example, have a markedly raised rate by comparison with those of seven or eight and this may be grounded in the developing cognitive abilities which accompany adolescence, when children can conceptualise the *possibility* of accidents or of trauma in their lives.

Current Life Circumstances

These circumstances include those of the school and neighbourhood and the influences which flow from them. As children develop and begin to take part in activities beyond the immediate family, so social experiences become increasingly important for them. The effect of having, or not having, friends is absolutely central to their well-being, particularly as they mature and spend less time at home and more in the company of their peers. There is substantial evidence that the peer group can be a force which fosters the development of pro- or anti-social behaviour.

Reasons why some children get into difficulties while others do not are to do with the way the interacting variables fall out for an individual child. For example, parents' *perceptions* of their children are very important: some parents told me that they felt they never did have control of their children; others, that they lost it within the earliest years of the child's life. Having once felt that control is lost they do not know what to do to change the course of events: they had *learned* helplessness. The studies of Harriet Wilson (1980, 1987) are instructive here. She compared the delinquency rates of children living in either the inner city or the suburbs according to whether the degree of parental supervision exercised over them was 'strict', 'intermediate' or 'lax'; she found that, after controlling for other variables, 'strictness', defined as parents' knowing where their sons were and exercising control over their activities, conferred protection against delinquency: within the inner city, for example, the delinquency rate of 'lax' families was over two and a half times that of 'strict' families. Patterns of parental supervision of their children are likely to be set in the early years of their children's lives and are thus an important component of prevention.

Socio-economic and Demographic Variables

In these respects, many factors have been shown to be involved. It is known, for example, from studies in this country and elsewhere, that the children of very young mothers experience greater stress than do those of older mothers, particularly where the mothers are unsupported by the child's natural father or indeed by their own family. Farrington (1995a) has drawn attention to many vulnerability factors; he writes:

> In Western industrialized countries, at least, early child-bearing—or teenage pregnancy—predicts many undesirable outcomes for the children, including low school attainment, anti-social school behaviour, substance use and early sexual intercourse.

Farrington also highlights the advantages which, the research indicates, of these mothers having continuing relationships with the children's biological fathers. This seems to offer protective factors. These situations have been explored widely by Hilary Graham (1993), who has confirmed the impact of isolation, disadvantage and lack of child care facilities upon young mothers.

It is also known that black children and children in care are particularly vulnerable in respect of difficulties in these early years. A report by Gardiner (1996) upon permanent exclusions from school reported in the *Times Educational Supplement* (November 1996) that:

> . . . 25.7% of all exclusions are from minority groups and that two-thirds of those excluded are below average ability.

She also cited the large number of children in care being excluded—about two-thirds of all exclusions. Thus the most needy of all children are those who experience further adversity.

Cognitive Variables

These refer to the factors which are inherent in the way a given individual perceives stimuli and decides to take action. For example, Dodge and Frame (1982) have explored differences between the ways in which children with records of aggressive behaviour and non-aggressive children process and respond to cues in the environment. These researchers found that aggressive boys were 'hypervigilant' in scanning their social environment for potential threat and that they responded to perceived hostility with aggressive responses far more readily than did non-aggressive boys. Discussing this work, Kendall (1991) writes:

> Aggressive boys have been found to be 50% more likely than non-aggressive boys to infer that antagonists in hypothetical provocations acted with hostile rather than neutral or benign intent (Dodge and Frame, 1982).

This work has been replicated in a series of studies, all of which confirm that aggressive boys attribute hostility to others far more frequently than is in fact the case. They also underestimate their own aggressiveness (Lochman, White and Wayland, 1991).

Situation Variables

These refer to the specific situations in which children display troublesome behaviour. For example, one little boy may be rude, aggressive and violent towards his mother, but be a model of courtesy and consideration towards his class teacher. Another little girl may be cheeky and impertinent to her father, but polite to and compliant with her grandfather. For other children, it may be certain times of day when their behaviour becomes unbearable and for yet others, it may be certain days of the week, such as Sunday nights, before school the following morning. All these possible contributory factors need to be considered.

Thus, reasons why some children get into difficulties while others do not are in part to do with the way social and cognitive variables fall out for an individual child and how they interact with each child's innate endowment. I would reiterate that to help children we need to be alert both to structural factors, such as unemployment, poverty and poor housing, and to the circumstances of each individual family and how its members interact. In other words, we need explanations for children's difficulties which encompass *both* sociological *and* psychological perspectives.

A RANGE OF APPROACHES FOR HELPING TROUBLED CHILDREN

There has been a great deal of research into strategies for helping parents whose children appear to be getting into difficulties: this chapter will draw upon the work of Alan Kazdin (1987, 1995) and others in order to examine which strategies appear to be the most effective.

The field of children's difficulties that has been most carefully surveyed in respect of the effectiveness of different models of intervention has been children's anti-social behaviour. No doubt this

Table 1.3: Processes of major classes of treatment for anti-social behaviour (after Kazdin, 1987)

Target of intervention	Type of intervention	Main focus	Key processes
Child	Individual therapy	Intrapsychic bases of antisocial behaviour	Relationship with therapist; insight
	Group therapy	Individual therapy and group processes	Relationship with therapist and peers
	Behaviour therapy	Problem behaviours	Learning new pro-social behaviours
	Problem-solving skill	Cognitive problem-solving skills	Teaching problem-solving skills
	Pharmacotherapy	To affect biological systems	Administration of medication
	Residential treatment	Range of therapies	Processes of other approaches used
Family	Family therapy	Interactions of the whole family	Communication and relationships in family
	Parent management training	Interactions between parents and children	Training of parents to manage their children
Community-based	Community-wide interventions	Activities to foster competence/relations	To develop pro-social behaviours

in part is because of its close association with offending behaviour. Kazdin (1987) has devised an extremely helpful table illustrating the various types of intervention that have been developed. He identifies three main foci of 'treatment': child-focused, family-focused and community-based. Table 1.3 is a simplified form of his table.

Kazdin considers that four main approaches to the management of anti-social behaviour are beginning to be adequately researched: parent management training, family therapy, problem-solving skills training and community-based interventions. The studies show, as one would expect, that families with many stressors fare less well whatever the model of intervention but that parent management training (that is, helping parents to manage their children with both personal support and skills training) showed benefits. Kazdin (1987) writes:

> Several features make PMT [Parent Management Training] one of the more promising treatments for conduct disorders. First, the treatment has been effective with conduct-problem children varying in severity of dysfunction. Treatment effects are maintained up to 1 year later and occasionally longer. Moreover, changes at home and at school bring deviant behaviour of treated children within the range of children functioning normally. Second, the benefits of treatment often extend beyond the target child; siblings profit from PMT. This may be an important advantage because siblings of anti-social youths are at risk for anti-social behaviour (Twito and Stewart, 1982). Third, along with outcome investigations, basic research on family interaction patterns has contributed to the understanding of the emergence of anti-social behavior. Fourth, a major advantage is the availability of treatment manuals and training materials for parents and professional therapists . . .

To add to this, Callias (1994), in a comprehensive review of the evidence concerning parent training and its subsequent effectiveness, also concludes that this approach has a good deal to offer. She highlights the desirablility of parent training being available as one of a number of supportive measures for parents of children with autism, developmental difficulties and other problems, as well as the importance of a range of other services to combat isolation, poverty and mental health problems, and regards the research evidence as encouraging. She writes:

With conduct-disordered children, behavioural parent-training pro-grammes have been shown to be more effective than family-based psychotherapy, discussion (attention placebo) and no treatment, family systems therapy and parent discussion . . .

Research into Parent Education and Training

Behavioural parent training has been widely investigated in many studies carried out across the world over the past decades. Gordon and Davidson, as long ago as 1981, reported 'the successful treatment of thousands of children with a wide variety of problems'. This 'wide variety' includes children with conduct disorders (Herbert, 1987), children who have been neglected or emotionally abused (Iwaniec, 1995), children with sleeping difficulties (Ferber, 1986) and children with eating disorders (Macht, 1990). Indeed, the body of research and research reviews is now so extensive that, as already indicated, the Committee of the House of Commons considering mental health services for children and young people has recommended that the approach should be supported by the Department of Health.

My Own Research: Further Evidence for the Effectiveness of Parent Training

It was because of this body of evidence of what can be done to help the families of young children that I myself undertook a substantial research programme (Sutton, 1992, 1995) in this field. After a pilot study with 11 families, which yielded encouraging results, I worked with 37 further families, all of whom were seeking help for their pre-school children who had previously been screened by professionals. Pre-intervention measures were taken and the families were se-quentially allocated to one of four methods of intervention:

- My working with them in a group context.
- My visiting them at home.
- My offering training over the telephone without meeting them.
- Being on a waiting list to see if the children's behaviour im-proved with the passage of time—so-called 'delayed treatment waiting list control'.

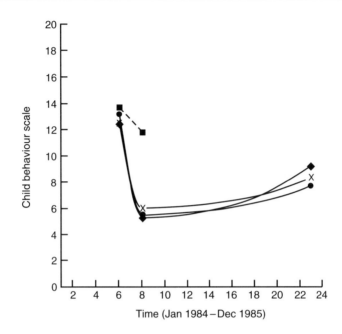

Figure 1.2:   Effect of parent training during training and at follow-up as measured by the Child Behaviour Scale (reproduced by permission of the British Association for Behavioural and Cognitive Psychotherapy from Sutton, 1992, *Behavioural Psychotherapy*, **20**)

Each training sequence lasted eight weeks, involving one meeting per week lasting about two hours for those parents meeting in a group, one hour for those whom I visited at home and an average of 45 minutes for those whom I trained by telephone. Each group received two follow-up 'booster' trainings. Figures 1.2 and 1.3 show the outcomes for the various groups on two of the main measures, both at the end of the eight weeks of training and 12–18 months later, when independent assessors visited all the families to see how the children were faring.

From this work I developed a number of conclusions:

1. It was possible to train the parents of difficult pre-school children to manage them effectively by means of eight weekly sessions of no more than two hours per week.
2. The children became more manageable by comparison with the children of parents who did not receive training.

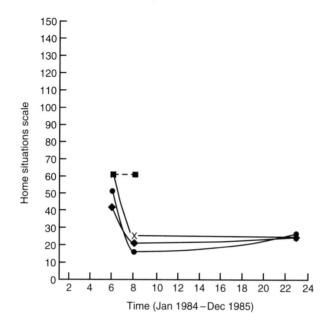

Figure 1.3: Effect of parent training during training and at follow-up as measured by the Home Situations Scale (reproduced by permission of the British Association for Behavioural and Cognitive Psychotherapy from Sutton, 1992, *Behavioural Psychotherapy*, **20**)

3. The effects of the training persisted at 12–18 months, as reported to independent evaluators.
4. There was a falling away, however, in the extent to which effects were maintained between post-intervention and follow-up. The telephone method showed most falling away.
5. There was little to choose between outcomes at any stage among the three methods of active training: group method, home visit method and telephone method.

Factors apparently central to success

The study was thus another piece of evidence of the effectiveness of parent management training, but I was able to go further than some researchers in identifying three factors apparently central to success:

1. *The availability of family or marital support.* While I did not ask parents explicitly about marital distress, it became apparent that those mothers who had the least or no success were those who were either without marital or family support or whose husband, partner or wider family actively disapproved of the methods being taught. A number of single parents were extremely successful, including several in the telephone method and even one with twins in this method. These parents had the support of someone who appeared to approve of the practices being taught, for example the child's grandparents. Where such people did not approve, or undermined consistent management of the children, the parents were virtually doomed to failure.

2. *Competence in using Time Out.* Many studies, for example Forehand and MacDonough (1975), found Time Out (from positive reinforcement) to be an effective strategy for managing a wide variety of childhood misbehaviour, while Hobbs and colleagues (1978) have shown four minutes to be the most effective length of sanction. I found that parents who were able effectively to place a child in Time Out and to keep him there were much more likely to achieve a positive outcome than those who found this difficult or who were inconsistent in so doing.

3. *The use of training manuals.* The use of eight brief manuals, distributed one per week for each of the eight weeks, was seen as central to the successful outcome. Feedback from the parents indicated that they had found them useful as a means of developing their confidence in practising the theoretical ideas being taught. Some parents, however, particularly those who could barely read, asked for simpler materials involving 'fewer long words'.

Clinical significance of the findings from this study

A number of other important points may be made:

1. *The falling away of the effects of training is a well-established phenomenon.* Patterson (1974), for example, found that half the families in his sample began to slip back into former patterns of parenting six months after completing their training. It was on these grounds that he recommended 'booster' sessions to maintain treatment gains. While I did offer 'boosters' two weeks and

twelve weeks after the completion of training, Figures 1.2 and 1.3 show that additional 'boosters' should be built in at regular intervals following the completion of training.

2. *Socially disadvantaged people can be effectively helped.* There was no evidence from my study that the training methods were more successful with the more well-to-do families. It was the availability of support and the ability to implement Time Out which were the key variables.

3. *Parents whose children have had a difficult start in life need additional support.* This emerged from examining the data for those children referred by general practitioners or paediatricians and who had had, for example, multiple hospital admissions in the first year of life. These children were among those with the most serious behaviour disorders (perhaps associated with the anxiety which their parents felt about them) and should not be allocated to a telephone method. The families may well need many booster sessions.

Further evidence from a partial replication of this study

Because I was surprised by the evidence that it was possible to train parents without ever meeting them or setting eyes on the child, I undertook a further study (Sutton, 1995) to replicate the telephone method of training. I worked with 23 families whose pre-school children had been screened by GPs or health visitors and trained with the parents entirely by telephone. Applications were randomly allocated, either to an immediate intervention group or to a delayed intervention waiting list control group, and pre-intervention measures were taken of the children's behaviour and of the level of depression of the mother. The programme of training as described above was replicated, but on this occasion it was carried out entirely by telephone. As before, measures were taken before and after the training. Figure 1.4 shows the effect of training as measured by the Child Behaviour Scale and Figure 1.5 shows the improvement in the mothers' levels of depression as their children's behaviour improved.

The results confirmed those of the earlier study and were in line with hundreds of other studies across the world. The second study made the distinctive contribution that such training can be

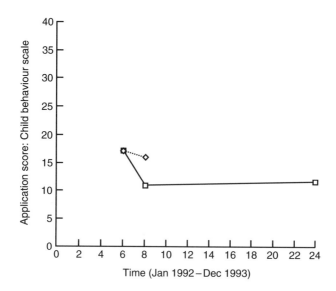

Figure 1.4:   Effect of parent training at pre-training, post-training and at follow-up as measured by the Child Behaviour Scale (reproduced by permission of the British Association for Behavioural and Cognitive Psychotherapy from Sutton, 1995, *Behavioural and Cognitive Psychotherapy,* **23**)

successfully offered by telephone, providing that an appropriate professional has screened the child for all the other possible factors which may be contributing to the child's behaviour difficulty.

In these studies several factors caught my attention which there was no space to report but which may form the basis of another researcher's enquiry. First, it seems that sheer inexperience of the role of the parent regarding how to manage a child is playing a part. The majority of children referred to me were first-born children and this is in line with the data given by, for example, Robins (1981), who found that the majority of children referred to child guidance clinics were first-born children. In my own case, I had scarcely even handled a baby before my first child was born and I had not the faintest idea of the way in which young children totally take over one's life. Second, very gentle, unassertive parents sometimes experienced more difficulties than others—especially where their child was demanding, high-spirited and wilful. There is no mystery here. If you are by nature a fairly quiet person, one who

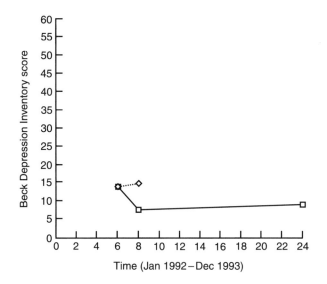

Figure 1.5: Effect of parent training on maternal depression at pre-training, post-training and at follow-up as measured by the Beck Depression Inventory (reproduced by permission of the British Association for Behavioural and Cognitive Psychotherapy from Sutton, 1995, *Behavioural and Cognitive Psychotherapy*, **23**)

dislikes arguments and values calm and peaceful relationships, and your child turns out to be a tearaway, there is a serious clash between how you wish to behave and how it seems that having a very lively child requires you to behave. It may just not be within your capacity to assert yourself sufficiently to manage a head-strong two or three year-old who is defiantly refusing your quite reasonable requests. It is highly likely that on at least some of these occasions the child 'wins the day', so reinforcing his or her asser-tiveness. Third, some parents confided to me that they longed so much for the love of their children that they feared that if they were 'too strict' the child would not love them. They believed that indulging the child would lead to gratitude from him or her; alas, the opposite was the case. Far from appearing to love and appreci-ate the mother more, the child exploited the indulgence to the full: demands became greater, arguments longer and sometimes even violence occurred as the child learned to persist, sometimes for hours on end in his or her wilfulness. Many of these situations were deeply saddening: parents longed to do their best for their children, but did not know what to do. They had tried all sorts of different strategies but, as one would expect from a knowledge of social learning theory, this inconsistency just made things worse. As we shall see, however, cognitive behavioural theory also supplied the key to improving the situation.

2

SOCIAL LEARNING/ COGNITIVE-BEHAVIOURAL THEORY

How do we begin to make sense of the complexity of the human situation? Of the many ways which social scientists have developed of conceptualising and coming to grips with this complexity, I wish briefly to consider here two: the first is of human beings as part of 'systems'; the second is of a range of 'perspectives' upon human beings.

WAYS OF THINKING ABOUT HUMAN BEINGS

Human Beings as Part of 'Systems'

A system has two main features. First, it is an assembly of parts or components connected together in an organised way; and second, the parts of the system affect each other—a change in one may well precipitate a change in another. Human beings are themselves 'systems', assemblies of closely integrated networks in which breathing, digesting food, circulating blood, reproduction and the other highly organised and integrated webs of activity together compose a living person. All the smaller systems contribute to the smooth functioning of the larger system, the body, and a significant change in one, such as catching 'flu, is very likely to affect the

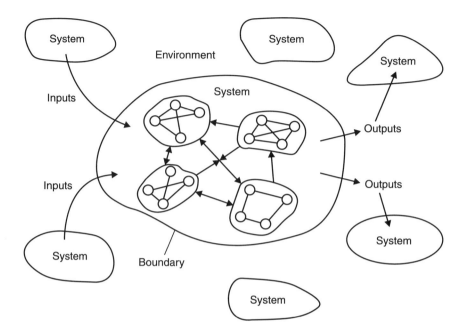

Figure 2.1: A system with sub-systems, interacting with other systems (reproduced from Open University, 1980, by permission of the Open University)

functioning of the others. Yet we ourselves are not only assemblies of systems; we also exist *within* systems: the family system, the education system, the political system, and so on. We are affected *by* others in those systems, such as our relatives and teachers, and we ourselves also affect other systems, for example other families and other organisations like schools and hospitals. We are all intimately connected in networks of relationships: no-one is an island.

Figure 2.1 shows a system, limited by a boundary, containing smaller systems in relationship. Other systems feed in and out of it. The larger system could represent either a person, composed of smaller systems and influenced by forces acting upon him or her, such as the events of family life, or it could represent a health authority or social services department, both affected by central government policy and consumer groups and affecting them in turn by decisions by voters and by letters to MPs.

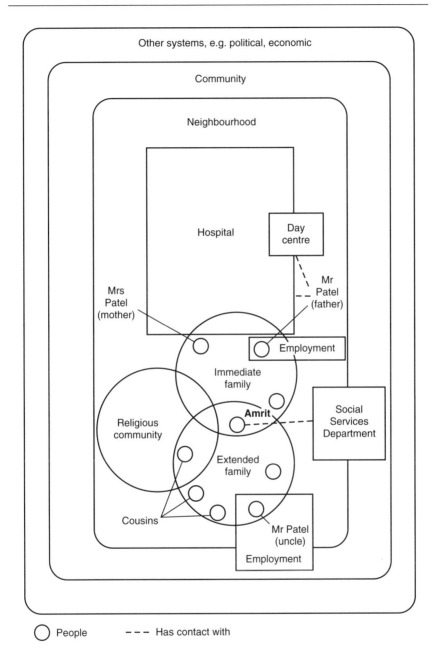

Figure 2.2: A child as part of many systems (reproduced with permission from Sutton and Herbert, 1992)

As I have written elsewhere (Sutton, 1994):

> Human beings, then, are inextricably linked with other human beings, since our deepest needs can only be met by other people. We are, however, also very different from one another. So we have this tension: human beings are at one and the same time both intimately bound up with each other and yet highly individual.

Figure 2.2 shows, in a schematic way, a child called Amrit Patel who, as a member of both an immediate and an extended family, is affected by the influences of people within those families and who are in turn affected by influences brought to bear, directly and indirectly, upon them.

A Range of Perspectives upon Human Beings

Psychology is a discipline whose focus is primarily upon individuals, families and small groups and their interactions—as distinct from sociology, which usually focuses upon larger groups and processes. In order to grapple with complexity, psychology has often taken different *perspectives* upon systems and upon human nature. The ideal, of course, is an 'holistic' approach, in which each person is perceived in his or her entirety, encompassing the physical body, development and learning, human experience, creativity, potential and so forth, but in order to keep things manageable, five perspectives upon the human being (Figure 2.3), often called 'models', have been developed. These are:

A. The *biological* perspective, this focuses upon the person as a biological phenomenon.
B. The *psychodynamic/emotional* perspective, including feelings, conscious and unconscious.
C. The *behavioural and social learning* perspective, including learning in a social context.
D. The *cognitive* perspective, including individual perceptions, thoughts and judgements.
E. The *humanistic* perspective, including the potential for development and growth.

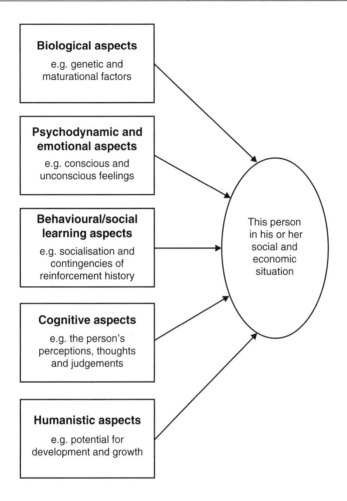

Figure 2.3: Five psychological perspectives on the human being

I shall briefly consider these perspectives, each of which overlaps and interacts with the others, before focusing upon the behavioural and cognitive perspectives, as research in these areas has been found particularly valuable in understanding and helping troubled children.

The biological perspective

This perspective focuses upon human beings as biological pheno-mena. It takes account of genetic influences and such processes as maturation and ageing. Genes govern the processes of growth and maturation and make a contribution to some of our psychological characteristics; they determine our biological sex and physical characteristics such as our eye, skin and hair colouring; and they may be implicated in some aspects of our health and mental health, such as sickle-cell anaemia and schizophrenia.

The study of how innate factors affect development is a very complex field indeed. One particular method is to investigate characteristics of identical twins, called monozygotic or MZ twins, meaning that they were born from a single egg, as distinct from dizygotic or DZ twins, born from two separate eggs and therefore not identical. In the past, identical twins were sometimes separated at birth and grew up in different environments; this allowed rare opportunities to distinguish innate effects from those acquired from the environment. As I have written elsewhere (Sutton, 1994):

> Major studies, such as that of Tellegen and colleagues (1988), who examined 44 pairs of identical twins separated in early infancy and subsequently brought together at an average age of 34 years, showed major similarities between the pairs of twins. The highest similarities were found on measures of sociability, intelligence and measures of stability or instability. These findings, which are in line with other studies, suggest that we inherit about 50% of our potential for these characteristics.

Other fields of human experience that seem to be underpinned by biological factors include the attachment of infants to their mothers or other caretakers, bonding between mothers and their infants and children, introversion or extraversion of personality, as well as responses to threat, such as aggressiveness and anxiety.

The psychodynamic and emotional perspectives

Sigmund Freud and his early followers, Jung and Adler, were among those who made the earliest attempts to ground the study of human experience upon a scientific, as distinct from a philosophical, basis. Freud (1856–1939) was a doctor and neurologist, and developed his theories as part of his research for a treatment for people who came to him in Vienna with disorders whose origin was inexplicable, such as sudden paralysis of limbs or the onset of blindness. In some instances, the opportunity to speak freely, expressing feelings of anger, resentment, bitterness or sexual desire, which were often kept hidden, especially in late nineteenth century Vienna, seemed to relieve the problem.

From his work, Freud developed a complex theory of psychosexual stages of human development. This has been very influential in its time, and in the past provided the main theoretical framework for trying to help troubled children, but has many critics, particularly among those who are aware of the multi-factorial underpinnings of human distress. Atkinson and colleagues (1990) have offered an objective appraisal of Freud's theories, pointing out that rigorously designed studies provide little empirical data in support of Freud's psychosexual stages; moreover, the sample of people upon whom he based his theories was far from representative. They consider, however, that he and his daughter Anna made at least three major contributions towards the understanding of human experience: first, devising the method of free association, that is, speaking whatever comes into one's mind in an uncensored way; second, elucidating the principle that much human behaviour is a compromise between our wishes and our fears and anxieties; and third, showing that much of our behaviour is influenced by processes which are non-conscious.

The behavioural and cognitive-behavioural perspectives

Behaviourism: In reaction to the claims of Freud and his followers that they had established a scientific basis for the study of human development, there arose a number of challengers. Many were concerned to place the study of human experience upon as firm an empirical foundation as the physical sciences had achieved, and J.B. Watson (1930), for example, in an attempt to employ a means of gathering information and evidence in such a way that it could be tested and verified, proposed *behaviour* as a phenomenon which could be observed, measured and recorded by observers. Building upon the work of Pavlov, he was able to demonstrate that a great deal of learning takes place via a process known as 'conditioning'. The term was used because it referred to the learning of a behaviour *on condition that* it was associated with another event. Two main forms of conditioning have been distinguished: classical conditioning and operant conditioning:

- *Classical conditioning* is the learning of a behaviour because it is associated in time with a specific stimulus with which it was not formerly associated. An example of this is the child who has had a hospital admission, who subsequently shows fear when he or she encounters someone in a white coat—say, when going to the butcher's shop. The white coat, formerly a neutral object, has become associated with distress and thus elicits the fear response in the child.
- *Operant conditioning* is the learning of a behaviour because it *operates upon* and is affected by the environment. In essence, if a behaviour is followed by an outcome or response which is pleasurable or rewarding to the person or animal concerned, the behaviour is likely to be repeated: if it is followed by an outcome which is not pleasurable, it is less likely to be repeated. If, for example, a shy student contributes in class and what is said is acknowledged constructively by the tutor, that person is likely to contribute again; if what is said is ridiculed, the student is less likely to contribute again.

Cognitive-behavioural theory—a development of social learning theory: Behavioural theory seems to present the person as the passive recipient of the conditioning process: cognitive-behavioural theory (deriving from social learning theory) incorporates what is known about the laws of how patterns of behaviour are learned but also places far more emphasis upon the context of that learning. Herbert (1981) emphasised that learning takes place *within a social context*; for example, Billy may come to understand the subtleties of the systems of which he is part and in the light of these think through various strategies for getting what he wants. Thus, while he may have learned that when he asks his Mum for sweets she just ignores him unless it is Sunday, he may also have noticed that if he asks on weekdays in a way that makes her laugh, he is more likely to get them. In these circumstances, Billy may learn to be a joker because the attention and rewards he gets from his joking teach him go on trying to make people laugh.

I shall consider very briefly three important concepts within social learning/cognitive-behavioural theory:

- Learning via reinforcement and feedback.
- Learning by imitation and modelling.
- Learning through cognitive processes.

LEARNING VIA REINFORCEMENT AND FEEDBACK   There is no doubt that parents, child-minders, teachers and all who have the care of children and young people practise the principles of reinforcing certain patterns of behaviour and sanctioning others. When Danny drinks up his milk and his mother tells him, 'You *have* done well!', she is rewarding his drinking up his milk and giving him positive feedback. When Jenny shows her mother a painting she has done at playgroup and her Mum says, 'We can't take messy paper home: you must leave it here', she may in effect be 'punishing' Jenny. She will certainly be discouraging her from painting pictures 'to show Mummy'. These little scenes capture the processes of feedback which parents and all those who have the care of children and young people offer those in their charge throughout the day. *The carers may or may not be aware of the consequences of their reactions and they may or may not intend those consequences, but they happen whether they are aware of them or intend them or not.* The meanings of the terms are as follows:

1. *A reinforcer.*   This is anything which has the effect of increasing the probability of the behaviour which preceded it occurring again. It can be positive or negative.
2. *Positive reinforcement.*   This is any event which has the effect of increasing the probability of the behaviour which preceded it occurring again; for example, appreciation, praise, thanks, promotion and salaries. A child commended for trying hard at her school work is likely to continue to try hard; a social worker thanked by her team manager for her support to the team is likely to continue to behave supportively to others in the team.
3. *Negative reinforcement/feedback.*   This may be hard to understand. Technically, it is any happening which, because it is unpleasant (e.g. the sound of a pneumatic drill), has a rewarding effect when it stops. It may therefore increase a behaviour. For example, if a toddler is whining and crying and, when her father shouts at her, she stops, this stopping crying is likely to increase the frequency of the father shouting at her. The stopping crying acts as a 'negative reinforcer' to the father's shouting. In popular parlance, the

expression 'negative reinforcement' is often, mistakenly, confused with and used instead of the more accurate expression
'punishment' or 'penalty'.
4. *Punishment, penalty or sanction.* This is any event which has the
effect of decreasing the probability of recurrence of the behaviour that preceded it. There are two types of punishment:
one is the occurrence of an unpleasant event following a behaviour; the other is the loss of a pleasant event following a
behaviour.

Watson and Tharp (1981) clarify the distinctions between negative reinforcement and the two types of punishment as follows:

• *Negative reinforcement.* 'Behaviour . . . escapes or avoids a (usually unpleasant) consequence; this strengthens the behaviour.'
Another example is that studying may be increased in school
children by removing threats of loss of pocket money, contingent upon behaviour.
• *Punishment, type 1.* 'Behaviour . . . leads to some unpleasant
event; this makes the behaviour less probable.' For example, a
child's hitting other children may be reduced by its being consistently followed by the child's being excluded from play with
other children.
• *Punishment, type 2.* 'Behaviour . . . leads to the loss of something pleasant; this also makes the behaviour less probable.' For
example, a child's swearing may be reduced by people walking
away whenever it occurs.

Both 'rewards' and 'punishments', however, are highly idiosyncratic, so that while for many children a smack may be a powerful
punishment and discourage the behaviour which preceded it, for
others, the smacks may be actively rewarding—since *for them, any
attention is better than none.* This is a very important theoretical
point. Box 2.1 illustrates the ways in which different patterns of
response to a given pattern of behaviour often act to increase or
decrease the probability of that pattern of behaviour occurring
again.
   Much learning seems to occur via a series of feedback loops, as
shown in Figure 2.4 (Emmet, 1987). For example, learning the
language of one's community, while underpinned by genetically
based factors, is obviously learned by the feedback a child receives.

Box 2.1: Behaviours, consequences and their probable outcomes
(reproduced with permission from Sutton, 1994)

Desirable behaviour	+ reinforcement (reward)	→	more desirable behaviour
Desirable behaviour	+ no reinforcement	→	less desirable behaviour
Undesirable behaviour	+ reinforcement (reward)	→	more undesirable behaviour
Undesirable behaviour	+ no reinforcement	→	less undesirable behaviour

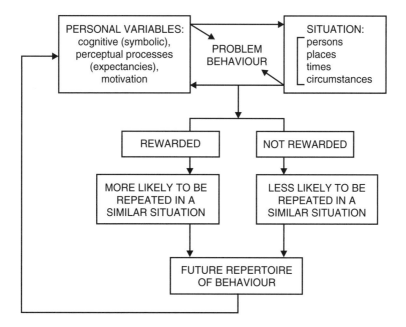

Figure 2.4: A feedback loop suggested by cognitive-behavioural theory
(reproduced with permission from Emmet, 1987)

Other behaviours, including problem behaviour, may be learned in similar ways. If, for example, a child is rude to a teacher and the teacher not only tolerates this, but the young person's friends admire him for it, then being rude to the teacher is likely to happen again. Such sequences can escalate into full confrontations and even violence.

LEARNING BY OBSERVATION, IMITATION AND MODELLING   Cognitive behavioural theory also takes account of 'modelling'—that is, the way in which people imitate others, particularly those with status and with influence over them. Parents or caregivers are likely to be the first models whom young children imitate—their language, their accents, their choice of words, as well as their customary ways of behaving and their attitudes. Children learn specific roles at least partly through imitation; for example, children tend to imitate the parent or caregiver of the same sex, particularly if the parent is seen as nurturant and influential. If girls see mostly men in positions of influence and authority, such as doctors, business executives, judges and politicians, they have little opportunity to imitate women in such roles and are more likely to take subordinate roles for themselves.

There is evidence that much behaviour, pro- and anti-social, is learned by imitation. The power of peer group pressure upon young people is well established, and many young offenders have learned their behaviour by taking influential members of their peer groups as models. There are good reasons for calling institutions for young offenders 'universities of crime'. Bandura (1986) has written extensively about these processes of modelling.

LEARNING THROUGH COGNITIVE PROCESSES   Mischel (1973) has considered some of the individual differences in thinking, judging and valuing which contribute to the very personal ways in which we perceive and behave in day-to-day life. He also emphasised the multi-dimensional interactions which are implicit in human affairs and incorporated this awareness into social learning theory. For example, while people are much influenced by their upbringing and socialisation experiences, they may become very aware and critical of them, and actively choose not to follow similar approaches in bringing up their own children.

The cognitive perspective

This perspective focuses upon the perceptual, thinking, judging and intellectual processes of human beings. It takes account of the evidence that we are not simply driven by unconscious forces or reacting to stimuli in the environment: we form opinions, we judge others' actions and attitudes, we consider other alternatives, we plan strategies and are creative in our efforts to make sense of the experience of being alive. According to this perspective, human beings gather and process information and take action on their view of this information.

Piaget (1896–1980), the renowned cognitive child psychologist, monitored the growth of children's cognitive capacities as they passed through various stages of development. These appear to correspond with stages of brain development, showing, for example, that these stages follow a predictable sequence in all children—although some children will pass through them more swiftly than others. There is no space here to consider the detail of Piaget's work, but it is important that health visitors and social workers are familiar with the concepts he developed so that they can understand the limitations of young children's capacities to grasp ideas—for example, *the notion that people really do see the world and things that happen in it differently*: they attend to different things, they remember different things and they put different interpretations upon what they have perceived; reality is, as I have already indicated, akin to 'seeing pictures in the fire'.

Further, children also make judgements about events which, because of their immaturity and inexperience or the ways in which they may have been told to interpret events, may be inaccurate and in some instances completely wrong. A child whose parent, in a moment of exasperation, says, 'You are a bad/horrible/wicked child', may believe what has been said into adulthood and beyond; another may witness sexual intercourse and believe that the people concerned are fighting and that someone is being hurt; while a third, who has been abused, may have been threatened that if she tells anyone about what has occurred she will get ill or will be 'sent away'. Young children are trapped in their perceptions and interpretations.

The humanistic perspective

This view of humanity is concerned with positive and optimistic features of human experience. Two psychologists who have re-dressed the tendency of researchers to focus upon human pathology and have reasserted a constructive view of people and their potential for growth and development are Abraham Maslow (1908–1970) and Carl Rogers (1902–1987). Maslow's (1970) hierarchy of human needs is familiar to many students. Rogers, his contemporary, believed that human beings demonstrate one basic 'tendency and striving—to actualise, maintain and enhance the experiencing organism'. He therefore sought to identify the circumstances and conditions that other people could provide, which would help them reach such potential. Rogers, together with those who have subjected his theories to detailed investigation, such as Truax and Carkhuff (1967), identified several features which seem reliably to contribute to helping people in distress:

- *Unconditional positive regard* by the therapist or worker for the client.
- *An attitude of personal warmth* towards him or her.
- *The capacity for empathy*, so that the person feels deeply understood.
- *Congruence*, the notion of being genuine, of not playing a part.

These concepts have emerged from repeated studies as key components of helpful counselling and are cornerstones of 'client-centred counselling'. This same sensitive regard for people in distress, and especially for troubled children, is taken for granted in what I am advocating. While our efforts to help children and their families will usually go beyond counselling, they are underpinned by the same attitudes of respect and concern for people in distress which have proved so beneficial within counselling.

EXPLORING PRINCIPLES OF COGNITIVE-BEHAVIOURAL THEORY

Having briefly introduced five main perspectives within psychology, I wish now to explore cognitive-behavioural theory in greater depth. This rather clumsy expression refers to a body of concepts and principles which incorporates both cognitive perspectives and those deriving from behavioural perspectives. As indicated, an earlier name for this body of concepts and principles was social learning theory, which emphasised that behaviours are learned in a social context, but the expression 'cognitive-behavioural theory' seems to be emerging as the preferred term.

We saw above (p. 49) that much behaviour is *learned*, both by imitation or modelling and in accordance with certain contingencies of reward and sanction. This understanding is extremely important: it provides us with the means of analysing undesirable patterns of behaviour to see if they are being maintained by the rewards which are, often unwittingly, being provided by parents or caregivers; alternatively, we can see whether desired patterns of behaviour, which occur only occasionally, are fading away because, unintentionally, parents are punishing them or failing to reward them.

Meeting Children's Needs for Attention

Children need attention. Children need a great deal of individualised attention and nothing in this book should be interpreted as suggesting otherwise. Light may be thrown upon the behaviour of troubled children in an important paper by Howlin (1998) upon autism, in which the author discusses how this condition makes it very difficult for affected children to have any clear impact upon their environment. Howlin cites the work of Durand and Carr (1991) and suggests that 'the five main functions of aggressive, self-injurious, stereotyped or other disruptive behaviours' are as follows:

A. To indicate the need for help or attention.
B. To escape from stressful situations or activities.
C. To obtain desired objects.
D. To protest against unwanted events/activities.
E. To obtain stimulation.

While these five functions of troubled behaviour have been distinguished in the context of the study of autism, I suggest that they are relevant to *all* children. In other words, many children with serious behaviour difficulties are seeking to meet one or other of the above needs. It follows that while it may well be impossible and inappropriate to try to avoid frustrating them or to give them desired objects whenever they demand them, this way of looking at children's behaviour does suggest that children seek and need extensive attention. *Adults have responsibility for responding to those needs, but in ways and at times which help children learn pro-social behaviour.* Thus, to attend extensively to Darren when he has just bitten another child at a playgroup will teach him that this is an effective way of gaining attention from adults; to ignore him or reprimand him briefly at that time but to give him individual attention at another available time is likely both to meet his needs and to help him learn to live acceptably with other children.

Box 2.2:   Patterns of young children's play (after Bee, 1992)

1. *Sensorimotor play.*   Children of about 12 months explore and manipulate objects, mouthing them, shaking them and moving them along the floor.
2. *Constructive play.*   By the age of two, children are building towers, making patterns with shapes, using blocks which fit together, twist and so on.
3. *First pretend play.*   Young children begin to 'feed Teddy' and 'put dolly to bed'. They experiment with roles by putting on hats or Mummy's shoes.
4. *Substitute pretend play.*   Around two or three years, children begin to let one thing stand for another: boxes become boats or cars; clay can stand for food; and imagination, given rein, can invent rich fantasy games.
5. *Sociodramatic play.*   Children begin to take on roles: Mummy and Daddy; farmer and farmer's wife; astronaut; teacher and child. Bee suggests that this play helps them relinquish their egocentric way of understanding the world.
6. *Awareness of roles.*   Around six years, children plan their play ahead and give out roles: 'You be the teacher and I'll be the child and then we'll swop'.
7. *Games with rules.*   As children enter primary or elementary school, pretend play declines and is replaced by more and more games with specific rules.

The importance of shared play

Many of the needs of children for this individual attention will be met via play (Box 2.2). Bee (1992) has suggested that while children show several different kinds of play at any one time, there are often regular patterns of play which are noticeable as children develop. Bee makes the point that:

> . . . in some very real ways, play is children's 'work'. Opportunities to manipulate and experiment with objects, pretend with them, play parts and roles, all seem to be important ingredients in the child's cognitive and social development . . . The key point is that children need to have *time* for play—time when they are not watching TV, not organized, not required to do anything 'constructive'.

Moreover, these stages will all be enriched if the child's parents, grandparents or other caregivers can make time, even if only for a few minutes daily, to share the child's developing world of play. These times can be low-key, involving no expensive bought games, but short periods when the child is allowed to lead in the play. So, he or she may choose whether to look at a story book together, to sit on the floor with bricks, to use home-made playdough or to wash up together. Not only do these short individualised times foster the cognitive and language development of the child, but also this nurturing attention builds trust and attachment: its importance cannot be over-estimated.

Behaviour Analysis

Parents typically make very general complaints about their children. 'Steven is lazy'; 'Joanne is a horrid child'; 'John's been nothing but trouble since he was born'; 'Sanjay is naughty'. It is sometimes startling for them when I ask, 'Exactly what does Steven/Joanne/John/Sanjay *do* that upsets you so?' They usually find it very difficult to specify exactly what their child *does* but this is a crucial step in using this body of theory. We need to know precisely which *behaviours* the child displays which so upset his parents, his brothers and sisters, his teachers and sometimes himself. With help, parents can eventually identify and work out a 'problem profile' for their child. These often include some of the following:

- Aggressiveness: hits other children or parents.
- Bites other children or adults.
- Tips over furniture.
- Will not stay in bed; or demands unnecessary attention in the night.
- Refuses to do what parents ask.
- Throws food.
- Does not settle to anything for more than a few minutes: short attention span.
- Demands mother's attention so that she cannot talk to anyone else.
- Swears at mother or visitors to the house.
- Spits at family members.

I also ask them if they can identify positive or pleasing aspects of their child's behaviour, aspects that they would like to see more of, and this is sometimes even more difficult for them. Sometimes they can suggest two or three things—the child's bringing home for them things made at play group; Dean's readiness to come for a cuddle; or the way Wendy, a terror while awake, sleeps all night through. Sometimes, very sadly, there is nothing that a parent can think of that they like about their child; they have already written him off at the age of three and 'can't wait until he goes to school'. Eventually, however, we are usually able to develop a 'positive profile', which may include an acknowledgement that the child:

- Occasionally carries out a request.
- Finds something which is lost.
- Feeds the dog.
- Eats well.
- Looks at picture/story books calmly.

This way of analysing what often seems to parents to be a blur of continuous misbehaviour, by distinguishing its component behaviours, at first mystifies parents but gradually they come to see the advantages of identifying specific behaviours and addressing them separately.

In my work it was necessary to ask the parents to collect two sets of behaviour counts, known as 'data' or evidence. The first record showed, on a day-by-day basis, the instances of one negative behaviour, the refusal to follow instructions or requests, while the second showed the instances of positive behaviour, carrying out requests (see Box 2.3). These records are necessary for a minimum of one week, to provide a 'baseline' or benchmark against which to measure subsequent change. They also provide the means of judging, over the weeks that followed, whether the behaviour is changing in the desired direction: that is, with negative forms of the behaviour decreasing and positive ones increasing.

Box 2.3:   Positive and negative forms of some specific behaviours

Negative form of behaviour
- Refusal/reluctance to follow requests or instructions within one minute.
- Aggressiveness; hits or bites others.
- Comes downstairs after being put to bed.
- Refuses to eat/throws food.
- Disrupts other children's activities.
- Speaks rudely to or shouts at parents.

Positive form of behaviour
- Begins to follow requests or instructions within one minute.
- Kind behaviour; shares/lends toys.
- Settles after being put to bed.

- Eats a small amount.
- Plays quietly with other children.
- Speaks calmly and quietly to parents.

Analysing the Antecedents–Behaviour–Consequence Sequence

The relationship between a behaviour and the events in the environment associated with it is called a *contingency* and it includes three components: the behaviour itself, antecedent events, both distant and immediate, and consequent events. It has proved easy to remember these important terms by referring to them as the A–B–C sequence, standing for 'Antecedents', 'Behaviour' and 'Consequences'. The term 'Activator' is sometimes clearer to use than 'Antecedent', and is useful in that it has connotations of being a cue or a trigger to behaviour. Since practice using principles of cognitive-behavioural theory involves analysing how behaviour may be affected by its antecedents, by its consequences, or by both together, let us consider some examples of each situation:

Examples of antecedents affecting behaviour

1. A Health Visitor asks a three year-old boy, who is said by his mother to be 'very naughty', to build some bricks into a tower for her. As the child moves to pick up the bricks, his mother says, 'He won't do it—he never does anything he's told to . . .' The child checks his movement towards the bricks . . .
2. A child is going back to school after being ill for a fortnight. As he gets his things ready, his father says, 'Now, are you sure you feel OK?' The boy pauses, turns pale and says he feels sick . . . He does not go to school.
3. A mother is worried about her child, who is not eating well. She prepares some food and brings it to the table. The child picks up her spoon. The mother says, 'Now, just you eat this all up!' The child puts down the spoon and turns her head away . . .

Table 2.1: Analysis of behaviour, with a focus upon *Antecedents*

Antecedent	Behaviour	Consequence
1. Health Visitor asks a child to add a brick; mother says, 'He won't do it . . .'.	Child checks his movement towards the bricks.	He does not do as asked.
2. Father says, 'Are you sure you feel OK?'.	The boy says he feels sick.	He does not go to school.
3. Mother says, 'Now just you eat this all up . . .'.	The child puts down her spoon . . .	She does not eat the food prepared for her.

Setting out the contingencies in the form of a table clarifies the analysis (Table 2.1). You will see that, in all the examples in Table 2.1, the child's undesired behaviour followed directly from what went before, the *Antecedent*. In effect, the child was cued to behave in the very way which the parents did not want. This is no-one's fault, or at least it was certainly not done with the intention of cueing the child, but it nevertheless had that effect. So there is no

Table 2.2: Analysis of behaviour showing *Consequences* affecting behaviour

Antecedent	Behaviour	Consequence
1. Dad told Danny to put the TV off.	He kept putting it on.	Eventually it was left on to give people a bit of peace.
2. Grandma told Jane to wear her blue jersey.	Jane said she wanted to wear her new red one.	Eventually Grandma gave way, so as not to seem horrid.
3. Paul was out with Mum. He demanded an ice cream. Mum refused.	He began to scream, 'I want one, you old cow!'.	Mum gave way, so that people wouldn't stare at her.

point in blaming people for being unaware of something which is extremely subtle. It is, however, how learning takes place, so it is helpful if parents and other people who look after children can come to see that sometimes we unintentionally and unwittingly *teach* children to behave in undesirable ways.

In the examples in Table 2.2 the children have learned from the *Consequences* of their behaviour that if they persist long enough and unpleasantly enough in demanding their own way, the adults will eventually give in! We may not be aware of what we are teaching children when we give in to their threats or their rudeness, *but we are ourselves teaching them to be rude and threatening just as if we told them in a classroom, 'It is right to be rude and threatening to people'.*

MAKING USE OF PRINCIPLES OF COGNITIVE-BEHAVIOURAL THEORY

Cognitive-behavioural theory is emerging from extensive research as a valuable resource for helping people. Box 2.4 draws on the work by Martin and Pear (1992) upon cognitive-behavioural approaches and also includes principles which I have found helpful in my own research. I shall then consider each one.

Box 2.4:   Cognitive-behavioural procedures (after Martin and Pear, 1992)

1. Taking account of principles of classical conditioning.
2. Getting a behaviour to occur more often with positive reinforcement or reward.
3. Encouraging perseverence through intermittent reinforcement: pitfalls of this approach.
4. Getting a behaviour to occur less often by avoiding rewarding it, so that it extinguishes or fades away.
5. Getting a behaviour to occur less often by actively penalising it.
6. Getting a behaviour to occur less often by 'response cost'.
7. Using modelling and rehearsal to affect behaviour.
8. Helping an individual child or young person to develop self-control.
9. Helping children and parents to 'take charge of' their own patterns of thought.
10. Using problem-solving approaches.

---

1. Taking Account of Principles of Classical Conditioning

The earliest formal account of this is still an excellent illustration. In 1920 two researchers, Watson and Rayner, sought to establish whether fears could be acquired simply by association. They worked with a little boy, Albert, aged 11 months, who showed no fear of a variety of objects placed on the floor near him; these included a white rat. Then, as part of the study, while Albert was watching the rat closely, one of the researchers banged a steel bar with a hammer just behind Albert's head, causing him to be startled and to cry. During two separate sessions, a week apart, the researchers linked the loud noise to the sight of the rat on seven occasions—causing Albert to show signs of great fear. Subsequently, whenever the rat appeared, Albert became very upset, trembled and cried—and these fears also spread or 'generalised' to other animals, including a dog and a rabbit.

The principle here, then, is that a neutral stimulus, in this case the rat, has acquired the capacity to elicit fear by being presented at the same time as a fear-provoking event.

An everyday example of this was suggested by a participant at one of my training events. A little girl who never objected to going to bed and who loved bedtime stories one evening was read a story which she found very frightening; thereafter, for many evenings, she became very fearful when she went to bed. Her bed, and the bedtime routine, which formerly had had neutral associations, had now acquired very frightening associations.

The means of reducing such an acquired fear is, happily, also based upon cognitive-behavioural principles. If we were seeking to help Albert overcome his fear of rats, a structured programme might be developed, as shown in Box 2.5.

This procedure is called *desensitisation*. We shall see the research evidence of its helpfulness in the chapter on helping children with

---

Box 2.5: A programme to help a child frightened of rats—little Albert

1. Albert sees other children looking at picture books of children, the seaside, farmyards and so on, while sitting on his mother's lap.
2. Albert joins other children looking at picture books.
3. Picture books containing photographs of animals are included among the books over the next few days.
4. Albert joins other children enjoying looking at photographs of animals, while with his mother who shows interest and pleasure in the photographs.
5. Over several days, Albert is taken for walks in the park where there are birds and perhaps squirrels in the distance.
6. Albert's walks include going closer to the birds and squirrels in a very calm, easy way.
7. Albert is taken past a pet shop where there are hamsters and other small animals in cages.
8. This walk is taken very frequently, in the presence of loving and unconcerned adults, who do not hurry him to overcome his fears. Rather, they are allowed to subside.
9. Albert and his mother look in the window of the pet shop where hamsters and rats are kept. They do this for several days.
10. Albert and his mother go into the pet shop and look briefly at the animals, including hamsters and rats in their cages. Everything is done lightheartedly and pleasurably.

sleeping difficulties (see Chapter 7). Similarly, in the case of the little girl who was frightened by the bedtime story, it was possible to ensure that once the origins of her fear were understood, her bedtime routine was kept calm and enjoyable, but without too much over-anxious reassurance and with only amusing and light-hearted stories when she wished for them.

2. Getting a Behaviour to Occur More Often by Means of Reward

Human beings are motivated to a very great extent by what they, individually, find rewarding. This statement may make people sound very unpleasant and selfish, but this is not intended. Sometimes the rewards are *tangible* or *material*: most people want money in the form of a salary or payment of some kind as a means to attaining both the essential and inessentials of life. How many of us, if our salaries were completely withdrawn, would continue to do the same work, or the same amount of work, for more than a few days? Many people also want certain possessions, a car, a house and things to go in it. Advertisers are constantly attempting to stimulate our readiness to want possessions by offering inducements to purchase furniture, clothing, jewellery or household goods. Children too seek tangible rewards—although, as we shall see, they are less motivated by these when they are little: they are *taught* to want material possessions as they grow older. We have learned to give things at Christmas and our materialist society seeks to teach us to place a value upon these things according to their cost.

Yet people are also motivated by *social* rewards: by the friendliness of other people, by concern and by affection. Many are also motivated by seeing the values which they hold advanced or disseminated. Some act as volunteers in activities which are important to them for years on end; others give generously to charitable causes where they will never meet the recipients. In such situations, it is the success of the projects which they support and the feeling that they are contributing towards the *furtherance of their aims and values* which is rewarding. Rewards are highly individual, even idiosyncratic, but they are nevertheless absolutely central to understanding human behaviour.

Other rewards are only available from other human beings: *we cannot be ourselves by ourselves*. We need friends and companions and contact with supportive people: these are profoundly important to our emotional well-being. To receive a letter or telephone call from a friend or an invitation from someone we like makes us feel valued, appreciated, while to have people in whom we can confide has been shown to be one of the necessities for good mental health (Brown and Harris, 1978). Thus, to receive acknowledgement of our contribution towards some success or to be thanked for a kindness is a very rewarding experience: indeed, we often feel under-valued or under-appreciated if our efforts are not acknowledged in this way. These needs are particularly acute for young children: the affection and attention of their parents or dependable caregivers are absolutely essential to their psychological well-being. It follows that nurturing attention and approval are powerful social rewards for children.

As we have seen in Figure 2.1, a behaviour which is followed by a reward, whether tangible or social, is likely to increase. This suggests that commendation or 'positive feedback' from people who are important in the child's world, parents, caregivers, teachers, is, whether they are aware of it or not, making it more or less likely that certain behaviours will occur again. If we attend positively to a child's learning to feed herself, to use a potty or to dress herself, and commend her for her achievement, she is likely to continue to practise these skills. If, however, we attend positively (and rewardingly) to a child's provocation, her swearing or her smearing and throwing food, then she is likely to continue to practise *these* activities too. A close analysis of the exact Antecedents and Consequences of an aspect of behaviour is often extremely informative and illuminating.

Consider an example. Children learn and work out *from their experiences* whether fighting other children is permitted or not. Suppose that Danny, a well-built three year-old and tall for his age, has discovered that children give up their toys to him when he fights with them:

1. If both parents and all the other adults in their world prohibit fighting by disapproving reactions and by sanctions against it, he is likely gradually to learn to inhibit fighting.

2. If both parents and others approve it, by saying to him, 'You're a real boy, aren't you!', he will soon learn to develop his fighting ability.
3. If his parents approve of his fighting but his teachers disapprove, he is likely to learn to inhibit fighting at school, but because of the tendency of behaviours to generalise from one situation to another—that is, from home to school—it will not be easy for the teachers to inhibit the fighting.
4. If one parent approves and one parent disapproves, Danny will be very confused. He is likely to react erratically to this inconsistency and to resort to fighting when situations become frustrating for him.

So if we want a behaviour such as fighting to change, we have to do at least three things:

1. Get Danny's parents and *all* the people who care for him to agree that they will stop him fighting and will not let him hit other children or to take their toys away.
2. Explain to Danny that fighting is not allowed either at home or at school.
3. Find opportunities to help Danny manage mini-situations (laying a table, giving out the crayons, putting away the Lego) without fighting and then commend him warmly for this.

In theoretical terms, Danny will need the following:

- First, every instance of this success should be commended (*continuous reinforcement*).
- Later, he will need commending only occasionally (*intermittent reinforcement*).

This example is valid for the promotion of all new learning, whether for children or adults. In all cases the new learning will be acquired most effectively and most enjoyably if early instances of the newly acquired behaviour are noticed, appreciated and commended by the teacher or instructor. If you doubt this, think back to your own learning in childhood: to read, to swim, or to ride a bicycle. Or think of learning a new skill as an adult: to drive a car or to use a word-processor. Try to recall whether this learning was accompanied by encouragement or criticism or perhaps by no feedback at all. Finally, remember what the effect of these various responses was upon your learning.

3. Getting a Behaviour to Persist Through Occasional Reward, but Noting Pitfalls

As children learn new skills, such as how to dress themselves or use cutlery or chopsticks, they are typically commended on most occasions at the outset by the smiles and praise of those who care for them: as indicated, this is called *continuous* reinforcement. This is as true for adults as for children. As learners become more proficient, however, teachers either consciously or unconsciously realise that only an occasional reassurance is necessary—'You're getting on well with that, Jane', or 'You're doing fine, Winston; keep going'. This is called *intermittent* or *occasional* reinforcement.

This principle operates, however, for good or ill. Children need much encouragement as they learn the skills required of them in the educational system and adults need much encouragement from their spouses, partners and relatives to continue with the demanding tasks of bringing up children to be constructive members of society. But the principle also operates in ordinary, day-to-day life. Indeed, thousands, millions of people regularly buy tickets in the National Lottery because they anticipate that one day they will win a substantial reward. Although their better judgement may tell them that this is unlikely, the pay-out of small, £10, rewards on an occasional basis keeps them buying lottery tickets week by week.

It is known from laboratory studies and from everyday life that behaviours which have been rewarded only occasionally tend to persist and are very hard to change. An everyday example of this is a child, Johnny, who has got into the habit of coming to his parents' bed at least twice a night. Sometimes they let him into their bed and sometimes they don't. His parents, short of space and weary, decide to encourage him to sleep in his own bed. They agree to return him to his own bed every single time he appears at their bedside and to commend him every morning for remaining in his own bed. They are eventually successful by using *continuous* reward. Perhaps, however, after several weeks of successfully following this plan, Johnny, awakened by chance, once again appears at their bedside at 2.00 a.m.; on this occasion the parents, being particularly tired, again allow him to get in and sleep with them. It is highly likely that Johnny will reappear the following night, for he has effectively been taught to do so on an *intermittent* basis—that is, he has been occasionally rewarded for coming to his parents' bed. To repeat, behaviours which are occasionally rewarded are very hard to change.

A participant in one of my workshops recounted how her young son, when she had said 'No' to something he very much wanted, pestered and pestered her to give way. Eventually, exasperated, she said to him, 'I have said No—you cannot do this. Why do you keep on trying to make me change my mind?'. The little boy replied, 'You did once'.

This theoretical issue is extremely important. *It is operating whether we are aware of it or not* and it underpins the importance of parents, teachers and caregivers attempting to be as consistent as possible in their ways of responding to children's behaviours. If they say one thing one day and another the next the child does not know where he stands: similarly, if one parent or family member reacts angrily to being sworn at one day, but lets the child get away with it the next, the child will persist in swearing.

4. Getting a Behaviour to Occur Less Often by Avoiding Rewarding It

If a behaviour is not rewarded, it will tend to die away; the technical name for this is 'extinguishing'. This, too, will happen whether people intend it or not or whether they are aware of it or not. For example, when I worked in a Child and Family Centre, a mother told me that her daughter's teacher was very upset by the behaviour of her daughter, aged seven. The little girl was much distressed by the death of her father and was very unsettled both at home and at school; she constantly left her seat to go to the teacher's desk seeking help with her work. The teacher, aware of the little girl's distress and anxious not to reject her, attended to her every time she went to her desk—*so, unintentionally, making this behaviour more likely to recur*. This situation was, however, both intruding upon the rights of other children to the teacher's time and causing the teacher acute conflict. Using cognitive-behavioural theory, we can see that the teacher was unwittingly reinforcing the very behaviour she wanted to discourage. The solution would have been to give the little girl the absolute minimum of attention each time she went to the teacher's desk, so that this behaviour gradually extinguished and to give her individualised attention when the teacher was in a position to give her time—for example, at the end of the lesson.

Here the principle for reducing the frequency of a behaviour is, first undertake the A–B–C analysis and then, when you have established which rewards are maintaining the undesired behaviour, withdraw those rewards altogether. If this is inappropriate then one should gradually reduce them so that the behaviour slowly dies away. This last is particularly relevant if the reward which is maintaining a behaviour is attention.

Many petty misbehaviours can be reduced and even eliminated in this way. Children's whining and demanding are particularly stressful to adults, but can be reduced by showing the child that you are not attending to them. Getting out a Hoover and actively attending to the dust on the carpet gives an extremely clear message to a grizzling child and can be done every time the whining starts!

5. Getting a Behaviour to Occur Less Often by Actively Penalising It

Some behaviours are too serious to be ignored. One cannot ignore a child's biting or hitting another child, nor deliberate disobedience, nor disruption of other people's or children's activities. Sometimes clear penalties are necessary. Consider the issue of smacking, still advocated by many parents as the best means of chastising children, but clearly contrary to the Children Act 1989:

Pros and cons of smacking
Pros: It is quick and the effects are immediate.
        It tells the child, Don't do that!
        It relieves the parent's feelings.
Cons: It provides the child with a model of aggression to imitate.
        It does not tell the child what he/she should do instead of the unwanted behaviour.
        It loses its effect if frequently used.
        It may become a reward if it is virtually the only attention a child gets.

Using Time Out/Calm Down

A *far* more effective penalty than smacking is to use the principle of withdrawing attention by placing misbehaving children in a situation where they are not receiving any rewarding attention at all. This is called placing them in Time Out, although the term Calm Down Time is increasingly favoured as explaining more clearly what is meant to happen during the period of being ignored. Webster-Stratton and Herbert (1994) have distinguished three forms of Time Out, of increasing effectiveness (Box 2.6).

Box 2.6:   Different levels of Time Out (reproduced with permission from Webster-Stratton and Herbert, 1994)

- *Activity Time Out,* where the child is simply barred from joining in an enjoyable activity but still allowed to observe it, e.g. having misbehaved, he or she is made to sit out of a game.
- *Room Time Out,* where he or she is removed from an enjoyable activity, is not allowed to observe this, but is not totally isolated, e.g. having misbehaved, he or she is seated at the far end of the sitting room or a classroom.
- *Exclusion Time Out,* where he or she is briefly isolated in a situation away from the reinforcing contingencies, e.g. in a hallway or empty room (unlocked).

Young children can be placed on a cushion or chair in the corner of the room; older children can be placed in a safe hallway. I myself recall being stood in the corner after some small misdemeanour; I was mystified and bored. I don't recall having it explained to me why I was being stood in the corner, or what I should do to avoid this boredom on another occasion. It is now known that such an explanation helps a child understand what is happening, and is now built into this work at the Planning stage. Other strategies which work to the same ends and which have been reported to me as effective during training sessions include:

- Holding a child who struggles against being placed in Time Out *very* firmly by the hand or wrist so that he cannot run off, but offering 'no speech, no eye contact'. The time period is two to

Box 2.7: Guidelines for using Time Out/Calm Down

1. If you decide to use Time Out, explain it to the child or young person beforehand.
2. Give one warning only before carrying it through.
3. Never threaten to use Time Out and then fail to follow through.
4. Never use a frightening place for Time Out; use a place that is safe, unrewarding and dull: see three forms of Time Out (Webster-Stratton and Herbert (1994), see Box 2.6).
5. Always check for safety.
6. Never lock a child in a room. Just keep returning him or her to the Time Out/Calm Down place, insisting that he or she stays, until the 'penny drops' with the child that you really mean it.
7. A useful rule of thumb for how long a child should remain in Time Out/Calm Down is the number of minutes corresponding to the child's age. Thus:
   A 2 or 3 year-old remains 2 minutes on each occasion.
   A 4–9 year-old remains 4 minutes on each occasion.
   A 10 year-old remains 10 minutes on each occasion, and so on.
8. There is no point in making the Time Out period very long. We are trying to help a child learn a new association between misbehaving and the inevitability of the penalty. He or she will learn this association best from having every instance of misbehaving followed consistently by a brief Time Out period.
9. If the child who has been placed in Time Out repeats the misbehaviour on emerging, he or she goes straight back into Time Out/Calm Down. If need be, repeat this as many as 15 (or more) times a day, so that a new association is learned as soon as possible.
10. The person who puts the child in Time Out/Calm Down takes him or her out.
11. Keep a simple record of how often you have had to use Time Out/Calm Down day by day. This will show if instances of the misbehaviour are increasing or decreasing.
12. *Things may get worse before they get better.* This is important. Having 'ruled the roost' for so long, the child will work hard and misbehave all the more to keep his or her dominant and controlling position. If you persist, however, the message will eventually be learned: *you* are in charge now.

three minutes. This is said to be effective for a young but obstreperous child in understaffed classrooms!

- Other children in a family or small class are asked actively to ignore the misbehaving child for the Time Out interval each time he misbehaves.
- The mother herself leaves the child without an audience and goes to the bathroom for the Time Out interval—having checked the room where the child is for safety.

A warning should always be given to the child so that he or she can anticipate what may happen, but if the misbehaviour persists then the warning *must* be acted upon. The term 'naughty chair' is increasingly frowned upon in educational circles: the 'thinking chair' (as providing an opportunity for reflection upon transgression) is apparently acceptable.

The optimum Time Out period for primary school children is four minutes (Hobbs, Forehand and Murray, 1978); a two or three year-old responds to two-minute exclusions, a four to nine year-old to four minute ones and thereafter according to age. A kitchen timer is useful here. The procedure should be explained to the child (see Planning, p. 118) who should be told that he cannot rejoin the other members of the family or group until the bell has rung and he has stopped crying. Whoever puts the child into Time Out takes him out. If the child will not stay where he is put, the parent can either be very assertive and insist that he stays until fetched or, if he cannot be stopped from rejoining the family, they should totally ignore him/her until the time interval has elapsed. Alternatively, a mother alone may explain to the child that she will go into the bathroom with a magazine for the specified number of minutes—this having the required effect of ensuring that the child does not receive gratifying attention. Guidelines for using Time Out/Calm Down are shown in Box 2.7.

6. Getting a Behaviour to Occur Less Often by 'Response Cost'

This is a variant of the above methods for reducing the frequency of a behaviour. The essence is that a person, child or adult, is awarded the full potential reward *before* the problematic situation occurs. For example, a child is given his/her pocket money on a

Saturday for the forthcoming week. It is made clear, by negotiation with the youngster concerned, that certain infringements of rules will lead to a fine; for example, five pence for leaving a coat on the floor; 10 pence for not putting dirty clothes in the laundry basket, and so on. The point is that each undesirable behaviour, clearly discussed and written down beforehand, has a cost—which should be exacted immediately. While this practice is obviously more suitable for older rather than younger children, the principle can be used at all ages, particularly if the adults get fined too. It can be a very effective approach: the same rules can be negotiated for adults as well as young people within a family, and it is helpful if someone neutral can act as arbiter. Further, there needs to be agreement that the money so gathered will be sent to a cause agreed by all the family—not to take them all on a family outing!

7. Using Modelling and Rehearsal to Influence Behaviour

Young children are natural imitators, as we have explored above. They copy the patterns of behaviour of the adults around them, whether they or the adults are aware of it or not. While having its problems and its embarrassments, this predisposition to imitate allows us to use it to help children who are experiencing difficulties. For example, a child who is afraid of the sea can be encouraged to watch how his more confident sister sits at the edge and allows the water to touch first her toes, then her ankles and finally to wash over her legs. Very shy children or those who find it hard to make friends can be guided to watch how more confident children approach other children and make friends.

Role play and rehearsal have much to offer as strategies to help children who lack confidence. I have spent many sessions helping students practise skills of speaking up in a classroom situation and discussing with them how, by first making simple comments and then, as the weeks pass, making longer or more detailed contributions, they can gain confidence in speaking in public settings. Absolutely the same principles can be used to help children who are withdrawn or who lack confidence. Similarly, I have worked with many parents, all mothers, who needed to rehearse giving their child a clear and forthright instruction. It is fun to do and typically accompanied by a lot of laughter.

8. Helping a Child or Young Person to Develop Self-Control

Although this approach may seem only relevant for adults who seek, for example, to lose weight or to take exercise, it can be appropriate for quite young children also. They can be encouraged to develop a routine to increase the amount of time spent on a desirable but demanding skill, such as learning to read or play a musical instrument. In such a case, a 'baseline' of minutes daily spent in practice can be kept for one week, and then the parents or a teacher of the child can help her to decide for herself how long daily she wishes to practise—advising modest and attainable goals! The point is that their approval should be secondary to that of the child herself; the child is the one who decides, for example, to do her practice or homework before watching television: the adult is there not to nag but to support and commend the child's self-management.

9. Helping Children and Parents to 'Take Control' of Their Own Thinking Patterns

This refers to the very substantial evidence that to some extent at least 'we are what we think'. We are all, often unwittingly, rehearsing thoughts about and views of ourselves, many of which, as discussed earlier, we heard in childhood and adolescence: 'I'm no good'; 'I'll never amount to anything . . .'; 'I am not lovable . . .'; 'I'll never be a good mother . . .'. Young children, in need of affection, attention and clear guidelines for their behaviour, often *have learned to misbehave in order to gain this attention*—so eliciting comments like, 'You are so naughty; there must be something wrong with you', and 'I've got two children, one good and one bad—and you're the bad one'. Such beliefs, frequently rehearsed, consciously or not, can undermine a child's confidence and self-esteem—for life. Sometimes they may surface in discussion with, say, an empathic counsellor, but more often they fester inside, their origin and their effect unrecognised.

Practitioners can use cognitive approaches to help both adults and children. We can ask them, in a simple way and not necessarily as part of a major counselling or therapeutic approach, what ideas and beliefs about themselves can they identify within their thought patterns. If, as is so often the case, a mother, say, can recognise her thought pattern, 'I'm a bad mother' or 'He'll never do what I say— I'm no good', understanding help can be given both in questioning such thoughts and in considering more helpful ones, for example:

I am *not* a bad mother; I have a lively three year-old whom I'm learning to manage.

He often does do what I say . . . I'm getting better at managing him.

I was unhappy as a child; my child seems much happier than I was. *I* achieved that!

No-one gets training to be a parent; I am doing a pretty good job, all considered.

Similarly, it is possible to help children practise to take control of their beliefs and substitute more constructive ones. I recently saw a video by Professor Carolyn Webster-Stratton in which she was coaching three young children, about to be excluded from school for unacceptable language, to say to themselves, 'I don't have to talk rudely; I can talk nicely to the teacher and then I won't be put out of school'. These approaches are certain to become more common as their effects enable unruly children to control themselves.

10. Problem-solving Skills

This strategy is surprisingly little known in view of its usefulness in a number of different situations, including ordinary, day-to-day difficulties. There is substantial evidence of its helpfulness in working with people with mental health problems, such as schizophrenia (Falloon, Boyd and McGill, 1984) and depression (Nezu and Perri, 1989). I believe it can be readily adapted to working with troubled children and their families.

According to Spivack, Platt and Shure (1976), problem-solving can be divided into a number of steps (see Box 2.8). This approach could readily be adapted to many of the difficulties experienced by families seeking to maintain good relaionships with their adolescents but could also be used to deal with disagreements between family members about how to deal with the troubles of younger children.

Box 2.8:   Steps of the problem-solving process (after Spivack, Platt and Shure, 1976)

1. Pinpoint the problem.
2. Gather all the relevant facts about the problem.
3. Formulate the difficulty in terms of a problem-to-be solved.
4. Generate potential solutions by means of a 'brainstorm'. Any ideas may be put forward; criticism is deliberately withheld.
5. Examine the potential consequences of each solution. How well does each one solve the problem? Agree on the best strategy/solution.
6. Plan how to implement the strategy.
7. Put the plan into action.
8. Review and evaluate the effectiveness of the plan. Adapt it as necessary.

SUMMARY OF SOME KEY PRINCIPLES OF COGNITIVE-BEHAVIOURAL THEORY

Box 2.9 shows well-tested principles arising from this body of theory. Reference will be made to those principles in later parts of this book.

Box 2.9:   Recapitulation of principles of cognitive-behavioural theory (after Martin and Pear, 1992)

Principle 1   A behaviour which is rewarded is more likely to be repeated.
Principle 2   A behaviour which is penalised is less likely to be repeated.
Principle 3   A behaviour which is consistently ignored or penalised is likely to fade away.
Principle 4   A behaviour which has been established, then ignored, but then rewarded again, is likely to start all over again.
Principle 5   A behaviour may be learned because it occurs in association with another behaviour.
Principle 6   A behaviour may be learned by imitating another's behaviour.
Principle 7   A behaviour may be acquired by thinking it through and practising it beforehand.
Principle 8   A belief can be examined to see if it is based upon sound evidence.
Principle 9   Beliefs can be tested out to see if they are accurate or not.
Principle 10   People can be helped to use problem-solving skills rather than 'rehearsing the problem'.

3

ENGAGING AND SUPPORTING PARENTS AND FAMILIES

No matter how sound the theoretical base for one's work and no matter how great the enthusiasm of the practitioner to help families in this way, it is essential that there should be a number of supportive structures in place before work can begin. It is no good expecting hard-pressed professionals, already carrying large caseloads, to take on the necessary work without additional time and resources. This is skilled work, requiring training for practitioners and time for them to do the extra work; if it is attempted without such resources, it will fail and matters will be worse than before.

Once these support mechanisms are in place, there are a number of principles for engaging and supporting families. Thus, this chapter will consider first, for some children, the statutory context provided by the Children Act 1989, and the organisational support necessary for working with children in preventive ways; second, what the evidence suggests in respect of the best methods for giving support; third, the difficulties of getting alongside families and collaborating with them; fourth, the importance of being aware of and responsive to cultural factors; and finally, the importance of developing a positive focus for the work.

CHILDREN WITHIN A STATUTORY AND ORGANISATIONAL CONTEXT

An extremely important group of troubled children fall directly within the scope of the Children Act 1989. Under Section 17 of the Act, local authorities have a duty to safeguard and promote the welfare of 'children in need'. They are responsible for supporting families in bringing up their children and must provide services, including accommodation, for them. The Act states:

> For the purposes of this Part a child shall be taken to be in need if:
>
> (a) he [sic] is unlikely to achieve or maintain, or have the opportunity of achieving or maintaining, a reasonable standard of health and development without the provision of services by a local authority under this Part;
> (b) his health or development is likely to be significantly impaired, or further impaired, without the provision for him of such services; or,
> (c) he is disabled.

There is very wide variation in the interpretation of the concept of 'a child in need' in local authorities in Britain (Colton, Drury and Williams, 1995), and in the resources made available to help families in difficulties. A Department of Health report, *Child Protection: Messages from Research* (Department of Health, 1995) summarised research in this crucial field and found considerable variations in practice—differing thresholds for action concerning the children, differing amounts of resources available to support families and, in cases of suspected abuse, different criteria for action. The authors of this report, Bullock, Little, Millham and Mount, considered how professionals can best protect children. While they were concerned with research upon children who have already experienced abuse, or who were seriously at risk of being abused, there is much overlap between these children and those we are considering. In my own work, for example, mothers explicitly said, 'I don't know how I keep my hands off the child' and 'I could put my hands round his neck . . .'.

Bullock et al (Department of Health, 1995) posed the question, '. . . what guidance does the research offer on how to ensure children's safety?', and they answer their question:

Although they approached the issue from different angles, it is significant that all the studies identified five pre-conditions of effective practice to protect children and promote their welfare:

Sensitive and informed professional/client relationships.

An appropriate balance of power between participants.

A wide perspective on child protection.

Effective supervision and training of social workers.

Services which enhance children's general quality of life.

If these conditions prevail, outcomes for children are generally better at all stages of the protection process. This is the key finding of the research programme.

The same pre-conditions of effective practice are also relevant to preventive work. First, however, I reiterate the necessity for carefully planned and structured organisational support being made available to offer the intensive help required by parents with troubled children, whether they have been abused or not and whether they are technically seen as 'children in need' or not. For example, in Leicestershire in the UK, specific teams of social workers, now named Intensive Support Teams, were initiated in 1980 as part of a larger Child Care Strategy. One of their key roles is to work with families in order to avoid the necessity of children being accommodated under the Children Act 1989. The teams, comprising several social workers and a team leader, work intensively with small caseloads so that, if need be, they can visit families twice or even three times weekly, in order to engage family members and offer them support. The evidence from these teams shows that they *are* able to prevent substantial numbers of children from being accommodated. The workers are now extremely experienced and are able to support both families and other practitioners within the authority and, if appropriate, to receive referrals from them.

Establishing such strategies requires the involvement and support of large numbers of people, specifically members of the Social Services Committee of the local authority. To move from offering a reactive to a preventive service requires major investment, both financial and organisational. Yet it is only common sense to help children before their troubles become entrenched. The logic of this argument is now being recognised at Central Government level, so it may in future be less difficult to achieve investment in preventive services.

DEVELOPING SENSITIVE RELATIONSHIPS

When working with families or parents, it is essential to offer them the unconditional positive regard which Rogers (1951) and his fellow researchers have shown to be central in the field of helpful counselling. Showing empathy, concern and respect underpins the work of parent education and training. Bullock et al (Department of Health, 1995) wrote, concerning child protection:

> The most important condition for success is the quality of the relationship between a child's family and the professionals responsible. Terms used in the research publications vary: alliance, empowerment, support and information all occur, but each implies a conscious attempt to incorporate the family into the investigation and protection plan . . .

This is precisely the approach which effective workers adopt when working to engage families with troubled children. Some of its components are considered below.

Using Listening Skills: Enabling Parents to Vent Their Feelings

As in any distressing situation, it will almost certainly help those with whom we work if we *listen* to them—often extensively. Some parents will need only the opportunity to express their anxiety, depression or distress but others may need longer as they test us out for understanding or trustworthiness. Wherever possible, it seems desirable to devote much of one's first meeting with a mother or father simply to being there and accepting the bitterness, anger, despair, fear or the sea of other emotions which parents experience when they have done their best to cope with troubled and often troublesome children.

This stage must not be rushed. If people are tense with anxiety and anger they are physiologically very 'aroused': their adrenalin levels will be high and this is experienced subjectively as very uncomfortable. If we are to help, we must give time for this level of tension to subside, typically by offering an opportunity to express or pour out the feelings and frustrations formerly held in check. Our response must be empathic, non-judgemental and must convey our active wish to be supportive. This response on our part often leads the way to the parent's becoming open to considering her child's behaviour more objectively—a step which may be almost impossible if we do not allow the time for parents' agitation to subside.

Often, of course, the feelings which are expressed do not relate solely to the child or children: they concern the parent's partner, parents, in-laws or even neighbours. Readers may reasonably ask where one draws the line between becoming over-involved in the many interlocking strands of history or current circumstances which together seem to contribute to the child's difficulties. I can only report my own experience in the research which I described above: because it was necessary for practical reasons to focus primarily upon the day-to-day interactions between parents and child, I listened as long as time permitted to the many difficulties described, but then gently brought the speaker back to the practicalities of managing the aggressiveness, destructiveness or other behaviour difficulties. This was in part because the work was a research study, with a tight structure and only limited time, but also partly because I could easily have lost my own sense of direction had I tried to address the many, many problem areas, practical and in terms of relationships, which the parents described.

Field social workers may have particular difficulties in this respect, in that many of them will visit families because of a referral in respect of a child and will come to realise, in the course of their assessment, that the child is experiencing either harsh or seriously inconsistent parenting or that he or she is being neglected. In other words, there are issues of child protection involved. I know from my own experience that there is no space within the caseload of a mainstream field social worker to incorporate time-consuming sessions on parenting in such situations. In these circumstances, social workers who have attended my training sessions on 'Parenting Positively' have proposed two ways forward: first, that the 'regular' social worker continues to deal with, for example, the statutory aspects of the work while a colleague undertakes a circumscribed piece of work with the parents of, say, eight weekly one-hour sessions with two follow-up sessions; or second, for a specialist worker whose work is primarily related to parent education and training to be appointed by the Social Services Department. Both strategies take a preventive rather than a reactive approach.

Getting Alongside Families

We need to show families that we are, or wish to be, alongside them in their efforts to help their children. Although the Children Act 1989 does not actually use the expression 'partnership with parents', this phrase has come to be seen as one of the cornerstones of the Act, as workers seek to empower parents to care for their children effectively and to avoid removing them unless there are the gravest of circumstances. This is easier said than done, for the fear of losing their children is so great among some families that there is an almost immediate negative reaction to those of us with statutory powers.

Experienced practitioners confirm that almost the only way forward with families who are hostile to us and to their children is deep empathy. This may well be inappropriate if there are serious issues of child protection, but if this is not so, then sincere empathy can sometimes reach the most rejecting and defensive parents. A highly skilled colleague of mine has described how she can say, genuinely, 'How have you coped with this situation for all these years?—I could not have done so', as she hears of parents who have spent five and six hours a night awake with their apparently tireless toddler, or 'You feel you've done your very best for your child, and all he can do is to call you foul names—how have you borne it?' This demonstration of understanding and empathy can act as balm to a parent who has given up all hope of gaining help for her child or for herself. As has been found in a counselling context, this non-blaming understanding and acceptance lays an essential foundation for subsequent work and opens the way to enabling people to unburden themselves of sometimes years of pent-up emotion.

With a strong relationship as a foundation, we can draw upon a range of strategies to support families. We can sometimes help parents who are having current difficulties by involving other parents who have successfully learned skills of parenting positively;

other parents often have greater credibility than professionals. Sometimes the word gets round that the health visitors or social workers who run groups for parents really do have a lot to offer. Sometimes, however, we can only continue to show reliability, honesty and goodwill and hope that this will eventually win families' confidence. In my own case, I speak briefly of my personal difficulties as a mother, as I find that this helps other mothers to accept that I am speaking from experience!

It may be useful during this early stage to find out what other forms of help families have already sought or received in connection with their child's difficulties. If they have met with a worker whom you know, and report that he or she was unhelpful, it is tempting to collude with the parent's view of the worker, but professional standards should prevail; one needs to note the parent's perception but to avoid reinforcing it. Other families may report similar views of our own practice on another occasion! Useful and important information may be forthcoming, however, concerning the types of help which parents have sought and from whom it has been received: medication in the form of sedatives or other drugs; various forms of therapy; counselling, as offered by general practitioners, psychiatrists or paediatricians, social workers, health visitors, school nurses and counsellors. This information should all be noted.

I am sometimes asked what language to use when families employ words local to their neighbourhood to describe their child or some aspect of family life. I try to use the same terms, for example 'pissed off', for feeling depressed or upset, 'a mardy child', for one who grizzles or cries a lot, or 'getting caught', for becoming pregnant. If we are meeting in a group, I tend to use the family word alongside one which other group members would recognise. The whole point is to put people at their ease but also to promote clear communication.

Emphasising a Collaborative Approach with Parents

It is vital when working with families to avoid giving the impression that we are the 'experts' in bringing up children. Each parent will know more about his or her child than we can ever hope or wish to know; they are the experts, but we have gathered some useful knowledge and skills by way of training and experience. The approach that has been found useful is essentially a collaborative one. Indeed, Patterson (1975) calls this empowering of parents the 'Golden Rule', and O'Dell (1985) advocates interventions which 'heavily involve the parent, seek his or her advice and treat him or her more like a co-therapist than a patient . . .'. We can acknowledge that we have received some relevant training or have had particular experience but in essence we are seeking to collaborate with families, to empower them, to pass on what we have learned, but also to learn from their experience in bringing up their child. The same point is made by Webster-Stratton and Herbert (1994) in their excellent book, *Troubled Families: Problem Children*.

DEVELOPING AWARENESS OF CULTURAL ISSUES

If we are to engage parents to work with us, then we need to develop our awareness of the cultural diversity of families in Britain. Here I am referring both to issues which affect families belonging to ethnic minorities and to those belonging to cultural minorities.

Awareness of the Wider Family Context

Each culture has its own ways of dealing with family difficulties: in some, it is the convention to seek help from outsiders to manage domestic tensions, so to go to a GP or to a family counselling organisation is natural and totally acceptable; in others, such a step is outrageous, deeply disloyal to the family and a cause of additional stress. The professional or counsellor cannot ordinarily know whether seeking help for an unhappy child is acceptable or not to the family of the child concerned, but we must be alert to every possibility. Increasingly, I have come to the view that as British society grows ever more diverse, we can make very few generalisations indeed: every single family is special, with its own culture and conventions. I have also concluded, however, that each person within each family seeks *respect* from others, both for him or herself and for the family of which he or she is part.

This attempt to be sensitive to individual families and to individual sets of parents places major responsibilities upon workers, for it means that we must make no assumptions. We must attempt to rid ourselves of preconceptions and, in particular, those which pertain to people who are often marginalised: lone parents, families where the sexual orientation of the parents is gay or lesbian, families in which fathers are the main carers for their children, families belonging to ethnic minorities. Forehand and Kotchik (1996) have published an important paper entitled 'Cultural diversity: a wake-up call for parent training'. This draws further attention to the fact that parent education and training must be sensitive to the beliefs and norms of an ever-widening range of community

---

Box 3.1: Questions to alert practitioners to parents' needs in a diversity of cultures (after Forehand and Kotchik, 1996)

1. How do you feel about going to a professional to help you deal with your children's difficulties?
2. What child behaviours do you most like in your child?
3. What child behaviours are most difficult for you as a parent?
4. What parenting behaviours work best in changing your child's behaviour?
5. What parenting skills do not work so well in changing your child's behaviour?
6. What would be some of the things that might keep you from taking part in a parenting programme?
7. What would make it more likely that you would take part in parent training?
8. Are there any really important things which we ought to bear in mind in trying to help you deal with your child?
9. How do family members feel about your seeking help in dealing with your child?
10. What is the best way to teach parenting skills to you?
11. What are the stresses that keep you from doing your best as a parent?
12. What are the most important characteristics that you would like in someone who helps you deal with your child's problem?

groups and cultures in the USA: the same is exactly true of the UK. Parents in all communities appear to need help, but unless there is sensitivity to the way in which such 'help' is perceived by parents and by community members, then it may not prove to be helpful at all. These authors suggest a number of questions (see Box 3.1) which can be usefully explored with parents in order to make practitioners more sensitive to the finer details of the work.

Further, it would not be good anti-discriminatory practice to assume that there will be a female figure or a male figure in the life of a given child: as children are increasingly brought up by lone parents or by lesbian or gay couples, there may not be caregivers of both genders available. We are reminded by the Children Act 1989, however, that many different people can contribute helpfully to the child's development: grandparents, aunts, uncles, cousins and distant relatives. In any case, as we shall see, it is essential that as many people as possible among those who make a significant contribution to a child's development shall be involved in cooperating to care for the child.

Gathering Information to Make an Assessment

As we shall see in the next chapter, and as professionals already know, it is necessary to gather extensive information about a child and his or her background to inform the assessment. According to the child's age, this information may well come from the child him or herself as well as from the child's caregivers or parents. Yet, as already indicated, it may be totally against family conventions to divulge information to outsiders: the child is not necessarily being stubborn if he or she chooses not to talk to a social worker or other practitioner, and his or her silence may not necessarily indicate that there are secrets which must be investigated: it may rather mean that the child has been instructed that he or she should not talk about private family matters to non-family members. If issues of Child Protection are involved, then enquiries may have to go ahead without the full cooperation of the family; if they are not, then it may still be a considerable time before we can gain parental cooperation in giving us a fuller understanding of the child's difficulties.

Working with Cultural and Religious Diversity

As the UK becomes ever more racially, culturally and religiously diverse, so it is extremely challenging for professional workers to familiarise themselves with this diversity. My discussions with students and practitioners from a wide range of community groups have led us to conclude that any kind of stereotype is inappropriate and, since it is almost impossible for any one individual to become familiar with the diversity within one estate, let alone one city, the most appropriate approach may be to convey one's wish to help, one's unfamiliarity with the background of the family or parents concerned, and to ask if they would tell you what their expectations are of their child. Sometimes these may be inappropriate in terms of the child's age or developmental stage, and in such cases we have an important educational role, but often we can note the parents' expectations—'If only he'd do as I say!'—and confirm that this is indeed a reasonable desire.

Building Credibility and Rewardingness

Skills in forming positive relationships and in developing active helping roles are essential here. Sometimes it will be our listening skills and empathy which will enable a hostile person to move from being defensive and resentful to being ready to make use of our suggestions; sometimes we may be able to demonstrate goodwill by showing the person concerned that they are entitled to more welfare benefits than they had realised. Sometimes only the passing of time will reassure them that we seek to enable them to care for their child themselves—not to remove the child.

It is right, however, to have confidence that one has knowledge and skills to offer, and referring to the fact that we have helped other families with similar difficulties to a successful outcome may raise our credibility. One very skilled health visitor in Fosse Health Trust has compiled a folder of 'success stories'. These are testimonials from families, identified only by initials, with whom he has been successful in resolving complex and long-standing sleeping difficulties: he has the permission of these satisfied customers to show the testimonials to newly referred families. This is a way of building one's credibility which can prove very persuasive.

DEVELOPING A POSITIVE FOCUS

With the foundations laid for a constructive relationship, we move towards making an assessment. The detail of this will be considered in more detail in Chapter 4; here I am concerned with the importance of adopting from the outset an approach which 'places the parents in the driving seat', so to speak. This can best be achieved by structuring our work so that the families set the direction and pace of the work.

Focusing Upon What the Parents Want to Achieve

Professor Martin Herbert, the leading psychologist in Britain in helping families with troubled children, suggests that we invite parents to set the goals for the work which they and the practitioner are undertaking together. He suggests saying words to the effect, 'If I had a magic wand, and if I were able to help you, how would you want your child to be behaving in a few months' time?'. This approach has a number of advantages:

1. It encourages parents to look forward rather than backward.
2. It helps them to begin to think in terms of specific behaviour.
3. It empowers them to identify their own hopes for their child—as distinct from those of some external expert.
4. Yet it does not guarantee change—as we shall see, the parents are the change agents.

According to the age of the child, the answers might be:

1. I want him to do what I say without constantly arguing.
2. I want him to go to school.
3. I want him to speak to me politely—not call me horrible names.

Each of these is a distinct *behaviour*, one which can be written down; it is also possible to monitor progress towards each one.

At this point I wish to emphasise that this book focuses upon children rather than adolescents, and it is my intention to illustrate the concepts by reference to pre-school and primary school-age children rather than to those in secondary school. This is because of my commitment to preventive work and because one short book cannot cover all ages of children and young people. However, once an assessment has been made, this same strategy of focusing upon desired patterns of behaviour is equally relevant to work with young people.

We shall see in Chapter 5 how this strategy of goal setting can enable parents and workers to be clear about the ends to which they are working—rather than becoming involved in non-specific 'therapy', without any clear idea of what they are trying to achieve. As we shall discuss, it is often difficult to enable parents to orientate themselves towards a more hopeful future, as their past has been, and their present is, so full of difficulty and hopelessness; such a forward-looking orientation, however, is both appropriate and constructive.

Recognising Positive Features of the Current Situation

One step which is often found helpful is to acknowledge those features of the present situation that do give grounds for hope and optimism. Parents who have experienced years of tantrums and arguments with their young child, or who have decided that their only course of action, if they are not to harm their child, is to ask for him to be accommodated by the local authority, may experience astonishment and relief on hearing a worker actively acknowledge their on-going care and concern for their child. Skilled and sensitive practitioners are able to say, genuinely and honestly, 'If you didn't really care about your child, you wouldn't have come to us' or 'It shows that you still care about him, despite all that has happened, if you are willing to talk to us about very personal and private things that have happened in your family'.

I am not suggesting that workers should give false hope or offer spurious reassurances that things will improve: I am suggesting, however, that when we recognise that underneath the outward anger with and rejection of the child, there is still the hope that the relationship can be rebuilt, then it is fitting to build upon this hope in a firm but realistic way. This is not based upon vague optimism, but upon a confident familiarity with the research literature which reports, as I have already explained, 'the successful treatment of thousands of children with a wide variety of problems'.

PRACTICE ISSUES: STRUCTURE AND SAFETY

A number of important points arise when seeking to engage parents, particularly in settings where safety may be an issue.

Keeping a Very Clear Focus for Oneself

In order to build confidence and trust in the parents, it is important to be extremely clear and focused in one's work with them and open to questions from them. I am not referring here to high standards of professional behaviour concerning punctuality and accountability—these I take for granted—but to setting very modest goals for our work together at each meeting and explaining these to the parent(s). 'Yes, as I said, I want this week to talk with you about Johnnie's bad behaviour and his good behaviour, and to give you a way of noting how often these happen. Are there any particular things you would like to talk about?' . . . 'Right. You'd like to talk about whether we should tell Johnnie's teacher about my being in touch with you: fine . . . Let's write these two topics down so that we don't forget them. Anything else?' To have very specific goals for the session gives confidence to parents and provides everyone concerned with a clear structure for progress.

Another means of engaging families which depends upon openness is devising a shared service contract. This is considered further in Chapter 12. In essence, the worker undertakes to offer a family structured support to help a troubled child by means of, say, a series of eight weekly meetings. The focus upon parenting may well be part of a much larger intervention involving alcohol abuse by the father, mental ill-health in the mother and concern about the well-being of a pre-school child, but a clear statement about the specific focus upon support in parenting the pre-schooler can clarify both the timing and boundaries of this work.

Being Honest with Parents

Nothing is to be gained by a dishonest emphasis upon the positive features of a situation. Indeed, the more worrying the situation, the more important it is to be straight, but not blunt, with the family. One example offered by a very experienced practitioner was, in appropriate circumstances, to say, truthfully but in a constructive tone, for example, 'Your child is on the Child Protection Register and unless we work together to improve the situation, he will stay on it'. This can have the effect of motivating some families to work hard to have this stigma removed.

Giving Supportive Encouragement to Parents

Given that many families with whom we work will have had deeply disadvantaged childhoods themselves, and given that nurturing children is largely a learned behaviour, we ourselves have the opportunity to offer the parents who now seek our help something of the encouragement and warmth that so many of them missed in early life. We can show empathy for their difficulties, appreciation of the problems they encounter in being positive to children whom they have come to dislike or even fear, and a sense of humour when everything goes wrong. In essence, we have to make the meetings with parents very rewarding events—whether they are in the privacy of someone's home or whether they are group meetings where everyone has his/her own personal agenda. For remember that each person is carrying out an implicit cost–benefit analysis (Sutton, 1994); each one is estimating whether it is more advantageous to meet with the worker or to pretend to be out when she calls—or whether it is more advantageous to them to come to that particular group meeting or to stay away. Part of our job is to make the meetings as genuinely rewarding as we can, partly by offering skills to help parents cope with their children helpfully but also by providing opportunities for laughing and for sharing the ups and downs of family life in a light-hearted way. You could say that we are offering some parents a mini-experience of being nurtured and parented all over again.

I have been asked whether there are not dangers of encouraging dependency in taking such a role: I have not found so. The time which I typically spend with the parents, eight weekly sessions of between one and two hours, followed by two follow-up meetings, is usually devoted primarily to discussing how to get a child up in the morning and off to school or to getting him or her to take notice of a parent's requests. We do not have long to spend on reflecting upon the parent's own childhood experiences. If anything, the difficulties I encounter are more linked with maintaining contact when the structured sessions are over, rather than in dealing with dependency.

HANDLING DIFFICULTIES ALONG THE WAY

Sometimes, despite our best efforts, parents are unmotivated to improve their child's misbehaviour or, having made some initial progress, lose momentum. These objections are very hard to deal with, but Box 3.2 shows some of the difficulties which health visitors in Fosse Health Trust have encountered and the range of solutions which they have tried.

Box 3.2: Common problems in engaging parents and possible solutions

Common problem	Possible solution
Getting started.	Promise, and give, regular support. Offer deep empathy. Boost mother's self-esteem. Show reports from other parents.
Keeping going.	'Buddy'/support group of other parents. Encouragement from us.
'I tried that and it didn't work'.	Checking exactly what they tried and for how long. Exactly what happened?
Getting parents to take responsibility.	Working out an agreement with them.
Parents say, 'He'll grow out of it'.	Emphasise that the research does not support this view.

INTER-AGENCY WORK

Finally, there are many advantages in working with other agencies in supporting families. For example, if a child's circumstances have already been considered by a case conference, it is likely that a 'core group' has been nominated to coordinate the child's welfare. The members of that core group, representing many different agencies, may well be able to provide encouraging and positive information concerning the child which can stimulate optimism about the future. For example, a nursery nurse may be able to report that a child has seemed calmer, more settled and more able to settle to play for a longer period of time after a parent has been trying to be more positive in her management of the child; this can provide crucial encouragement to the parent herself and can motivate her to continue her efforts.

From the point of view of management, group work appears to have advantages in that it is not only more cost effective than individualised home visiting, but it may be possible for, say, a community worker to respond to the interests of a group of isolated young parents: first via a focus on, for example, health, sport and leisure activities, so establishing trust and involvement in the group, and then at the request of group members for a health visitor, social worker or other practitioner to focus upon issues of parenting. A range of ways of working is required, allowing families choice in their preferred way of gaining support.

METHODS OF GIVING HELP: EVIDENCE FROM RESEARCH

I have already described, page 34, the three different methods I have used in my work for dealing with pre-school children having serious behaviour difficulties—working with parents in a group, visiting them at home and supporting and training parents by telephone—were found to be equally effective. Other researchers have investigated other strategies of support for parents. An important study by Puckering et al (1994) focused upon 21 mothers with severe parenting difficulties. The study was group-based lasting four months. Psychotherapy was available 'to allow mothers to come to terms with past and present stressors'. This work had positive results, with 10 of 12 children whose names were on the Child Protection Register having their names removed—and this compared well with figures in a control area. It will be noted that this admirable work lasted over four months and involved at least five practitioners, by contrast with my own work, in which I met with parents for two hours weekly over eight weeks and worked alone.

The point I am making is that this is a relatively new research field and we do not yet know all the details of the best ways of working to support families reporting serious problems in their children; only further research will provide this. The parents themselves will have had hugely varying experiences of being parented: some will have had positive experiences and need only minimal guidance and support before they can employ new strategies for managing their children; others will have had deeply unhappy experiences, deprived of the affection which brings security and cared for by people who rejected and punished them. Yet with so many children in difficulties, research into the optimal ways of helping their parents to help them is urgently needed. So my own position is that while counselling or psychotherapy for parents may be highly desirable, only a tiny fraction of them are going to receive it. We need to find a way of undertaking preventive work with families which is both effective and cost-effective and the research programme towards this goal is only just beginning.

We see, then, that engaging and maintaining the engagement of families who have troubled children is no easy matter. Only a small proportion of those who come to our attention are strongly motivated: many are reluctant participants and readily lose heart. Yet, as these ways of helping families become better known, so their positive features will also become better known; and as we practise positive methods of interacting with the parents, emphasising their strengths and their concern for their children, so a benign circle of constructive relationships can be established.

4

ASPIRE—ASSESSMENT

I wish now to introduce a framework for practice which is attracting a good deal of attention as helpful to students and practitioners. I developed it with Professor Martin Herbert in an earlier book which we wrote together (Sutton and Herbert, 1992) and it is proving its usefulness to a range of practitioners: counsellors, social workers, group workers and community workers.

ASPIRE: A PROCESS FOR PRACTICE

ASPIRE is a mnemonic, composed of the first letters of other words. It is chosen because these letters represent stages in working with people which offer a useful reminder of the process at times when we may feel overwhelmed by information or events and need to find our bearings again. Box 4.1 shows the four stages of the ASPIRE process. These stages are particularly relevant in working with parents with troubled children—and indeed with anyone who is experiencing life difficulties or challenges—

Box 4.1: The ASPIRE process (after Sutton and Herbert, 1992)

AS	Assessment
P	Planning
I	Implementation
RE	Review and Evaluation

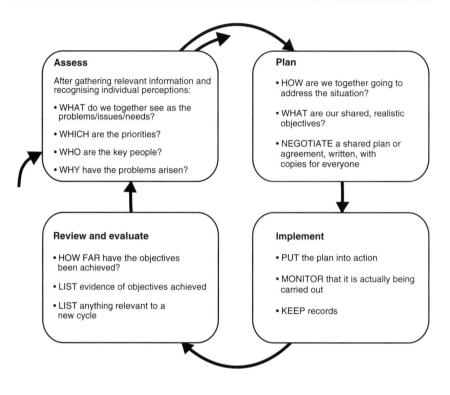

Figure 4.1:   The ASPIRE process as a cycle

whether as an individual, as a member of a group or as members of a community. The first and most important stage is that of Assessment, and this chapter will be devoted to it. The later stages will be considered in Chapter 5.

The way in which the ASPIRE process is set out in Box 4.1 implies a simple, linear series of steps and of course life and practice are never as simple as that: the process is more likely to be cyclical (see Figure 4.1).

WHAT IS ASSESSMENT?

To 'assess' means to judge or estimate something; the comparable word in a medical context is to 'diagnose'. There are, however, major differences between 'assessment' and 'diagnosis'. As I have written elsewhere (Sutton, 1994), in a medical context a doctor typically diagnoses judges what is amiss with systems internal to the person's body: a person trying to help a family with a troubled child typically tries to understand and help the child directly but also via the systems of which he or she is a part: family, school, friendship, cultural and others.

Accurate assessment is the key to effective intervention. As Herbert (1978) has written:

> . . . difficulties and failures in treatment of children's behaviour problems can be frequently traced back to lack of precision during the crucial assessment (or diagnostic) phase of a therapeutic contact.

Assessment in this context is the activity of gathering information concerning the circumstances of a troubled child and of making a judgement about possible links between those circumstances and his or her difficulties. It is not a once-and-for-all judgement but a *process*—so that the assessment can be changed or adjusted as new information comes to light. Thus, we aim to understand the child's history, the key people who have featured in his/her experience and how the life events of those people or of the child may have played a part in the child's troubles. The people will include the immediate caregivers as well as others who may be geographically distant. They may even be dead, but may still continue to be of profound importance.

Practitioners are increasingly working in multi-disciplinary teams. While people trained in the context of one particular profession, be it medical, psychiatric, health visiting or social work, are likely to perceive a child's difficulties initially through the spectacles of that professional group, this move to multi-disciplinary teams is facilitating a broad-based view of children's difficulties. Where teams are working well and there is respect among the members for the knowledge and skills which each profession can offer, there can be highly integrated approaches to assessment.

Aspects of Assessment

It is essential to locate any child's troubles within a developmental framework. That is, a psychologist, psychiatrist, social worker or other professional must be sufficiently familiar with the research literature on the main developmental features for the majority of children to be able to judge when, for a given child, there is a significant departure from normal. For example, it is known (Ollendick and King, 1991) that children aged five and six show characteristic fears of animals, ghosts and monsters and that these typically fade as the child grows older. Similarly, workers of all professions need to be familiar with the evidence that severe mis-behaviour in young children is a very worrying sign, particularly if it occurs both at home and in settings outside the home.

The process of information-gathering and formulating an assess-ment will be on-going throughout one's contact with a child or family. I attempt to visit a family at home at least once so that they are likely to feel more comfortable and secure, but even a meeting of up to an hour is seldom sufficient to enable me to feel that I have enough information to proceed. Of course, during the initial meet-ing one is doing much more than gather information: one is de-veloping relationships, meeting other family members who come in part-way through, winning confidence, recognising risk factors and establishing confidentiality or its boundaries. More specifi-cally, one is enabling some of the anxiety of the parent to subside— anxiety underpinned by increased adrenalin secretion, leading to physiological arousal, raised heart-rate, increased stomach secre-tions and emotional agitation. Yet I also know that for overworked health visitors or social workers to give this amount of time is a luxury, and is often found at the expense, not of other needy people, but of the workers themselves or their families.

I have said that assessment is a process. As such, it is provi-sional, tentative and couched in such a way that it can be easily adjusted. When we meet with families with troubled children it is wise to convey this tentativeness, this provisionality, partly in order to avoid being invested with the mantle of 'expert' and so be expected to solve huge and long-standing difficulties at a stroke, but also partly to engage families on as equal a footing as possible in what is essentially a problem-solving exercise. Our shared task is to engage in understanding answers to the question, 'How has this situation come about?' and the parent(s) will have crucially important information, ideas and hunches which we necessarily lack. An advantage of working in this open way is that it permits

Box 4.2: The 10 steps of the ASPIRE process

Step 1   Introduce yourself: build supportive and empathic relationships.
Step 2   **ASSESS** (AS of ASPIRE process):
          ● Gather information in the usual way
          ● Check that child has been screened, for example for allergies, etc.
          ● Help family to identify stressors in child's life and in parents' life
Step 3   Identify problem behaviours: i.e. problem profile:
          ● What are the difficulties?
          ● Which are the priority problems?   ⎫ Use scales to
          ● When do they occur?   ⎬ identify behaviour
          ● Who is involved?   ⎪ problems if
          ● Why do parents think they happen?   ⎭ appropriate
Step 4   Identify positive profile:
          ● What behaviours would parents like to see more of?
Step 5   Discover desired outcomes; write them down for future reference.
Step 6   Explore tentative rationale for child's/family's difficulties:
          ● Stressful events in child's/parents' earlier experiences
          ● Factors intrinsic to the child; e.g. hearing impairment
          ● Day-to-day difficulties: suggest you can offer useful skills to help parents manage these
Step 7   Ask for one week's counts of one negative ⎫ Introduce
          behaviour and one positive behaviour   ⎭ A–B–C
Step 8   **PLAN** (P of ASPIRE process).
          Empower parents by exploring plans:
          ● To relieve any specific stressor for child/parent
          ● To practise skills for managing day-to-day difficulties
          Teach A–B–C sequence; lots of examples; no blame to parents
          Explain which skill to use when negative behaviours happen; when positive behaviours happen
Step 9   **IMPLEMENT PLAN** (I of ASPIRE process):
          ● Put plan into action: lots of encouragement for parents
          ● Ask parents/caregivers to continue to keep records
          ● Trouble-shoot difficulties
Step 10   **REVIEW** and **EVALUATE** (RE of ASPIRE process):
          ● Provide boosters to maintain progress

new information or new perspectives to be taken into account in our attempts to understand a child's difficulties; so the process of assessment is gradual and cumulative, not fixed and final.

The aim, then, is to arrive at a *provisional but shared view* of the situation, so that all those concerned are broadly in agreement about the nature of the difficulties. In my experience family members are likely in these early stages still to be seeing the difficult behaviour of a child, his/her anxiety or disruptiveness, primarily as located *in* the child—the 'There's something wrong with him' perspective.

THE STEPS OF ASSESSMENT—AND BEYOND

Box 4.2 shows an outline of the steps for undertaking an Assessment. For clarity, the steps to be undertaken under Planning, Implementation, Review and Evaluation are also included in Box 4.2, although steps 8–10 will be discussed in Chapter 5. Let us look at these steps in more detail.

Step 1—Building Supportive and Empathic Relationships

As already discussed, the first steps in making contact with the parent(s) of a child with difficulties are, after introducing oneself, to show warmth and respect, a readiness to listen, concern for their distress and a capacity to offer empathy. Readers will recognise the features and approaches identified by Truax and Carkhuff (1967) from their detailed examination of 'thousands of research studies' as characteristic of effective counsellors and therapists: empathy, warmth and congruence—that is, the counsellor is all-of-a piece. Together, these characteristics convey an absence of threat, an unmistakable valuing of the person concerned and a readiness to attempt to understand the person's experience from his or her standpoint. This can be deeply reassuring to anxious families, who typically want to help a troubled child but do not know how to do so.

Practitioners are increasingly recognising the urgent necessity of active efforts to enhance the self-esteem of parents who are experiencing difficulties with their children. Often the needs of the parents are as great as those of the children, as their troubled and troublesome children bring increasing criticism from neighbours, teachers and relatives. If we, too, join the ranks of the critics, we are adding to their difficulties. We must remain non-judgemental, recognising parents' achievements and strengths and adding our own encouragement and support to strengthen their wilting motivation.

Community workers on deeply disadvantaged housing estates have told me that it sometimes takes them weeks or months of contact with families who have previously been bruised by their contact with the statutory services to begin to establish trust in anyone in any role of authority. The premature offer of training in parenting skills would lead to the worker being shown the door!

This can be draining work for practitioners. In a sense, we are attempting to offer nurture and encouragement to people who may have had little of either, and it can be very exhausting. We must avoid fostering dependency, and having very specific goals agreed with parents assists in this. Yet we, too, need our support systems and means of recharging our own batteries.

If possible and acceptable, it is helpful to meet as many people who have contact with the child as possible, as well, of course, as the child. In this way one can gain an impression of the difficulties as perceived by a number of family members. Moreover, I always try to avoid situations in which a young child hears one or both parents talking about his misbehaviour or his unhappiness to me— a complete stranger. This is likely to cause an already difficult situation to get worse.

It is important to clarify the expectations of those we are seeking to help. In the various settings in which I have worked, some people are very frightened that their child will be accommodated or removed from them while, at the other ex-treme, some are actively wanting their child to be accommodated or removed from them! In either case, it is helpful to try to find out their hopes and fears, to correct the inaccurate and confirm the well-founded.

Step 2—Gathering Information to Inform the Assessment

An early step will be to ask, 'How can I help you?' or words to that effect. There is likely to be an outpouring of complaints and/or distress about the child or young person which may seem intense, exaggerated or, by contrast, very mild. It is here that an empathic response, albeit of a general kind, is most helpful—along the lines of, 'This experience has upset you very much, hasn't it?'. It is a good idea to request permission to write down key information at this stage, undertaking to show the information given to the person concerned at the end. A pro forma which allows much detail to be gathered is included as Appendix 1. One can sit side by side with the person so that each can see the questions and complete them together, rather than across a desk or in such a way that he/she cannot see the questions or what we are writing down. I have found that showing what one has written both imposes a discipline upon the notes I take, and contributes to the development of trust between myself and the people I am meeting.

Predisposing factors

These will be identified from information given by parents about when they first noticed that their child appeared to be tense or worried—indeed, what they noticed about him/her as a baby and toddler: was he/she tense then, or did this tendency develop later? What have been the occasions through the child's early life when the family members noticed the child's distress? These should be written down, in chronological order.

There are two sets of 'life events' to be considered: those affecting the child and those affecting the parents—and, indirectly, the child also, although parents may be unaware of this effect. In respect of major events in the child's life, parents can sometimes pinpoint a date or an event which they think contributed significantly to the child's difficulties: an accident, an admission to hospital, a move to a new school, a bereavement or the separation of the child's parents. Some children, however, may be reacting to a life event whose significance is either not recognised by the parent or about which nothing can be done. Appendix 2, concerning Life

Events, may be useful here and can form the basis of a useful discussion with parents about important happenings in their own and their children's lives: experiences at school, the loss of a close friend, being bullied or being the target of racism or name-calling. Older children can report the events themselves; parents may or may not know about them. The practitioner will have to seek the child's permission to tell the parents what he or she is coping with, but a skilled worker who follows the child's wishes faithfully and so maintains trust can often be of enormous help in such situations. The point is that this greater understanding can facilitate non-blaming communication between the child and parent: it opens the eyes of each to the emotional realities of the other.

One approach to understanding major events in the experience of the parent(s) is to invite them to complete the Life Events Scale devised by Holmes and Rahe (1967) (see Appendix 3). This gives people 'permission' to understand the extent of the difficulties with which they are dealing and to appreciate the level of stress they have dealt or are dealing with: serious illness in themselves or in another family member, a marital separation, a relationship breakdown, or bereavement. A total score of 340 or more indicates a high level of risk to one's health. Talking of these events in a sensitive and supportive relationship may give much relief— which in turn relieves the pressure upon the child. In some cases it may be necessary to refer the parent(s) to a counselling organisation for individual supportive help.

Organic and developmental factors

These include all those factors which make it intrinsically more likely that the child will experience stress. Here will be recorded the developmental factors which may be playing into the situation: hearing or visual impairment, developmental delay, as well as being taller or shorter, fatter or thinner than most of the children in the neighbourhood or classroom. Here too will be recorded a child's medical difficulties, epilepsy, heart problems, as well as eczema, asthma and all the other conditions which make life hard for children. In my own work, I require that parents ask a GP, a school nurse or a health visitor to examine the child, not only to rule out organic factors but to talk to the child about things which he or she may worry about, such as protruding ears, skin blemishes or being overweight; the significance of these may be dismissed by parents but can be a cause of acute distress to a child. Often a good deal can be done to help.

It is increasingly understood that a child may suffer from racism or bullying because of the colour of his or her skin or other features linked with ethnicity. In such circumstances, which may not have been disclosed to the parents, help will be needed both to approach the child's playgroup or school so that the bullying and name-calling stops and to help the child take pride in his or her ethnic identity.

An area which is attracting much attention from speech and language therapists is the extent to which a child's poor receptive language abilities, that is, the ability to understand and make sense of messages, may underpin slowness in, for example, complying with requests. A recent paper by Cross (1997) makes this point clearly: she writes:

> It is significant that children with previously unsuspected language problems might be perceived as more 'difficult'. Cohen et al (1993) found that those with unsuspected language deficits were more likely to have externalising behaviour problems; for example, oppositional behaviour, hyperactivity and aggression. . . . Generally expressive problems are relatively easy to spot, but parents and medical professionals tends to underestimate receptive problems . . .

In addition, there are the whole array of difficulties which fall on the spectrum of hyperactivity: while those at one end may be extremely apparent, milder forms may be harder to spot and a child who has substantial difficulties in sustaining attention or in controlling restlessness or impetuosity, may simply be labelled as 'naughty'. Similarly, many children suffer from serious impairments in respect of their social interaction skills: for example, their difficulties in making and maintaining eye contact. These crucial abilities have their roots in the earliest years of life, when the exchanges with caretakers of 'gaze, touch and talk', by which attachment and all that goes with it are established, have not taken place adequately, if at all. Skilled and detailed assessment is essential if the deep-rooted difficulties of these children are to be identified and help given.

Table 4.1:   A framework for key information relevant to an assessment

PARENTING POSITIVELY

Helping parents improve children's behaviour

Key information relevant to an assessment

Name of child _____   **Date** _____

Predisposing factors for this child/family

  1 ....

  2 ....

  3 ....

Organic/developmental factors affecting the child

  1 ....

  2 ....

  3 ....

Immediate factors

Behaviour difficulties:

  1 ....

  2 ....

  3 ....

A–B–C analysis:

	Antecedents	*Behaviour*	*Consequences*
	1	1	1 ....
	2	2	2 ....
	3	3	3 ....

Table 4.2:   An example of gathering information to inform an assessment

1. *Predisposing factors for this child/family*
   (a) Parents separated when the child was three.
   (b) Mum has lost touch with her family; feels very isolated.
   (c) Family has moved frequently.
2. *Organic developmental factors affecting the child*
   (a) Child has a mild hearing impairment.
   (b) He is asthmatic.
3. *Immediate factors: difficult behaviours within the family (A–B–C)*
   (a) Child makes many demands. Child says, 'If you don't give me what I want, I shan't love you'. Mother cannot bear this and gives in to demands.
   (b) Child does not do anything he is asked. Mum threatens to punish him but does not carry through threats.

   A–B–C analysis:

Antecedents	*Behaviour*	*Consequences*
a) Child demands new toy. Mother refuses.	Child says, 'I shan't love you'.	Mum gives way.
b) Child is asked to put his toys in the box.	He takes no notice.	Mum says, 'Do what I say or there'll be no TV'.
c) Child looks at her.	He grins at her.	She laughs, puts the TV on. Later *she* puts the toys away.

Immediate factors

The next step is to identify some of the main behaviours which are causing problems. This leads to an analysis in terms of Antecedents–Behaviours–Consequences (this is sometimes called a 'functional analysis' because it shows what *function* the behaviour is serving for the child). As discussed on pp. 60–61, this includes:

(a) Pinpointing the specific problem behaviours.
(b) Identifying possible Antecedents which may be triggering the behaviour problems.
(c) Identifying the Consequences which may be rewarding the behaviour problems.

Appendix 5 may be useful for this analysis, enabling the details of a child's behaviour to be identified, together with the Antecedents to and Consequences of that behaviour which may be contributing to it. This important issue will be examined in greater depth in later chapters.

A summary of key information relevant to an assessment

Table 4.1 provides a very simple summary framework which one can bear in mind when compiling information to understand the child's difficulty. It is included as Appendix 4. Knowledge of predisposing factors in the life of the child and family, awareness of organic or developmental variables together with an analysis of the child's day-to-day behaviour are, when integrated, likely to throw considerable light upon the behaviour of a troubled child.

Step 3—Identifying the Problem Behaviours: Developing a Problem Profile

As shown in Tables 4.1 and 4.2 the next step is to develop a 'problem profile' (Herbert, 1991). This is a statement of the specific things a child does—so an appropriate enquiry might be: 'What exactly does Chris *do* which is so upsetting?' The replies are likely to be very general: 'He's so difficult', 'She's impossible . . .', 'We think there's something wrong with him', or 'I can't get a civil word out of her . . .' We need a more precise description of the behaviour. We might say, 'You say, "He's so difficult . . ." Can you give me some idea of what Chris actually *does* when he's being difficult? What would I *see* if I were there?'. People need help in describing their child's difficulties in terms of *behaviour*, but eventually a mother or father might specify:

1. When I ask him to do something, he never does it.
2. He hits and kicks his sister and sometimes me.
3. He is very rude to my mother and sister when they come to the house; they say they won't come any more.
4. He is very demanding, always pestering me for biscuits, sweets, or TV.

For a withdrawn child, they might be:

1. She seldom goes out to play with the other children on the street.
2. She sits for long spells staring into space.
3. She bursts into tears a lot—even though we try to comfort her.

The order of priority for the parents should then be negotiated, but remember that everyone needs to succeed in these early days, so a simple behaviour which might be allowed to fade away (extinguish) is probably the one to start with. So the above lists might be re-ordered. For the aggressive child:

1. He is very demanding, always pestering me for biscuits, sweets, or TV.
2. When I ask him to do something, he never does it.
3. He hits and kicks his sister and sometimes me.
4. He is very rude to my mother and sister when they come to the house; they say they won't come any more.

For the withdrawn child, they might read:

1. She bursts into tears a lot—even though we try to comfort her.
2. She sits for long spells, staring into space.
3. She seldom goes out to play with the other children on the street.

Now it will be apparent that each of the above behaviours can be recorded and counted—whether it be instances of biting or hitting other children or of bursting into tears. Families will need suitably designed charts upon which to record their child's behaviour—see Appendix 5, which is a recording sheet, on which one behaviour should be entered. Practitioners will need to clarify carefully exactly what is to be recorded; they should also anticipate some puzzlement or resistance on the part of parents, as this will probably be a novel way of thinking of their child's behaviour.

This step of targeting specific behaviours corresponds to the *immediate factors* (see Tables 4.1 and 4.2). In the past, a great deal of time has often been spent in discussing any predisposing variables in the belief that by exploring their impact, an improvement will follow in the child's difficulties. There is very little evidence indeed to support this formulation. There is much more evidence that while it is important to understand any predisposing factors, it is often by understanding and intervening in respect of the immediate variables that one can really begin to help children (Herbert, 1991). As we shall see, many interventions will begin by helping parents try to transfer their attention from the child's misbehaviour to his/her good behaviour.

In some situations the behaviour is apparently antecedent to or follows certain situations which the child finds hard to cope with. If, for example, a child is always difficult after returning from a visit to his father and step-mother, this suggests that an exploration of how these visits affect him is likely to be helpful. Many children hide, or attempt to hide, fear, anxiety, confusion or hurt from their parents but an opportunity to confide in someone they trust can lead to misunderstandings being resolved and fears subsiding. I remember, for example, one boy, the child of a lone parent, who became increasingly reluctant to go to school. He was labelled 'school phobic'. A careful enquiry by a skilled school nurse gradually revealed, however, that he was not school phobic in the usual sense of the term: rather, he had heard his mother complaining of feeling unwell and his fear was not of going to school, but of leaving home, lest he lose his sole remaining parent.

Older children, once their confidence has been won, may be able to convey the causes of their unhappiness, either directly in conversation or indirectly through painting, drawing or story work; younger children are likely to be unable to articulate the causes of their distress as clearly.

Using a standardised scale for assessing behaviour

The practice of using a standardised scale for the assessment of a child's behaviour, in both its negative and positive forms, is gaining ground. A new scale, the Strengths and Difficulties Questionnaire, has been published by Dr Robert Goodman (1997) and he has generously given permission for this to be reprinted as Appendix 6 of this book. The scale can be used by parents, teachers and young people themselves to identify both problem behaviours and positive behaviours. It is suitable for children from 4 to 16. The particular value of such validated questionnaires is that they can be used, if appropriate, as measures before and after a programme of intervention and, indeed, at follow-up some months or years later. This demonstrates whether there have been any effects of training the parents or caregivers to manage the child's difficulties and whether any improvement has persisted.

A number of sub-scales are incorporated in the questionnaire:

1. Emotional symptoms score.
2. Conduct problems score.
3. Hyperactivity score.
4. Peer problems score.

These, added, produce a Total Difficulties score. Also incorporated is a Prosocial behaviour score. Goodman has also prepared a number of associated materials for use with particular groups of children: three year-olds, and children from a diversity of minority groups. His address is also given.

Step 4—Identifying a Positive Profile

At this stage it is extremely important to gain a picture of some feature(s) of the child or his/her behaviour which the parents actively value and appreciate. So the question, 'Now that you've told me about some of your child's shortcomings, is there anything that he does that you really like?' is important. Some parents, surprised, will say, 'Oh yes, he has days when he's wonderful—he'll do anything to help and he's really nice to be with', but others will say sadly, 'I can't think of anything I like about the child . . .'. This is an emergency—one where all our efforts are needed in an attempt to prevent the hostility between parents and children spiralling down into total rejection. So it may be helpful to say something appreciative about the child, something which values and validates the contribution which the parent has made to the child's development which we, as members of the outside world, have noticed. Without sounding patronising, we can say something like, 'I noticed he was polite when he came in . . .', or 'His teachers told you that, when he's on his own, he's a very thoughtful child, didn't they?'—something, almost anything, is needed to 'prime the pump' of enabling parents to consider their child positively! I cannot over-emphasise the importance of this—

although clearly one should avoid getting into an argument about whether the child has or has not any redeeming features or behaviours. If all else fails, then one can use pro-social items on the Strengths and Difficulties Questionnaire or problem behaviours which have low scores. The point of this is that we need gently to redirect the parents' attention to the child's remaining positive behaviours so that he or she may receive the nurturance and positive attention which are absolute essentials for any child. Typically, these few remaining positive behaviours have been all but overwhelmed by the attention paid to the misbehaviour.

Step 5—Discovering Parents' Desired Outcomes: Targeting Hoped-for Behaviours

Now is the time to attempt to establish the main concerns as perceived by the parents or caregivers and as perceived by oneself in one's professional role. I have learned that most parents of children who have a sleeping difficulty are likely to say that this takes precedence over all other concerns, and indeed, once a pattern of sleeping regularly has been established, many other difficulties of irritability, low attention span and general fractiousness are likely to diminish.

So one urgently desired outcome may be:

1. 'I want him to sleep through the night—or at least until 5.00 a.m.'

The threat of exclusion from nursery or school is likely to be seen as an urgent priority by many families, since this may also threaten the capacity of a parent to continue in employment. Social workers and health visitors may have different priorities from parents, however, and any pattern of behaviour which angers the parent to the point where they may perpetrate some form of child abuse, such as attacking the child, is likely to be *their* focus for concern. A mother said to me, 'I'll swing for him . . .', while others have said to social workers, 'What do I have to do to get help—punch him or beat him up?' In this case an urgently desired outcome may be:

2. 'I want him to stop hitting other children'; or, phrased positively, 'I want him to play calmly with other children'.

Other parents know that they are at breaking point if their child is persistently rude to them or to other adults. This 'shows them up' in a humiliating and embarrassing way and causes intense family stress. In these circumstances a desired outcome might be:

3. I want him to speak quietly to me and to people who come to the house, using no swear words.

Other target outcomes which parents have frequently identified are:

4. 'I want him to do what I ask him—simple things, like coming when I call'.

5. 'I want him to eat his meals without throwing food or deliberately messing with it'.

6. 'I want him to settle to play alone for at least five minutes at a time'.

Box 4.3 shows the actual list of positive behaviours, phrased as goals, which one mother worked out in discussion with me concerning her little boy, Paul. Now this was a pretty wild little boy, aged two and a half at the time of referral, living in a maisonette

---

Box 4.3:   Positive behaviours targeted for Paul

1. That Paul will do as he is told, whether by his Mum or his Dad, *almost* every time he is asked.
2. That Paul will not have more than one temper tantrum, lasting three minutes or less, each week.
3. That Paul will accept his Mum's saying 'No' when out shopping without having a temper tantrum.
4. That Paul will sit on his potty when his Mum asks him.
5. That Paul will leave his Mum and Dad alone and play by himself for three spells of 10 minutes, when told, 'Leave me alone—I'm busy'.
6. That Paul will not hit or bite other children, or his Mum or Dad, more than once a week.
7. That Paul will not interfere with, or disrupt the games of, other children more than once a week.
8. That Paul will not tip things over in the lounge.

with no garden or outdoor play space on an inner city council estate and driving his mother frantic. She had 'tried everything' and, as she said, 'Hitting doesn't work. I've been hitting him for two years and I know it doesn't work'. The lengthy list in Box 4.3 reflects his behaviour and her exasperation.

Readers may protest that it is relatively easy to improve a two year-old's behaviour and that in any case there are too many goals. My answer is that it is *not* so easy to improve these young children's behaviour without a structure, a set of principles for doing so. A great many parents are dealing with so many difficulties that, as Paul's Mum did, they 'try everything' and then, when nothing seems to work, they give up, living in despair from day to day. We included a lot of targeted behaviours partly because I am very confident that these principles are effective and partly because I have found that when parents begin to have success in one area, this often generalises into other areas. People new to the field, however, may find it more manageable to focus upon about three behaviours to be improved.

Step 6—Attempting a Formulation: Making Sense of the Child's Troubles

This is the most demanding step of the assessment. It is the time when all the information is brought together and an attempt is made to make sense of the child's troubles. It is our responsibility to compose this preliminary assessment in such a way that it is *shared* with the people concerned and that it makes some kind of sense to them. If we are fortunate and the situation is not too complex, they may arrive at a similar understanding themselves, but it is more probable that we shall need to go extremely slowly at this point, explaining that we are speaking provisionally and tentatively. Our ways of expressing ourselves should seek to engage people, not to alienate them—even if, as may happen, we feel angry at some aspect of their behaviour.

So to say to a mother, Stephanie, something along the lines of, 'From what you have told me, it sounds as though you have all been coping with a lot of stress for a long time. You've mentioned your loss of your sister in a road accident just before David was

born, and how things got off to a difficult start for you both . . .
And then you've told me that he was a baby who never slept, so
that you wondered how you would keep going . . . And you've
told me that David's Dad said he couldn't stand all these crying
kids and walked out when David was still a toddler. All these
things must have been very difficult for you—but you kept going
because you cared about David and Joanne. So now, when David
cheeks you, you see red and feel you might lose your temper and
hit him quite seriously . . .'. This sort of approach shows the practitioner's empathy with Stephanie, and so is likely to win her cooperation in any plan to help her and David.

There are often three components in this formulation:

1. Locating the child's and family's difficulties in the context of the
   stresses which they have all been experiencing, both in the past
   and in the more immediate period before encountering the practitioner. Exploring these in a supportive way allows for the
   release of tension and for the parents to feel understood, not
   criticised. *This, in turn, avoids triggering the 'fight' component of the
   'fight–flight–freeze' response to threat which lies deep within the brain.*
2. Acknowledging, and if necessary making plans for referring the
   child for further checks or active treatment with, any organic difficulty the child is experiencing. So, if you are unsure that a child
   understands what he is being asked to do, it might be possible for
   a speech and language therapist to assess the child in this respect.
   Similarly, medical and other checks may be the best means for
   getting appropriate treatment for a wide range of conditions.
3. Conveying to the parents that there are some skills of managing
   children's behaviour difficulties which are known to be helpful,
   that these principles can be taught to parents, and that research
   shows that they can help bring about marked improvement in
   children's behaviour.

So, in respect of the little child considered on p. 113, we might:

Acknowledge the impact of several upsetting life events upon
the child, such as his Daddy walking out, leaving his Mum
unsupported.
Highlight the necessity of having the child's hearing rechecked
and of ensuring that people who speak to him gain his attention

by saying his name, placing their hands on his shoulders and giving a short and clear instruction (see p. 233).

Explain to his mother that it is vital that once a reasonable request has been made, he should be required to comply.

At this stage we are being very tentative and are considering possibilities (hypotheses) only. At this stage too, however, it is fitting lightly to introduce the A–B–C sequence of analysing children's behaviour, corresponding broadly to the more technical term, the 'functional analyis'. As we have seen, this terminology refers to the attempt to understand *what functions the difficult behaviour serves* for the child. For example, in the example of child who ignores his mother's instructions—say to find his school bag before leaving for school:

1. He is able to continue watching one of his favourite television programmes for a few more minutes.
2. He avoids the chore of searching for his bag.
3. His mother does the work of finding the bag and giving it to him—again.

Early in our contact with them, however, parents may well find it very difficult to accept that they themselves play any part at all in their child's difficult behaviour; typically, they have located all the problems *in* the child, and any suggestion on our part that they are implicated in any way may be totally unacceptable. It is important, therefore, that we are sensitive to their reaction when we introduce the idea that the consequences of a child's behaviour may make a crucial contribution to the probability of that behaviour's being repeated or not.

This has to be *very* tactfully done. A very skilled health visitor known to me asks parents if they have noticed mothers in the supermarket buying children sweets or chocolate if they demand it—so as to keep them quiet? She asks them what they think of this practice. Sometimes the mother says how silly it is to reward children for behaving badly! The health visitor then wonders if there could be anything similar going on with the child in question . . .? Often 'the penny drops' at this point. If not, it is best not to make an issue of it at this stage: there will be opportunities to return to it later.

Step 7—Gathering 'Base-line Data' for One Negative and One Positive Behaviour

In order to test any of the above ideas we need a 'base-line', a benchmark, against which to measure the present situation and change in the future. To that end we need to provide families with a means of recording the number of instances of that behaviour over a number of weeks: how otherwise are we to know whether there is evidence to support any given hypothesis or not?

In my own work I often ask parents to collect records, counts of whether a child does or does not follow a request. 'Obedience' and 'disobedience', to use old-fashioned terms, are major preoccupations of parents and they are often ready to follow my suggestion that we start with them. Appendix 7 is an example of a recording sheet; Appendix 8 is a blank recording sheet upon which to enter counts of behaviour, and Appendix 9 provides a means of logging the weekly records. This is an essential step. If parents are uncomfortable with written record sheets, then they can put buttons in two jars, one positive and one negative, matches in two boxes or stickers on the fridge—anything, so long as at the end of this first week there are two counts of the child's behaviour, one positive and one negative.

If no specific behaviour presents itself which can have both a positive and negative form, as does 'compliance' and 'non-compliance', then two other behaviours, one positive and one negative, must be selected. Families known to me have chosen:

Negative	*Positive*
Hitting or biting other children.	Comforting a hurt child.
Restless, impulsive behaviour for five-minute intervals.	Sitting quietly with a book or game for five-minute intervals.
Rude, cheeky behaviour to a child or adult.	Speaking quietly and nicely to child/adult.

When this base-line information is available, we can begin systematically to test the ideas that have been derived from the formulation and in collaboration with the parents to explore which one(s) most accurately help us understand the child's unhappiness or troublesomeness.

We now move to the stages of Planning our intervention, Implementing the plan and Reviewing and Evaluating its effectiveness.

5

ASPIRE—PLANNING, IMPLEMENTATION, REVIEW AND EVALUATION

Planning takes place on the basis of the formulation and the ideas or hypotheses which have flowed from it. I have found in my own practice that at this stage parents can grasp only a few key ideas of what I am trying to share with them; they are still too involved emotionally in the distressing events associated with their child's difficult behaviour: broken nights, family rows, threats from neighbours and sometimes the threat of a major relationship break-up. However, we should clarify what we are doing at every stage in the hope that, as the child becomes less troubled, there will be a logic and coherence about what happens and things will 'make sense'.

THE STAGE OF PLANNING—WITH PARENTS OR CAREGIVERS

The practitioner at this stage is probably trying to plan an intervention on three 'fronts':

1. Dealing with issues arising from any predisposing stressors: for example, conflict between separated parents about access to the child.

2. Taking into account organic factors in the child; for example, arranging for a hearing test for a toddler who pays little attention to instructions.
3. Developing a response to the upsetting day-to-day behaviours.

All three require involving the parent(s) and trying to keep them involved.

Step 8—Planning (P of the ASPIRE Process)

Involving parents in dealing with predisposing stressors

For some children it will be apparent that they have experienced many tensions in their short lives and that these are still causing distress. Some children may have had repeated experiences of separation because of, say, hospital admissions, leading to acute anxiety, unsettled behaviour in the child and an undermining of the parents' capacity to manage the child calmly and firmly. Other children may have special needs and be unable to interpret the instructions and guidance of parents and caregivers as readily as children without disabilities. In yet others, the children may be the focus of intense competition for their loyalty among contending partners or families in a divorce or separation; they may find it hard to know what is expected of them and have learned to play one parent off against another. Many others live in profound disadvantage, with multiple demands made upon their parents, who are so stressed that their child's needs for consistent management come very low on the agenda.

We should respond to these predisposing stressors with every resource available to us. We shall be drawing upon community resources such as family centres and day nurseries to give parents respite from the full-time care of their children; referring families to welfare rights agencies to ensure that they are receiving their full financial entitlements; and enlisting the support of community agencies such as Homestart, which can introduce befrienders to needy families.

Some children's troubles can be helped by having worrying events or circumstances that they do not understand explained and discussed with them *as far as they concern themselves and their security.* Four and five year-olds cannot grasp why marriages or relationships of great importance to them come to an end, nor why they have only one parent while their friends at playgroup have two. They cannot understand why they have to live with grandparents when someone whom they have been told is their sister lives with the mother or father. They may not understand their colour: why are they of darker or lighter skin colour than other children within the family and what are their relationships to these other children? They can, however, benefit greatly from adults being open with them, answering their questions, without overloading them with too much, or too emotional, information. Many children worry acutely, and the open-ended questions suggested by Herbert (1991) can help them deal with these worries (see Chapter 6, p. 147.

Planning: responding to the special circumstances of a given child

The life experiences of some children may call for specialised therapy. Children who have been abused, emotionally, physically or sexually, children who have witnessed a parent or sibling being raped, assaulted or murdered and children who have been traumatised in a range of other ways, are all likely to manifest their distress through behaviour difficulties, either of the anti-social or the withdrawn variety. The book by Oaklander (1988), *Windows to Our Children*, may offer practitioners much assistance in helping these children.

Many children will have particular needs in respect of help with language and communication. Some receive such lengthy and complicated instructions from their caregivers that they simply cannot understand what they are being asked to do. These parents—indeed almost all parents—need help in giving very simple and clear messages to their children. For ideas on how to do this, see p. 233.

In order to ensure that each child receives the individualised, nurturing attention for which many of them are clamouring, I ask each parent to spend about 15 minutes every day with each preschool child—and indeed with older children too, if possible. For young children, the natural medium for this special time is play—

with toys, games, clay, paint, dressing-up clothes, but it may be a time to look at something growing in a pot or in the garden: the child will usually know what the activity should be. This time is *not* meant to be educational in the narrow sense: it is nourishing the child with nurturing loving attention. It makes the child's spirit grow. Some parents find this hard to agree to: they say they do not know how to play or feel silly playing; if so, to look at a story book together and talk about the pictures offers the same opportunity for individual attention. Alternatively, they might feel able to spend 15 minutes daily with the child talking about simple events in the child's life: a visit to the park, a ride on a bus, going to the supermarket. These activities offer time both for closeness and intimacy and for extending the child's language and ability to use ideas.

For some children, our hypothesis may be simpler: the child is proving troublesome because he/she is not experiencing sufficient physical activity on a day-to-day basis to employ high levels of energy. Some young children are exceedingly lively—without falling into the 'hyperactive' category (see Chapter 8)—and become frantic if cooped up indoors in very cold or wet weather. Here the plan will include the child being given an opportunity for physical activity, for spending, say, 15 minutes daily at a park where running, climbing and chasing will use surplus energy. Some families may enjoy testing out a hypothesis, for example:

> A daily visit of 30 minutes to the park over four weeks will enable Stephen's behaviour to calm down—this change to be measured by the number of incidents in one week of his throwing himself on the floor or jumping off the furniture before and after the visits to the park began.

Helping parents to manage day-to-day interactions

Not all children's behaviour difficulties should be seen as stemming from major earlier life events, or from circumstances intrinsic to the child. *In many cases, it is rather that the day-to-day interactions between parents and children have become increasingly negative, so that a vicious downward spiral of misbehaviour, argument, criticism and rejection has developed. In any case, helping parents develop more positive styles of interaction with their children can only improve relationships.* In these circumstances, we need to teach skills of parenting positively.

Teaching the A–B–C Sequence

We saw in Chapter 2 how behaviour is embedded within a network of Antecedents and Consequences. If we have not already clarified this process with parents or family members, now is the time to do so. In essence, because Consequences of behaviours are so powerful, we are trying to help them understand Table 2.2 (see Chapter 2) and, gradually, Table 2.1. We may need to spend considerable time in helping parents think through their interactions with their child in the light of these principles. It may be that they can grasp readily that they are often themselves rewarding the very behaviour of which they are complaining: if not, we need supportively to help them grasp it. It must *not* be a matter of confrontation.

Teaching step-by-step or teaching principles?

There is a big debate among researchers about whether we should be teaching in a step-by-step way—'When he does that, you do this'—or whether we should be teaching principles, that is, the key concepts of the importance of rewarding and penalising behaviour, of being consistent and of knowing when to ignore. After discussing this issue with many practitioners I have come to the conclusion that this is a sterile debate: the consensus seems to be that we shall almost certainly need to start by giving some direct guidance to demoralised and depressed parents, but that we *should work towards* their understanding the principles and making them their own. If they can understand the principles they have them for the rest of the child's life and for the lives of their other children.

Key Ideas for Parents

Sometimes, however, the detail of the A–B–C sequence is too complicated for families to grasp amid the confusion of their child's constant misbehaviour and many families prefer a simple statement of key ideas. Some of the main ones are given in Box 5.1.

Box 5.1:   Some key ideas for parents

1. Children learn to repeat behaviours which are rewarded.
2. They learn not to repeat behaviours which are not rewarded.
3. Attention is a powerful reward for children: being ignored is a powerful penalty.
4. Even attention which seems unpleasant ('negative attention') can be rewarding.
5. It is very important to be consistent: try to keep all promises and threats.
6. Children learn by copying behaviour—our own and that of other children.

Examples for teaching these key ideas

1. Children learn to repeat behaviours which are rewarded

(i) Ask parents to recall the familiar scene of children screaming for sweets in the supermarket. Ask them to recall or imagine the children being bought sweets to keep them quiet. Do they think it likely that these children will scream for sweets the next time they go to the supermarket? Most parents say that they will. We can then ask if they see anything similar in the fact that their own child shrieks and constantly interrupts when visitors come, when the mother is talking to neighbours or when she is watching television? Often 'the penny will drop' at this point, but if not we can ask, if the child is not shrieking for sweets, for what might he be shrieking? The child is probably shrieking for attention, and while it is right that he should receive attention at suitable times, he must learn not to demand attention by interrupting visitors or parents speaking on the telephone.

(ii) Ask parents about their experience of being taught a skill: for example, driving, swimming, painting or using a word-processor. Did they have teachers who encouraged them or ones who criticised them? How did they react to the teacher who encouraged them and how to the teacher who criticised them? Parents may need support in accepting that they play any part in their child's behaviour, good or ill; this may be a difficult and unwelcome realisation. It is important to emphasise two things at this point: first, that children come into the world differently, with differing temperaments and predispositions; second, that parents cannot be expected to know how these principles work—that attending to a behaviour, good or bad, rewards it—since scientists are only just beginning to tease out these details, just as they are unravelling the story of how genes contribute to our overall make-up and development.

2. Children learn not to repeat behaviours which are not rewarded

(i) Ask parents how they would go about teaching a child who had constantly been 'bought off' with sweets in the supermarket that his mum couldn't afford to do this any more. Their replies will probably be sound and in line with behavioural theory. For example:
  - They would explain beforehand to the child that Mummy had no pennies for sweeties.
  - They would ask the child to behave quietly in the public place.
  - They would take along a toy or dolly to amuse the child.
  - They would tell the child they were pleased if he/she behaved quietly.
  Encourage all the ideas which do indeed offer solutions but avoid encouraging very threatening reactions.
(ii) Ask parents what sanction or punishment does seem to be effective with their children. Typically, they will say, 'Being denied television', or 'Being kept in when the other children are playing outside'. If the sanction is in line with principles of behavioural theory, encourage them to explain to their child that this will be the standard penalty for misbehaviour and then to use it absolutely consistently when the circumstances arise. Helping parents to find their own solutions will enhance their problem-solving abilities in the future and build self-esteem.

3. Attention is a very powerful reward for children; being ignored is a powerful penalty

(i) Ask parents what they think keeps actors or pop stars performing on stage. They will probably at some point say, 'The money', 'The applause' or 'The attention they get'. Then say something to the effect of, 'So what do you think keeps your Darren always wanting to be centre-stage?'

(ii) If the child is present at the time of this discussion and if, as often happens, keeps interrupting or pestering for attention, consistently ignore the child yourself and ask the parent consistently to ignore him. Eventually the child will lose interest and wander off to do something else. Explain that this is one of the main ideas you are talking about. One very skilled health visitor known to me persists in carrying out her interview with the mother however much the child is interrupting; she manages to avoid speaking or even looking at him and invariably he eventually wanders away.

(iii) Ask parents what their own experience of being attended to was, when they were little. Did they feel they received the attention they needed? Build on their replies to illustrate how children all need and seek attention but at some times it is appropriate to give it them and sometimes it is entirely inappropriate.

4. Even attention that seems unpleasant ('negative attention') can be rewarding

(i) To illustrate this idea I usually describe the mother referred to previously, who said of her little boy, Paul, 'Hitting doesn't work: I've been hitting him for two years and I know it doesn't work'. I explain how this little boy had learned that the only way to get attention was to misbehave; his mother, who still loved him dearly, did what she believed was the right thing to do, she smacked him. *This is 'negative attention'—that is, gaining attention even though it is of a negative kind.* Happily, it was a fairly straightforward matter to guide her to ignore, or briefly penalise, the child's misbehaviour and to attend warmly but consistently to the few instances of positive behaviour which he did display. In line with the theory, these gradually increased while the instances of misbehaviour decreased. These principles are brought together in Box 5.2.

5. It is very important to be consistent: keep promises and threats

(i) The example which seems to register with many parents and caregivers is to enquire if they had ever had the experience of

---

Box 5.2:   Practical guidelines for parents

Parenting Positively: Some Notes for Parents

1. Work out some house or family guidelines: for example, 'All toys must be put away before bedtime'. Everyone helps everyone else to carry out the guidelines.
2. Find three behaviours each day for which you can praise a child. Catch them behaving well!
3. Reward behaviour you want to encourage by attending to it and showing how pleased you are with it.
4. Ignore small misbehaviours: whining, pestering, tantrums. Turn your back on the child.
5. Try to be consistent. If you promise or threaten something, you must carry out the promise or threat.
6. Speak directly and firmly to your child when giving instructions.
7. Encourage others who care for the child to use these same guidelines.
8. Take a day at a time. Put yesterday behind you.
9. You'll have some bad days. Try to commend yourself for what you have already achieved.
10. Try to find someone you can confide in when it all seems to be falling apart. Don't give up.

---

being promised something and then of that promise being broken? Most *have* had that experience and remember the confusion, anger and deep disappointment which accompanied it. It is then fitting to say that this is the same sort of confusion which their own child probably feels if parents make promises which are then not kept. We all do this on occasion, for sometimes circumstances are beyond our control, but children learn from this inconsistency; they learn to take no notice of what their parents say.

(ii) We can also discuss the more serious learning which occurs when parents make threats which they do not keep. 'Do that again, Jimmy, and we shan't be going to the park'. 'If you speak to me like that again, you won't be going out after tea'. The child does it again, or speaks rudely again, yet still goes to the park or out after tea. He learns that threats are meaningless, are never carried out and can be safely ignored.

6. *Children learn by copying behaviour—their parents' and that of other children*

Here we can illustrate how children learn their own main language—English, Welsh, Chinese, Urdu—largely by using skills of imitation. If they can learn a complicated skill like speaking a language by imitation, they can easily learn patterns of behaviour by imitation. We can then ask parents if they have noticed their child copying them in any way, by the way they talk to their dolls, by the things they say, by their likes and dislikes or in any other way. We can then point out that children may be imitating more serious patterns of behaviour which they experience around them: swearing, aggressiveness, even domestic violence. Clearly, much tact is needed in exploring these issues.

Making use of examples of record keeping

Some parents want to see examples of how these principles have been helpful to other families. I am therefore including Figure 5.1, which was drawn up in a research study for a little boy who was driving his mother frantic. It may look rather 'clinical' but it illustrates how, in an admittedly unusually determined family, children's misbehaviour can reduce and their desirable behaviour increase.

This little boy's misbehaviour, shown by the dotted line, initially intensified in line with the common finding that *behaviour frequently gets worse before it gets better*, but then began markedly to improve. Correspondingly, his positive behaviour also improved as his mother began to commend and praise him for doing as she asked. It must be acknowledged that the improvement is seldom as simple or as clear cut as this; there are often many ups and downs as parents, relatives and teachers try to get to grips with a new style of child management.

I also tell parents about the little girl who, for so-called 'eating problems', gained a great deal of attention in the form of discussion of her behaviour with other adults while she was present. She had learned a very effective method of manipulating the anxiety of her mother by toying with her meals, demanding different dishes and then not eating them and all the while 'holding centre-stage'

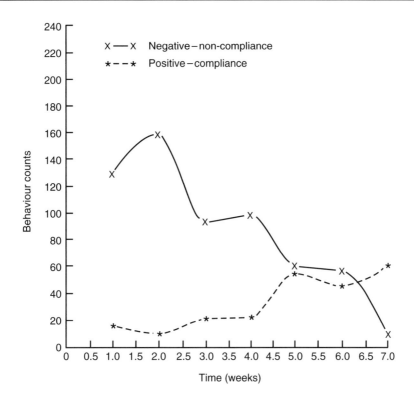

Figure 5.1: Plot of behaviour counts for R.B. over the period of the study. A record of one little boy's pattern of compliance and non-compliance

among her family and relatives. Happily, here too, after due assessment, it was possible to plan with the parents to ignore the inappropriate attention-seeking behaviour, to give her nurturing and affectionate attention at other times and to give her reasonably balanced and varied meals alongside her mother's and father's. Her plate was removed when theirs were and no further food at all was available until the next meal-time. She was also quietly commended when she did eat but the attention was low-key and calm. This long-standing difficulty resolved in less than a week.

Identifying and Working with One Pair of Behaviours

This has already been touched upon in Chapter 4, when pinpointing the behaviours whose frequency should be recorded. It is here that inexperienced practitioners should seek support and guidance from their supervisors or practice teachers. Practitioners need to establish their credibility quickly with parents or teachers, hence the need for choosing a difficulty known to extinguish fairly readily, such as whining or grizzling behaviour. I recommend attempting to work with only one pair of behaviours at the outset, when everyone may be new to one another and to this way of working. Another pair can be added later.

Recall that we need at least a week's counts of one negative behaviour and of one positive behaviour to act as the 'base-lines' against which to measure subsequent change—and that while the parents are recording this they should not try to make any changes at all in their ways of responding to the child. If this is a fairly straightforward task, easily accomplished, then in the following week the parents can begin to collect base-line information for the second pair of behaviours—say, those associated with sleeping. If the family insist that they want help with sleeping difficulties before anything else, then if you are inexperienced at least be in touch with a colleague with experience in this field; this is *essential*. Beware, too, of being pressurised to give guidance before you have firm base-line data against which to measure subsequent change.

Let us suppose that a pair of behaviours has been identified:

Negative: Samantha whines and grizzles if she does not get what she wants.
Positive: Samantha sometimes accepts quietly that she cannot have something she wants.

Or, if a misbehaviour has been chosen which does not have a simple counterpart:

Negative: Stephen punches his mother when she will not do as he wants.
Positive: Stephen occasionally helps his mum clear the table after tea.

Having obtained the base-line for one of the pairs of behaviours, and having ensured that you have introduced family members to the A–B–C analysis for understanding behaviour, discuss how in the next week they can avoid reinforcing the child's negative behaviour while ensuring that positive behaviour is attended to and rewarded. Some people understand the point immediately and make very relevant suggestions; others may need supportive guidance.

> *Negative*: Samantha whines and grizzles if she does not get what she wants. (Probable appropriate response: parents should turn away and ignore the whining, giving 'no speech, no eye contact').
> *Positive*: Samantha sometimes accepts quietly that she cannot have something she wants. (Probable appropriate response: parents should warmly but quietly commend her for accepting 'No').

As parents begin to understand the theoretical concepts in the light of their experience, they themselves can often suggest what steps to take with a given difficulty. It is then possible to move from the 'when he does that, try doing this . . .' approach to one based upon cognitive-behavioural *principles*. Typically, given that a minor misbehaviour has been chosen as the target misbehaviour, and either its mirror image or some other instance of desirable behaviour has been identified as the positive behaviour, they should:

1. Attempt to pay no attention at all to the misbehaviour—or give the least possible attention to it.
2. Notice each instance of the positive behaviour, for example behaviour not accompanied by whining, and praise the child for it ('I like it very much when you talk to me so nicely, Jane; well done', or words to that effect).
3. Continue to keep records of counts of each behaviour, positive and negative.

Involving Children in the Plan

When planning a clear change in the manner of handling a situation, it will be helpful to explain this to the child or young person concerned. This prepares him or her cognitively for what is to follow and enables him or her swiftly to make sense of the changes in the parents' behaviour. For example, a mother might explain to her four year-old that:

1. From now on, Mum and Dad are not going to keep on saying 'No' to requests for sweets when they are out. Mum (or Dad) will say 'No' once, and after that they will not even answer. Sweets will be available only at home on Saturdays—or whatever other arrangement the family chooses.
2. Even if her friend's Mummy allows her daughter to see a lot of television, Lucy will be allowed to see only specific programmes at home.
3. Meal times have become unhappy for everyone. From now on, Mum will not ask James what he wants to eat; she will prepare one meal for everyone, and if James does not want this, he can have bread and butter or go without.

Primary school age children may need a more 'thought-through' clarification at this Planning stage. If a practitioner has discussed with parents the strategy of using Time Out (see Chapter 7, p. 230) to manage endless bickering between her children, aged five and seven, and this has appealed to the parents, then the rules for Time Out should be explained calmly and quietly to the children

---

Box 5.3: A plan which a parent might negotiate with her son

1. Mum will have a talk with Stephen about:
   (a) How much pocket money she can afford to let him have each week.
       ● What will have to be bought from this amount.
       ● When he would like her to give it to him.
   (b) What, in return, he will do to help out in the household, for example:
       ● Emptying the rubbish daily.
       ● Taking the dog out each evening.
2. She will explain that once she has given him his pocket money, she will not be able to afford to give him any more, however often he asks and whatever he calls her.
3. She will thank him for small things he does around the house: e.g. hoovering.
4. Stephen can earn money for additional jobs that his mother wants done; she will work out a tariff: so much for . . . . and so much for . . . .
5. She will go on keeping records of targeted positive and negative behaviours.

---

concerned, so that when the new approach is used they recognise what is happening. They will still object, but at least they will understand. If they refuse to go to Time Out, then their television viewing time will be reduced—and so on. The parents *must* see through what they have said.

It is very helpful to write down the key ideas which have been discussed and the key steps which will be taken (see Appendix 10). This is supportive to the family when the practitioner is not immediately available. For older children, more in need of explanations, it may be necessary to show parents how to write an agreement in order that there shall be minimal disagreement at the stage of implementing the plan. Agreements are discussed in Chapter 12, p. 299 and forms for writing agreements are included as Appendices 14 and 15. For example, a parent, supported by a practitioner, might plan as shown in Box 5.3.

Devising the Plan: a More Complex Situation

In more complex situations, where there has been a substantial period of assessment leading to a number of hypotheses to be tested, a fuller plan may be necessary. For example, a number of key points arise from the assessment of the difficulties of Kevin Jackson, a troubled five year-old.

Predisposing factors:
1. Kevin has been much upset by the loss of contact with his dad, who left six months ago.
2. His mother, Elizabeth, says she is depressed.
3. Kevin may be feeling very much on his own; he does not seem to have friends.
4. Kevin does not like going to school; he says he is being called names.

Organic and developmental factors:
1. Kevin is very tall and strong for his age.

Immediate behaviours causing difficulty:

Negative: 1. Kevin throws and breaks things when he is fed up, e.g. ornaments.

  2. Often he comes home late from school; he will not say
     where he has been.
  3. He sometimes kicks his mother when frustrated.

Positive: Kevin can be helpful: for example, he sometimes clears
            the table.

Mrs Jackson and the practitioner agree to start with a week of
recording one negative and one positive behaviour. They choose
kicking his mother for the negative behaviour and clearing the
table for the positive behaviour (Table 5.1).

Negative: Kevin kicks his mother (base-line of eight instances in the
            first week).
Positive: Kevin helps clear the table (base-line of two instances in
            the first week).

Thereafter, a plan to help the Jackson family is drawn up (Box 5.4)
the positive and negative behaviours are charted for the next eight
weeks (Figure 5.2).

SHOWING THE INCREASE OR DECREASE WEEK BY WEEK

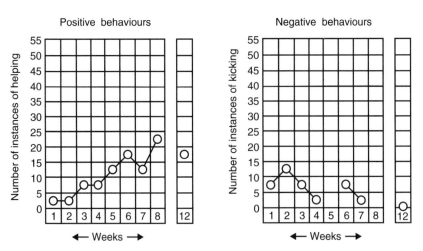

Figure 5.2: Kevin's positive and negative behaviours over eight weeks
and at three months follow-up

Table 5.1: Number of instances of Kevin's positive and negative behaviours over one week

CHARTING BEHAVIOURS				Name: Kevin Jackson			Week beginning: 17 October Week 1	
Behaviour	*Sunday*	*Monday*	*Tuesday*	*Wednesday*	*Thursday*	*Friday*	*Saturday*	*Total*
Behaviours to encourage and praise—Clearing table								
Morning								
Afternoon								
Evening			✓		✓			2
Behaviours to discourage—Kicking mother								
Morning					✓		✓✓	8
Afternoon			✓	✓				
Evening	✓	✓✓						

Box 5.4:   A plan to help the Jackson family

Plan for helping Kevin, aged five

This plan is drawn up by:
Mrs Jackson and Melanie Jones, Educational Welfare Officer, on 12 March

The main objectives of the work are:
1. To reduce the number of times Kevin, aged five, kicks his mother.
2. To reduce the number of times Kevin throws things.
3. To make life happier for Kevin, as he seems very upset and miserable.

Key points arising from the planning sessions:
1. Mrs Jackson will let her former husband know how much Kevin seems to be missing him.
2. She will ask him to try to see Kevin regularly, even if only once a fortnight.
3. She will talk with Kevin and say that even if he is upset, he must not kick her.
   (a) She will try to find out if anything further, e.g. at school, is upsetting him.
   (b) She will explain she will keep a record of the number of times he kicks her.
   (c) Every day Mrs Jackson will spend 15 minutes with Kevin in whatever way he chooses: e.g. looking at football cards, talking about school or his interests.
   (d) Each time that Kevin kicks her he will be sent into Time Out and there will be no television at all that day.
   (e) Mrs Jackson will actively look out for aspects of Kevin's behaviour that she can praise and commend. Kevin can remind her if she forgets to do this.
4. (a) This plan will be discussed with Kevin (and his ideas about it taken notice of) and with Melanie at her visit in a week's time (19 March).
   (b) Melanie will undertake to meet with Kevin and understand more about the school situation. She will try to explore whether he is being bullied and/or being called names.

IMPLEMENTING THE PLAN

During this stage, which can follow directly from the base-line stage of at least one week, the agreed, written plan should be put into action.

Step 9—Implementation of the Plan: Principles to Be Observed

1. Parents should be supplied with charts of a standardised kind on which to collect counts of children's behaviour.
2. They should actively attend to the things in their children's behaviour which they want to see more of and, as far as possible, pay as little attention as they can to small misbehaviours. In terms of the theoretical principles, they should attempt to reinforce existing positive behaviours, while ignoring or penalising existing negative behaviours. Thus, Mrs Jackson is asked to thank Kevin for clearing the table, expressing her pleasure warmly, while penalising Kevin's kicking her by instantly sending him to Time Out for four minutes on each occasion (see Chapter 7), and refusing him any TV that day.
3. Parents must be warned that 'things may get worse before they get better'. In my own research about 50% of the children did show this deteriorating behaviour before there was evidence of improvement. This period can be extremely difficult for hard-pressed parents to accept but it is better that they should be alerted to what may happen and find it does not, than that they should not be alerted and find that it does! To be able to anticipate this possible deterioration also raises the credibility of the practitioner very agreeably.
4. The practitioner should telephone or send a postcard part way through this second week to encourage the family to persist with their new strategy. Part of the task of the professional at this stage is to troubleshoot, encourage and exhort the parents not to give up now!
5. The practitioner should meet with the family at the end of the week and consider the records with them. If, as already

Table 5.2: Problems and possible solutions at the implementation stage (with acknowledgements to the Health Visitors and School Nurses of Fosse Health Trust for many excellent suggestions)

Common problem	Possible solution
Keeping going—that is, maintaining momentum with the new way of responding to the child.	Encouragement and support from us. Boosting self-esteem. Help with assertiveness.
Conflicting advice from others.	Emphasise research underpinning.
Extended family has different views and treats child differently.	Try to get all the family together and explain that the child is confused.
Too many other demands on parent.	Focus on just one area of difficulty, and give much encouragement to parents to continue.
Mum says she can't see it through.	Involve other support: sister, relative?
Another crisis happens.	Put programme 'on hold' but fix restart date.
Neighbours complain.	Talk to and explain plan to neighbours beforehand.
Pressure from school regarding the child.	Talk to and involve school.
Difficult to be consistent.	Help parents to commend themselves for being consistent . . . 'I did it! I saw it through . . .'
'This way of working is weak— what he needs is a thrashing . . .'	'It's a gentle approach, but it takes a lot of strength to put it into effect . . .'
Spouse/partner sabotages plan.	Acknowledge the rejecting feelings, but ask spouse to 'opt out' for four weeks, while you work with main carer. Then evaluate.
Parents lose heart.	Show file of success stories from parents.
Unable to manage Time Out.	Help negotiate 'family rules'. Involve children of four and older in planning sanctions.
Parent not complying with guidance.	Say, 'I *can* help, but only if you do as I suggest. Please phone me if you need me'.

discussed, the child's misbehaviour *has* got worse, parents can be commiserated with but also reminded that this was anticipated. If the behaviour improved, parents can be commended for their persistence but warned that much work remains to be done.

6. The counts of desirable and undesirable behaviour should be entered upon a simple graph (see Figure 5.2, Appendix 9 for a chart) to display the changes in patterns of behaviour for all to see.

Table 5.3: Rewards and penalties across the life span (with acknowledgements to a group of very creative practitioners, health visitors, teachers, social workers, nursery nurses and a family therapist who met in Bexley, Kent, in 1998)

Age	Rewards	Penalties
0–4	Cuddles, hugs, kisses. Approving attention. Praise and admiration. Simple outings: to a friend, to the park.	Being disapproved of. Being ignored. Criticism and blame. Being taken home from outing. Calm Down time (see Chapter 7).
5–11	All the above, plus: Stickers. Staying up late. Family outings, e.g. swimming.	All the above, plus: Loss of TV. Loss of privileges. Extra chores.
12–18	All the above, plus: Favourite meal. Extend coming home time. Friend invited for a meal. Friends invited to stay night. Friend invited for family outing.	All the above, plus: Ban on use of phone. Make coming home time earlier. Friends not permitted to come, for example for three evenings. Being collected from a party. Being 'grounded', i.e. required to stay in.
Parents	Choice of TV programme. Chance to meet friends. Uninterrupted time to yourself. Having ironing done. Having a meal cooked for you. An appreciative note about child from school.	Long arguments. Loss of friends. Constant interruptions. Not being listened to/heard. Being taken for granted. A complaint from school.

7. Parents often ask whether their child should be allowed to see the records. I suggest being very relaxed about this. They probably will see them in any case, and will ask what they are for. It seems best to say, in a non-committal way, 'Oh, I am just recording how often you do what I ask you . . .' or words to that effect. It is best not to make a big issue of the matter.

Managing the Implementation Stage

There are inevitable difficulties in the Implementation stage. Table 5.2 shows some of the most common of these, together with approaches that at least some practitioners have found to offer solutions. At this stage, too, the parents may say that they, too, would welcome some reward for all their efforts to be consistent and to ignore difficult behaviour. To this end, one of the groups I have worked with has suggested the list of both rewards and penalties, not only for children but for their parents and carers too, which is given in Table 5.3.

REVIEWING AND EVALUATING THE PLAN

This stage takes place at a date agreed beforehand by all concerned. Discussion will take place informally about progress or the lack of it as the weeks pass but at a fixed point, usually six to eight weeks after the start, there needs to be a shared examination of the evidence—which should be available on a simple graph.

Reviewing and Evaluating: How Do They Differ?

The process of reviewing is essentially that of monitoring progress, or the lack of it, as the practitioner collaborates with the parents or family members. It is an on-going process which takes place during the course of the implementation of the plan. By contrast, evaluation takes place once, right at the end of the intervention, but both use *evidence* as the basis for discussion.

Step 10—Reviewing the Intervention

This requires the latter to review (literally, look at again) with those concerned how they are faring in respect of progress towards the desired goals in respect of each of the child's difficulties written in the problem profile. Is there evidence to support one or more of the hypotheses? If the plans drawn up after the assessment have been followed, then there should be information or reports from, say, other professionals such as speech therapists or audiologists to consider, as well as letters from a child's school or from counsellors. In addition there will be evidence arising from helping the parents interact with their child differently—typically in a more positive way.

In my own research many of the major difficulties were reported as much improved, while several of the lesser problems had disappeared completely—*and these would have been forgotten had they not been written down.* Both quantitative and qualitative evidence are likely to be available, together with views of grandparents, teachers and, of course, the parents and the practitioner as well.

It is crucial to *maintain* an approach based on cognitive-behavioural theory. Very often, when parents report that some behaviours continue to be a problem, they have unintentionally again begun to attend to a pattern of behaviour which they had formerly learned to ignore. This is one of the major areas of difficulty in implementing principles of cognitive-behavioural theory: having been involved in years of arguments over demands which they cannot grant or do not think it fit to grant, many parents find that with support from the practitioner they *can* manage to ignore them; *however, the parents' original pattern of responses to their child has been so deeply learned that it readily resurfaces in stressful circumstances*—and before they know it, they are back into the old, distressing but familiar routine of rows and arguments with their child. If they can be persuaded to continue to keep records, however, this lapse will show up on the record sheets and can be explored by the practitioner in reviewing progress.

Sometimes, reviewing progress throws up other factors which are impeding progress and about which something must be done. This is the skill of 'trouble-shooting'. I have experienced three particular areas of difficulty: the first is the impact of the behaviour of other people who influence the child's behaviour strongly; the second is lack of confidence on the part of one or both parents, leading to difficulties in making confident requests to the child; and the third is difficulties experienced by parents in implementing the Time Out strategy. Let us consider each in turn.

The impact of people in the wider environment: It is obvious that as a child grows older, his/her life is influenced by ever-widening circles (systems) of people. Initially, it may be only the parents, childminders or nursery staff who have direct influence upon the child, but soon other children and other relatives have their impact—for good or ill. People typically want to be helpful, but as they do not understand the principles of cognitive-behavioural theory they do not always make constructive suggestions. They say things like, 'We had to eat everything on our plates when I was a child', or 'Boys will be boys; you don't want to make a cissy out of him!'. One major source of difficulty can be a family member who actively disagrees with what the practitioner is suggesting about how to respond to the child, saying, 'Don't take any notice of what that health visitor/social worker is saying; what does she mean—to praise the child more? What he needs is a good thrashing!'.

Other people, perhaps grandparents, again with the best of intentions, can sabotage new strategies of managing a child by actively undermining what the parents have requested—for example, that he should be ignored when he misbehaves. Grandpa may instead seek to divert the child by producing a treat or a diversion whenever he becomes obstreperous—so teaching him that to behave in this way is the very thing most likely to prove rewarding. I found in my research that for a parent, particularly a mother, to lack someone who actively supported her or, more seriously, to have someone who deliberately undermined her, was a recipe for failure. Lone parents, by contrast, were often very successful: they could follow the guidance given without anyone undermining them.

A particular example of this from my research was one family's difficulty in managing three year-old Danny. His uncle Bill, wanting to be constructive, taught him 'play-fighting' when the family visited each weekend. Danny loved this and took what he had learned into his nursery, where he found it made him a very powerful fellow indeed; he could take whatever toys he wanted and the other children did whatever he told them. It took a good deal of insistence on the part of Danny's parents to stop Uncle Bill from teaching Danny to play-fight—because Danny had come to look forward to all this attention and wanted the 'games' to continue. When the play-fighting was eventually stopped, however, and with further calm management on the part of Danny's parents, his aggressive behaviour at nursery also gradually died away— because it was no longer rewarded.

The effect of gentle, unassertive parents or caregivers: Practitioners should be alert to the possibility that very gentle, unassertive parents may find it extremely difficult or perhaps contrary to their values to impose their wishes on their child—and indeed, may see this as the 'imposition of adult dominance upon impressionable children'. A typical scenario is a young, rather gentle mother who happens to have given birth to a tearaway; she may be a lone parent or she may have a partner who either dissociates himself from the job of bringing up children or, because he himself has not the slightest difficulty in getting the child to do as he is told, regards his wife or partner as ineffectual or stupid. He typically makes little effort to help her manage the child and indeed, their different ways of handling him may itself lead to arguments between them. In these circumstances, it is essential to be tactful both in acknowledging that the father has few difficulties with the child and in helping the mother to develop strategies which are both effective and acceptable to her.

It is important to insist that the child really does 'need a clear message' from her if he is first, to attend to it and second, to act upon it. I have spent much time, either in face-to-face situations or over the telephone, coaching these loving but unassertive parents, in delivering these 'clear messages' to their child—in a firm and confident voice. The parent plays him/herself and I play the child; after a minute or so of role play, in which I'm asked to 'Find my shoes as it's time to go out' or to 'Come into the kitchen' I respond according to whether I felt my 'mother' really meant business. If I receive a clear, firm and assertive request, I comply: if the request was unclear and unassertive, I ignore it. In these latter circumstances, we have another go, until I (as the child) can report that I feel, 'She really does mean what she says this time: I'd better do as I'm told!' It is all very light-hearted and we laugh a lot. Sometimes I have to reassure parents that it is all right to be as firm as this; that is, this is not being domineering to the child—he needs to know that there are boundaries and that he is safe.

Difficulties in implementing the Time Out procedure: A third conclusion from my research, which links with the other findings, was that where parents could not implement the Time Out procedure (see Chapter 8) there was very little hope of their achieving a successful outcome. For their children had learned, sometimes over several years, to expect and to gain the limelight on every available opportunity and seriously to misbehave if this attention or their whims were denied. Extensive research has repeatedly shown that the most successful strategy for dealing with these insatiable demands is a few minutes in Time Out—that is, denying the child for very brief intervals the very thing that he demands— so that he can learn that positive attention is contingent upon his attending to other people, their needs and their guidance. It is no easy task, however, particularly for a lone mother, effectively to ignore a rude and aggressive child, especially if he is strong and has no respect at all for her or the rights of other people. However, ways *must* be found to ensure that the child is ignored—often by use of the Time Out procedure. This issue is considered in greater depth in Chapter 9.

Evaluating the intervention

This takes place right at the end of a series of weekly meetings or conversations, and is an opportunity for the family to offer a final judgement upon work undertaken together. The evidence of progess or otherwise will be to hand and it should be a simple matter to compare the final situation with the starting point and to judge whether there is evidence of improvement or deterioration against each goal. As when reviewing, a number of different forms of evidence will be available.

Alternatively, this may be time for a fresh Assessment: to consider what has been overlooked in the first assessment, or what has happened to throw an initially good programme of intervention off course. In one situation in which I was involved, things had started well, and the mother reported excellent progress. In week 5, however, she reported that 'Everything has fallen apart: he's worse than when we started'. I was at a loss but then remembered to ask whether anything out of the ordinary had happened since I had last spoken with her. 'Well', she said, 'We've had Easter and he did get seven Easter eggs . . . I thought I'd let him get them over with, so he ate them in two days . . .!' Here we had a completely different variable directly affecting the child's behaviour. When the effects of the chocolate wore off and the mother regained her confidence in how she was learning to manage the child, he resumed his pattern of improved behaviour.

It is important at this stage to ask the parents to complete once again the measures which they completed at the outset, using the Strengths and Difficulties Questionnaire (Goodman, 1997) or whatever measure the practitioner has employed. It is likely that the child will receive a lower score on this post-intervention measure. If the work is being evaluated quantitatively, the data for the children's pre- and post-score can be analysed using a number of statistical tests. If only qualitative data is being gathered, statements about the child's behaviour before and after the intervention can be compared. Similarly, data concerning the depression level of the parents can be compared, pre- and post-intervention, and a bank of data built up to show the impact of the 'Parenting Positively' programme.

II

HELPING FAMILIES WITH SPECIFIC DIFFICULTIES

6

HELPING FAMILIES WITH CHILDREN WHO ARE ANXIOUS OR DEPRESSED

DEFINITION OF EMOTIONAL DISORDERS

We saw in Chapter 2 that emotional disorders were reported by Rutter (1987) to be common among children. He defined them thus:

> Emotional disorders, as the name suggests, are those in which the main problem involves an abnormality of the emotions, such as anxiety, fear, depressions, obsessions, hypochondriasis and the like.

This chapter will focus upon anxiety and depression in pre-school and primary school-age children.

PREVALENCE OF EMOTIONAL DIFFICULTIES IN CHILDREN

Some of the best known studies of the incidence of emotional disturbance among children are those by Rutter et al (1975a). These compared 1689 10 year-olds growing up in an Inner London borough with 1279 10 year-old children living in the Isle of Wight. The Inner London children showed almost double the rate of disturbance of the Isle of Wight children. Both these and later enquiries have shown a range of 4 5–9.9% of 10 year-olds as experiencing emotional disorders, depending upon the location of the study. The figure for major depression among children is in the range 0.5–2.5% (Department of Health, 1995). (See Table 1.1 p. 16.)

Variables Protecting Children from Emotional Difficulties

Because not all children apparently equally stressed by their circumstances experience emotional or behavioural difficulties, research has been directed towards establishing what factors may give some protection. Rutter et al (1975a, b) noted the following protective circumstances:

- A low stress level within the home.
- Good circumstances compensating for stress at home, e.g. at school.
- Temperamental features of the child: easy, adaptable children are less vulnerable than awkward, negativistic ones.
- Heredity: some children may be genetically less likely to succumb to environmental stress than others.
- Good relationships with at least one parent.

This work has been built on by Garmezy (1983), who reviewed studies of acutely disadvantaged children in an attempt to pinpoint what made them able to function well despite living amid poverty and prejudice. He found that black children, growing up in urban ghettos, benefited from:

- Features of the child's disposition: the children were perceived as stable, competent and with a positive sense of self.
- Family cohesion and warmth: even where fathers were absent, mothers offered a well-structured environment and generous personal praise.
- Support figures, e.g. in school, who served as positive models for the children.

These studies, together with others, e.g. Werner and Smith (1982), who studied the development of vulnerable children, converge on the following evidence as offering protection:

1. Features of the child's temperament and disposition.
2. Family cohesion and warmth.
3. Supportive figures in the school or local environment.

Thus, in summary, it seems that psychosocial stress, such as growing up in a family where there is poverty, unemployment and overcrowding, together with marked discord between parents or caregivers, *particularly where these stresses are cumulative*, can place a child at risk of major difficulties. Nevertheless, the protective factors noted above can substantially reduce this risk.

We shall now consider the research concerning children and anxiety and children and depression separately.

RESEARCH INTO CHILDREN AND ANXIETY

Studies of Prevalence

As the quality of research improves, so more specific data are becoming available from international sources about the prevalence of children's troubles.

Forms of Anxiety

The *Diagnostic and Statistical Manual*, 4th edition, 1994 (DSM-IV) of the American Psychiatric Association classifies three anxiety disorders of childhood:

1. Separation anxiety disorder.
2. Avoidant disorder.
3. Over-anxious disorder.

Herbert (1991) reports:

- *Separation anxiety disorder* is characterised by 'excessive anxiety concerning separation from those to whom the child is attached'.

A child with separation anxiety disorder may be reluctant to go to school in order to stay near his/her mother or with some other important attachment figure. Headaches and stomach aches and other physical symptoms are also common.

- *Avoidant disorder* is characterised by 'excessive shrinking from contact with unfamiliar people that is of sufficient severity to interfere with social functioning in peer relationships . . . Such a child is likely to appear shy, socially withdrawn, embarrassed and timid when in the company of peers and adults. Of course, these behaviours may be appropriate at specific stages of development.

- *Over-anxious disorder* is characterised by 'excessive or unrealistic anxiety or worry'. An over-anxious child tends to worry excessively about school work and future events, and usually appears nervous or tense. The child has an incessant need for reassurance or comfort. Further, he/she complains of a variety of physical ailments (e.g. nausea and dizziness) and shows frequent self-consciousness.

Herbert goes on to clarify that in addition to these primary types of disorder, some children also experience both phobic disorders (persistent fears of specific stimuli, such as animals) and obsessive-compulsive disorders (in which certain rituals have to be

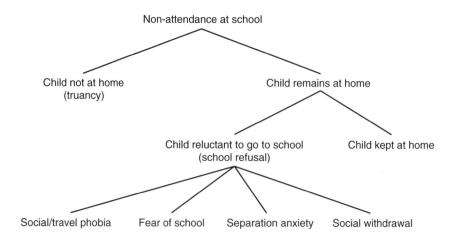

Figure 6.1: Non-attendance at school (reproduced with permission from Rutter, 1975)

frequently repeated to allay the child's anxiety). Such anxieties are often found among pre-school and school-age children, especially shy and conscientious ones. The indications are that children coping with these difficulties often come from homes particularly concerned with cleanliness, etiquette and morality. Some children with these anxieties also lack social skills. This can lead to increasing isolation from normal group activities, leading to misery which can intensify the obsessive symptoms.

School phobia is an anxiety-related disorder (Rutter, 1975), but it is a complex response which may be precipitated by a number of possible factors (Figure 6.1). The figure also shows distinctions to be made between forms of non-attendance at school; this highlights the need for very careful assessment and intervention.

Origins of Anxiety in Children: Natural Developmental Phenomena

It is entirely natural and normal for young children to be anxious and fearful. Ollendick and King (1991) suggest that:

> ... children experience a wide variety of 'normal' fears over their development and these fears appear to be related to their level of cognitive development (King, Hamilton and Ollendick, 1988). Young infants are afraid of loss of support, loud noises and strangers, as well as sudden, unexpected, and looming objects. One and two year-olds show a range of fears, including separation from parents and fear of strangers. During the third and fourth years, fears of the dark, being left alone, small animals and insects emerge. Fears of wild animals, ghosts and monsters come to the foreground during the fifth and sixth years; and fears of school, supernatural events and physical danger emerge in the seventh and eighth years. During the ninth to eleventh years, social fears and fears of war, health, bodily injury and school performance become more pronounced.

Most developmental fears, then, are transient. It appears that, under favourable circumstances, they fade away as a result of two main influences: first, children's naturally maturing cognitive processes, so that they come to understand that monsters, such as dinosaurs, are no threat to them; and, second, those who care for them *avoid reinforcing their fears* by giving simple explanations of upsetting noises like thunder and also by *avoiding showing fear* themselves. Thus, an understanding of cognitive-behavioural theory is of key importance in helping anxious children.

Origins of Anxiety in Children: Specific Events

Hersov (1985) has highlighted the specific impact of certain events in a child's life, such as a car accident or being the object of abuse, physical or sexual. Some children observe things which happen to other people, child or adult, such as loss of a parent via separation or bereavement, which brings the realisation that this could happen to them. In yet other cases there is 'contagion of anxiety' from chronically anxious parents (Eisenberg, 1958).

There is increasingly encouraging evidence (Kendall, 1991) of the impact of cognitive-behavioural strategies in helping children and young people. These include, after due assessment, correcting inaccurate or faulty cognitive interpretations or misunderstandings, training in physical relaxation and developing coping strategies through self-encouragement or behavioural rehearsal.

HELPING FAMILIES WITH ANXIOUS CHILDREN

Parents whose children are anxious or depressed are often deeply unhappy themselves: indeed, sometimes there is a vicious spiral of emotional distress in which each family member intensifies the difficulties experienced by the others. The sequences of the ASPIRE process (see Chapter 4) lend themselves to assessing, planning and intervening to reduce that distress.

Assessment

Anxious and depressed children are likely to find it very hard to communicate their difficulties—partly because they may feel that they will not receive a sympathetic hearing, partly because they are often shy and inarticulate, and partly because adults, caught up in their own worries, do not notice that they are unhappy or isolated. It is all the more difficult, therefore, for us to come close to them and to gain their confidence sufficiently for them to try to put their unhappiness into words. As with adults, a relationship-building approach showing concern and empathy is likely to be helpful.

Play and other activities as aids to assessment

It is, of course, essential to meet with the child and to gain his/her view of the situation as far as the age of the child permits. Children may be able to describe their fears or sadness and the situations which give rise to them—'I am afraid that now Mummy has left, Daddy may leave too'—but they may not. Sometimes there is an opportunity to convey something of their difficulties in drawing or painting and play materials should always be available to children. Oaklander (1988) describes some sensitive and imaginative activities in which it is possible to engage young children so that they may be able to express something of their troubles. There are many possible media: sand, clay, paint, papier maché, as well as dressing up, drama and writing. There is danger, however, in adults' interpreting a child's play or creative activity: it is usually

---

Box 6.1: Sentences for completion by troubled children (reproduced with permission from Herbert, 1991)

'I like to . . . .
'What I most dislike . . . .
'My best friend . . . .
'I wish . . . .
'My mum . . . .
'My dad . . . .
'If only . . . .
'In my home the nicest thing is . . . .
'The worst thing is . . . .
'I wish I knew . . . .
'I wonder . . . .
'The thing I worry about most is . . . .

better to seek the child's account of the significance of a painting, a poem or story.

Children willing to meet with the practitioner alone can often be much helped by a calm talk in which the worker makes it clear that he or she wishes only to help, and how it may be possible to do so. Herbert (1991) has proposed a number of open-ended statements which can help a younger child to indicate in an indirect manner something of the troubles or worries (Box 6.1).

As part of the attempt to understand a child's anxiety or depression, the practitioner will ask how the parents have attempted to deal with the situation. Often, understandably, they will say that they have talked to the child, told him or her that there is nothing to be afraid of or depressed about, asked him or her each morning how he or she is feeling and generally tried to reassure him or her. What they may not have thought of, and which is only becoming apparent because of research within the framework of cognitive-behavioural theory, is that they may be unwittingly reinforcing anxious or depressed behaviour in their child by unduly attending to it. This is, of course, likely to be only part of the story, but it is a significant part and the removal of this attention can, of itself, reduce the child's level of distress.

In all these situations of assessment, the constructive nature of the relationship between worker and parent(s) is paramount—based upon fundamental principles of counselling: empathy, warmth, genuineness and unconditional positive regard. This is **Step 1**.

Step 2—Information gathering

An holistic approach must be adopted—that is, one which considers the child's physical, social and psychological well-being and which acknowledges the impact both of maturation, such as increasing cognitive capacity to worry about the future as well as the past, and of events in the child's environment. As has been described in Chapter 4, careful assessment of the child's difficulty within the overall family and, as appropriate, the school system is necessary. Initially, however, the parents or caregivers will need time to unburden themselves of their own distress associated with the child's difficulties. Sometimes, talking to the practitioner in a calm and confidential setting will be the first opportunity parents or caregivers have had to speak freely of a situation without feeling that they are being implicitly criticised. This listening, as has been emphasised, is essentially a component of counselling and can markedly reduce tension for all concerned. A systematic approach (see Table 4.1) is helpful; see Appendix 4, which shows:

- Predisposing factor.
- Organic factors and developmental factors.
- Immediate variables: analysis of events in the child's daily life in terms of antecedents, behaviour and consequences (A–B–C).

Predisposing factors: These will include information from parents about when they first noticed that their child appeared tense or worried—indeed, what they noticed about him as a baby and toddler. Was he tense as an infant, or did this develop later? What seemed to distress the child in early life? When does the anxiety seem worse and when better? In respect of life events, parents can sometimes pinpoint a date or an event which they think contributed significantly to the child's difficulties: an accident, an admission to hospital, the move to a new school, or a separation of the child's parents. How has the child responded when they asked what was the matter?

Organic factors: These include variables which interact with physiological systems and which make it intrinsically more likely that the child will experience anxiety: for example, a tendency to be self-conscious and self-preoccupied leading to a tendency to blush, to wet him or herself or to develop a rash in stressful situations. Some children experience deeply painful shyness, so that they literally cannot look at another child or adult and are forever glancing past them or looking away. This social anxiety may be genetically underpinned or it may have been learned, either as a result of infrequent contact with the hurly burly of young children's play or of a very upsetting rejection. It will be important to ask how the parents understand or make sense of their child's anxiety or depression—but remember that parents or family members are unlikely to be familiar with the concept of 'anxiety' and its connotations—although they *are* likely to have encountered the idea of 'stress'. The child may be described as tense or worried, but is unlikely that parents will have an understanding of the physiological underpinnings of anxiety or depression or of how, for example, there can be generalisation of anxiety from one situation to other apparently very different situations.

The example of Marianne, a very anxious little girl: Consider Marianne, whose mother, Natalie, is asking her health visitor for help with her little girl's behaviour. Marianne is just four, an only child, who will not let Natalie out of her sight. The little girl follows her mother *everywhere*—all round the house, into the garden, even to the bathroom. Her mother feels increasingly annoyed with the little girl. If Natalie visits a friend, Marianne stands by her throughout the visit, rejecting all encouragement to play with other children. She insists on sleeping in her mother's bed.

Box 6.2:　Initial information concerning Marianne to inform the assessment

1. *Predisposing life events for this child and members of this family*:
   (a) Marianne's Daddy died in a road accident when she was three; she still asks for him.
   (b) Her mother is still grieving deeply.
   (c) Marianne's grandparents try to be helpful, but she will not stay with them.
   (d) Marianne has had little contact with other children, apart from a dancing class once a week. She will not stay at a playgroup or nursery.

2. *Organic factors, such as developmental stage or any disability or relevant illness*:
   (a) Marianne has always been 'shy'.
   (b) She had a number of allergies when a toddler, but these seem to have improved.

3. *Interactions within the family (A–B–C)**:
   (a) Marianne receives a great deal of attention when she behaves fearfully.
   (b) There are not many opportunities for her fearfulness to diminish as she meets few adults and fewer children.

*Natalie may not understand this concept, but it is useful to introduce it at this stage.

Further information comes to light as the asssessment proceeds; it can be entered on the summary sheet as shown in Box 6.2.

Step 3—Identifying problem behaviours

It is likely that Natalie will need help in beginning to think of her little girl's difficulties in terms of her *behaviours* but let us assume that she is able, with support, to identify the following:

1. Marianne cries a great deal.
2. She does not play with other children.
3. She screams when left with a neighbour or at playgroup.
4. She follows her mother round all the time.

When asked to list these behaviours in order of the distress they cause her, Natalie acknowledges that although she feels upset by her little girl's unhappiness, it is being followed about which irritates her most. So the list emerges:

1. Marianne follows her mother round all the time.
2. She cries a great deal.
3. She does not play with other children.
4. She screams when taken to a playgroup.

Step 4—Identifying positive features of a child's behaviour

This request may also surprise Natalie, but she is able to distinguish her little girl's strengths and qualities, although she probably needs help in stating them in terms of *observable behaviours*:

1. Marianne paints and draws readily: she is very imaginative.
2. She can pick out tunes on the piano: she seems very musical.
3. She goes readily to a small ballet class for five little girls; Natalie has to stay too. Here she smiles and occasionally laughs. She has one friend, Josie.

Step 5—Discovering desired outcomes

To the question of what target behaviours would Natalie like her little girl to show more frequently, she works out, with help, the following:

1. To allow Natalie to leave the living room for the kitchen or bathroom without Marianne following her.
2. To go to a nearby playgroup three mornings a week; Natalie to stay if necessary.
3. To let her Granny look after her for a day without screaming.

Step 6—Arriving at a formulation/rationale for the difficulties

When the practitioner has gathered as much relevant information as possible, or as much as she has time for, then it should be possible, drawing upon material offered by Natalie, to formulate some provisional rationale for Marianne's difficulties. For example, the following analysis might be helpful:

Predisposing factors:
1. Marianne was deeply upset at her father's disappearance and is still very upset.
2. She has seldom been cared for by anyone else.
3. Her mother is also still deeply sad and depressed.
4. Once, when her mother was very ill and was admitted to hospital, Marianne's Granny came from Scotland to care for her. Marianne was very upset and took many weeks to settle down once her mother returned home.

Organic and developmental factors:
1. Marianne seems temperamentally to be a very sensitive child.
2. The allergies she had as a baby, although less troublesome now, still cause difficulties.

Interactions within the family (A–B–C):
In discussion with Natalie, some of these could be tactfully considered in the way shown in Box 6.3.

This formulation of the difficulties might need much discussion, for while the predisposing and organic factors may 'make sense' to Natalie—indeed, they are obvious precipitants of anxiety in a young child—the examination of Marianne's behaviour when her mother is on the telephone or when she is taken to the playgroup, in terms of Antecedents–Behaviour–Consequences, may seem irrelevant and even irritating. The practitioner needs to help Natalie to understand that, with the best of intentions, she may be playing

---

Box 6.3: Preliminary assessment of/rationale for Marianne's difficulties

Antecedent	*Behaviour*	*Consequence*
1. Natalie is talking on the phone with her friend.	Marianne begins to cry piercingly.	Natalie interrupts her telephone call and reads Marianne a story to calm her down.
2. Mother takes Marianne to the playgroup.	Marianne soon screams and says she wants to go home.	Natalie takes her home.

---

into her little girl's difficulties. Together they can try out different strategies.

Natalie may not understand that by taking Marianne home from the playgroup she is reinforcing her anxiety that a playgroup is not a safe place. At this point we are simply sowing the seeds of her looking at Marianne's difficult behaviours both from her understanding of her little girl's grief but also from the slightly different viewpoint of what patterns of behaviour she is herself unwittingly reinforcing. There is no need to insist on one perspective: instead, one can suggest testing a number of hypotheses—or 'possibilities'; the number is likely to vary according to the age of the child. In respect of Marianne, they might be:

(a) Marianne's overall anxiety will diminish in frequency and intensity as she learns from repeated experience that her mother does not abandon her.

(b) Marianne's anxiety will reduce if it is possible for her to talk about her Daddy.

(c) Marianne's episodes of crying will diminish as Natalie manages to avoid attending to them—for example, when she is on the telephone.

(d) Marianne's anxiety will slowly diminish as, by very gradual steps, she becomes less sensitive to formerly stressful circumstances, such as the playgroup.

(e) Marianne will gain confidence if she is able to spend more time with her friend, Josie.

Table 6.1:   A scale for parents to estimate levels of anxiety in their young children

0	5	10
Generally calm, relaxed behaviour	Generally calm, some episodes of tension, clinging	Generally tense, panicky behaviour

In order to test these hypotheses, probably one at a time, it is desirable to have some measure of her present level of distress—a yardstick or benchmark against which to assess progress or deterioration. One can ask parents to estimate their child's average anxiety level over the past week, using a 10-point scale such as the one in Table 6.1. Parents can then estimate any changes in their child's average daily anxiety level as the plan takes effect. These can be charted simply and any changes monitored and discussed.

Step 7—Seeking one week's counts of a positive and a negative behaviour

Natalie can then be asked to identify a pair of behaviours, one negative and one positive, whose frequency she can record over the next week. She can be helped to identify one positive feature of Marianne's behaviour and one negative feature. She may choose as follows:

Negative behaviour: Marianne cries for a spell of three minutes.

Positive behaviour: Marianne draws or paints for three minutes.

When the information identified above is available, say within one week, it might look as shown in Table 6.2.

Step 8—Planning—with the Parent(s)

The practitioner and parent(s) are partners in a shared endeavour to help Marianne. Some of the ideas which have to be discussed may be very difficult for them: for example, Natalie may be find it

Table 6.2: Number of instances of Marianne's positive and negative behaviours over one week

CHARTING BEHAVIOURS		Name: Marianne				Week beginning: 16 May (Week 1)		
Behaviour	*Sunday*	*Monday*	*Tuesday*	*Wednesday*	*Thursday*	*Friday*	*Saturday*	*Total*
Behaviours to encourage and praise—Amusing self (e.g. by painting)								
Morning								
Afternoon				✓		✓		2
Evening								
Behaviours to discourage—Following mother								
Morning		✓✓		✓✓	✓	✓✓	✓	
Afternoon	✓	✓	✓✓✓	✓✓✓	✓✓	✓	✓✓✓	24
Evening			✓	✓			✓	

very painful to talk to Marianne about her Daddy. She may need support in doing so, not in an intense way but in a supportive way, in which she herself may weep and show her distress. Despite her own pain, she will probably understand that to show her own natural emotion is, in the long run, in her little girl's best interests.

Marianne, too, can be involved as fully as her understanding permits—so that it can be explained to her that Mummy and the health visitor/social worker know she gets very upset that her Daddy is no longer able to be with her. There are organisations to support children and parents with bereavement, and it seems that talking about the lost person, and asking any questions as and when they arise, is most helpful to a bereaved child. Parents will want to give explanations in line with their own views or beliefs; the important thing seems to be that the child shall be dealt with openly and truthfully, as far as is possible. Marianne will also need reassurance that it is understandable that she is frightened when she thinks her Mummy is going to leave her, but Mummy is *not* going to leave her; she will continue to look after Marianne. Once this has been confirmed, the topic should not be returned to again and again. This might easily increase Marianne's anxiety.

In respect of the immediate variables, it is crucial that we explain what is known about desensitisation from the standpoint of cognitive-behavioural theory. Most people are familiar with the idea of taking very small steps when gaining confidence in a new skill; it can be clarified that just as we advise adults to 'avoid

---

Box 6.4:   Gradual steps for introducing a child to a dentist

First step—They accompanied me when I was having a check-up. They were allowed to sit in the chair for a moment or two.
Second step—They accompanied me when I was having my teeth polished. They were allowed to have a very brief inspection.
Third step—They accompanied me when I was having one small filling. They were allowed to have a brief polish.
Fourth step—I took them when I made an ordinary visit; each had a brief check.
Final step—I took each one separately for a proper check; no treatment was necessary.

running before they can walk', and just as we teach children to swim not by throwing them in at the deep end but by gradually helping them to trust themselves to the water, so anxious children gain confidence by taking *very* small steps.

I sometimes tell parents and children of our dentist's way of introducing children to dental treatment (Box 6.4). To the children, the whole thing was intriguing. The dentist told me to tell our children that sometimes drilling did hurt a bit, but it soon wore off. Going to the dentist became a matter of great interest and even enjoyment!

Helping the parent explain the plan to the child

There will probably be at least two important things to explain to Marianne and these must obviously be pitched to her level of understanding. First, her Mummy knows that Marianne is afraid that her Mummy will leave her. She will not leave her, but she is not going to say this over and over again. Second, it is really important that Marianne lets her Mummy go to the loo without interrupting her. So, in future, when she wants to go to the lavatory, she will get out the crayons and paper or a jigsaw for Marianne and say once, in a matter-of-fact way, that she will be in the bathroom for a short time.

Plan of action

The details can be worked out with Natalie and Marianne and their suggestions taken into account, for example:

1. Marianne can use her crayons while her Mummy, Natalie, goes to the bathroom.
2. If Marianne amuses herself and does not cry, Natalie will read her a short story as soon as she comes out of the bathroom.
3. If she does cry, however, there will be no story and no cuddles at that time.

This explanation will help the little girl understand why her mother has changed her pattern of reactions to her; she is likely to respond positively within a day or two. Natalie, too, is likely to begin to understand the logic of the approach. She is to explain to Marianne, in effect, that *she intends to reward Marianne for desirable behaviour and avoid rewarding her for undesirable behaviour*. Reassurance will come as the little girl learns to trust that her mother will do as she said and as she gains no additional attention for her anxious behaviour. One can confidently predict that, so long as the assessment has been sound, and so long as the mother remains calm and avoids reinforcing her little daughter's anxieties when looking after her, Marianne's fearfulness will gradually fade away or 'extinguish'.

In other situations, for example at other people's houses, if Marianne cries, she should be ignored—so as not to reward her screaming with attention. However, when Marianne amuses herself with her paints or drawing for a spell of three minutes, she should be told gently (not over-enthusiastically) how well she has done.

Step 9—Implementation of the Plan

Marianne's mother is likely to be ready to try the suggestions offered, but there may well be problems in implementing the plan. Marianne has learned to control her mother so effectively over so long a period, as a means of managing her fears, that she is likely to put up heavy initial resistance to her mother's changed way of managing her. Her fearful behaviour may become worse rather than better for a few weeks and her mother may find it necessary to seek support from the practitioner, either face to face or by telephone. In my own research (Sutton, 1992, 1995) I was able to show that contact by telephone for many children's difficulties was as effective as face-to-face contact and brought about equally good results. In any case, I have found it is good policy to take the initiative in contacting parents, either by letter or telephone. A two-minute telephone call can be extremely economical, in terms of both time and money. This plan can be adopted for the next month, with access to the practitioner at least twice weekly initially and then once a week as Marianne becomes less anxious. Information such as that shown in Figure 6.2 is very commonly obtained. Marianne and Natalie will both need commendation and encouragement.

As the new strategies begin to take effect and as Natalie sees their impact, so systematic work upon a new pair of behaviours is

SHOWING THE INCREASE OR DECREASE WEEK BY WEEK

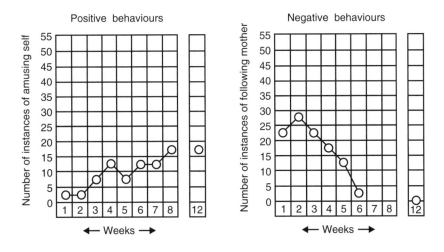

Figure 6.2: Marianne's positive and negative behaviours over eight weeks and at one month follow-up

called for—in Marianne's case, increasing the amount of time she spends amusing herself and avoiding attending to her crying in *any* setting. If, however, no progress is made and Marianne's distress has not diminished by the end of the agreed time, in this case a month, then another plan must be considered. Sometimes one finds that although the parent has intended to be consistent, in a moment of irritation she has said to the child, 'I can't stand much more of this: I'm going to send you to Scotland again and get a bit of time to myself'. The next moment she regrets her words, but the damage has been done and Marianne's fearful behaviours may re-intensify. Sometimes, we hear about such unintended lapses; at others we do not; we just hear that the plan for helping Marianne didn't work!

Step 10—Review and Evaluation

Ordinarily, one can anticipate that, so long as Marianne's mother is patient and does not attempt to rush things, her little girl's anxiety will decrease. As she gains confidence, the plan can be extended to making short outings from the house, taking plenty of time over each step. Soon they can plan their outings—perhaps next to a shop, where a small treat may be purchased for Marianne *and* for Natalie. Over the course of time, Marianne may go with her mother to a park, and then, gradually, to the local playgroup, where the staff are aware of the need for a very gradual introduction for this little girl to the buzz of a playgroup.

In my own years as a playgroup leader and before I had ever heard of cognitive-behavioural theory, I spent many hours carrying small tots around the room, while their anxious mothers first walked round the hall in which the group was held, then a week later went to the lavatory alone—sometimes the first occasion in which they had done so in years—and then, gradually, extended the period when she was out of her child's sight until the child could manage alone for a whole morning. It was wonderful to see the changes in both parent and child as the confidence of both gradually rose.

At another level, of course, the practitioner is likely to support Marianne's mother in ensuring that her own needs are met, perhaps by seeking counselling in respect of her bereavement and of her needs to develop aspects of her own life.

RESEARCH INTO CHILDREN AND DEPRESSION

Prevalence of Depression

Rutter (1986) reported that in the Isle of Wight study of 10–11 year-old children:

> . . . 13% showed a depressed mood at interview, 9% appeared pre-occupied with depressive topics, 17% failed to smile, and 15% showed poor emotional responsiveness.

The data from the Department of Health (1995) reports that major depression in children spans a range of 0.5–2.5%, according to the location of the study. Hersov (1977) has suggested that there is probably an interaction effect between genetic factors and life circumstances, and that this contributes towards whether a given child will respond to a difficult life event, such as parental separation, with depression or not. However, other studies, for example Wilde et al (1992), found that many children's depressions were associated with chronic and long-standing difficulties as much as with specific life events. So a 10 year-old may say, 'Mummy is always saying she can't afford things: I'm afraid that there soon won't be enough food for us'; or she may say, 'I can help with looking after Danny (a brother with Down's syndrome) now, but what will I do if Mummy gets ill?' Many of these worries have their origins in reality and all the resources of Health Authorities and Departments of Social Services are needed to help the children concerned.

Indicators of Depression

Depression is a condition characterised by disturbance of at least three systems:

- *Affect* or emotions of sadness or misery.
- *Behaviour* marked by slowness or lethargy.
- *Cognitions* or thoughts of hopelessness or sometimes suicide.

Herbert (1991) offers a checklist (Box 6.5) of the main signs of depression in children and young people. There is evidence

---

Box 6.5: Main signs of depression in children and young people (reproduced with permission from Herbert, 1991)

- A demeanour of unhappiness or misery (more persistent and intense than 'the blues', from which we all suffer now and then).
- A marked change in eating and/or sleeping patterns.
- A feeling of helplessness, hopelessness and self-dislike.
- An inability to concentrate and apply oneself to anything.
- Everything (even talking and dressing) is seen as an effort.
- Irritating or aggressive behaviour.
- A sudden change in school work.
- A constant search for distractions and new activities.
- Dangerous risk-taking (e.g. with drugs/alcohol; dangerous driving; delinquent actions).
- Friends being dropped or ignored.

(Bernstein and Garfinkel, 1986) that depression may also be accompanied by severe symptoms of anxiety, so Herbert emphasises that the assessment must be comprehensive enough to allow for the identification of both disorders.

Origins of Depression in Children

Harrington (1994) reports three major types of research into the factors contributing to depression in children and young people. First, there are those which study the impact of parental depression upon children: in this area several studies, notably the review by Rutter (1988), have shown the association between the mental disorder of parents and children's emotional and cognitive development. This depression in mothers is likely to lead to reduced mother–child interactions and may indeed contribute to depression in the children. (In my own research, 11 of the 23 mothers studied scored 15 or above on the Beck Depression Inventory at the pre-intervention stage; at post-intervention only four of 22 mothers reached this score, while at 12 months, follow-up only two of 18 mothers did so.)

The second set of studies are those in which three kinds of risk factor have been isolated:

1. *Acute life events*, such as loss of a parent. Rutter and Sandberg (1992) have shown that it is not only the loss *per se* but also the associated reduction in parental care which renders children vulnerable.
2. *Chronic adversities.* Wilde and colleagues (1992) showed that depression was often as much associated with long-standing problems as with a sudden life event.
3. *Vulnerability factors.* Brown and Harris (1978) showed that early experience of loss of mother before the age of 11 years rendered children vulnerable to subsequent depressive disorders.

The third type of approach is to study children who have experienced a specific 'life event'. Harrington (1994) reports that:

Depressive symptoms have been found in association with many types of adverse life experience, including divorce (Wallerstein and Kelly, 1980; Aro and Palosaari, 1992) . . . and disasters (Yule, Udwin and Murdoch, 1990). Bereaved preschoolers often have depressive symptoms and Weller et al (1991) reported that around one-third of bereaved prepubertal children met criteria for depressive disorder.

Depressive symptoms have also been found in association with both physical abuse (Allen and Tarnowski, 1989) and sexual abuse (Goldston et al, 1989). Depressive disorders have been said to occur in about 20% of maltreated children.

In seeking to explain the mechanisms by which these life events lead to the internal mood state of depression, Harrington (1994) suggests that the concept of 'learned helplessness' (Seligman and Peterson, 1986) provides the best explanatory framework. According to this model, the child (or adult) experiences *powerlessness* in the face of uncontrollable life circumstances and therefore comes to adopt a negative cognitive set (Beck, 1976). He or she develops a negative view of him or herself, of the world and of the future.

Harrington also reports the evidence of low social competence as being implicated in the development of depression in children and young people and cites the work by Patterson and Stoolmiller (1991), who found that:

Rejection by peers was an important correlate of depressed mood in pre-adolescent boys from at-risk families and it may be that peer and/or parental rejection mediates the link between antisocial behaviour and depression in young people.

Box 6.6:   Life events which may predispose a child or young person to depression

1. Loss by bereavement of or separation from a person emotionally important to them: mother, father, brother, sister or other close relationship.
2. Anticipated loss: for example, family separation.
3. Beliefs that they carry responsibility for a major life event within their family: for example, father leaving the household.
4. Social unacceptability: leading to loneliness and isolation.
5. Lack of friends.
6. Disability, both its direct impact and also its indirect effects, such as associated isolation from the peer group.

What Children get Depressed About

The events or beliefs listed in Box 6.6 appear frequently to lead to depression.

HELPING FAMILIES WITH DEPRESSED CHILDREN

You will recall that in the Isle of Wight studies, 13% of 10–11 year-old children were found to be depressed, and although the issue is beyond the scope of this book, it is distressing that at follow-up at age 14–15 *over 40%* of the same young people 'reported substantial feelings of misery and depression'. These are deeply disturbing figures—particularly when it is recalled that the employment situation for young people has sharply deteriorated since these studies were conducted. This situation for these young people is reflected in the serious increase in suicide in young people, particularly young men, over the past decade.

This book focuses upon children of primary school age, so cannot address the issues of adolescence, but the same basic approach is adopted for all children. First, as always, a comprehensive assessment is essential but this will be made more effective if, as **Step 1**, a supportive relationship with the parent is developed.

Assessment—the Example of Amrit

It will be necessary to interview parents and caregivers of depressed children in an effort to understand their view and knowledge of the child's life experience. This should start from their perception of the child as a toddler, characteristic patterns of shyness or of outgoingness, sensitivity or other temperamental features, as well as friendships and their disruption by changes of school or other factors. It will be necessary to gain their view of the onset of the depression, whether gradual or sudden, and what they believe were its precipitants. These may include bereavement or other major losses of family or friends, accidents which have left them with major physical or other difficulties, family break-up or experiences at school or elsewhere which have left the youngster feeling vulnerable.

It will, of course, be necessary to talk with the child separately, to see whether his/her views accord with those of the parent(s). Few children will be so articulate as to be able to identify the direct cause of their unhappiness, but again responses to open-ended questions may offer clues as to the contributory factors.

The following example of Amrit an Asian little boy sets out the various illustrative steps.

Step 1—Building supportive and empathic relationships

Amrit, aged nine, has been noticed by the school nurse as a lonely and apparently unhappy child. She has gained his confidence and has had one meeting with his mother, Smita, who says she has two other children, is on Income Support and is depressed herself; with two other children, she can't cope with Amrit's moods. However, she agrees to meet with the school nurse again. On this occasion, Smita explains that she is a lone parent; she was knocked about by Amrit's Dad, who is white, and she doesn't want to talk about him. She realises Amrit is very unhappy, but can't see that telling Amrit about what his Dad did to her and why she left him will help Amrit at all. She used to be very cross with Amrit if ever he got noisy or at all aggressive, as she was afraid that it was his Dad coming out in him, but now she wonders if she curbed him too much.

Step 2—Information gathering

In the course of gathering information (Box 6.7), the nurse learns that Amrit's Dad is in prison and that his Mum doesn't want him back. She is making something of a new life for herself with a new partner, Roy.

Step 3—Identifying the problem behaviours

Smita understands well that Amrit may be missing his father, and says she will do what she can to help him. When asked to identify the particular patterns of behaviour causing concern, she can state several:

Box 6.7:   Initial information concerning Amrit to inform the
assessment

1. *Predisposing life events for this child and members of this family*:
   (a) Amrit's father has had several spells in prison.
   (b) Amrit sees his Dad only very rarely—every three or four months.
   (c) Roy, Smita's new partner, and Amrit do not get on well.
2. *Organic factors, or those intrinsic to the child, e.g. developmental
   stage, disability*:
   (a) Amrit is a child of dual heritage.
   (b) He is beginning to put on a lot of weight.
   (c) He seems to have low self-esteem.
3. *Immediate variables: interactions within the family (A–B–C)**:
   (a) Smita admits she 'nags' Amrit when he eats a lot; then he eats
        more!
   (b) Amrit often spends all weekend in his bedroom. Smita lets him;
        she gives him his meals there on a tray.

*Smita may not understand this concept, but it is useful to introduce it at
this stage.

---

1. Amrit keeps saying he's 'No good'.
2. He is overweight for his age.
3. He spends much of his time alone.
4. He has few friends.
5. He has started to avoid going to school.

Play and other aids to assessment: As with anxiety, a variety
of aids can be helpful in enabling a child to reveal something
of his unhappiness, but here too interpretations by the worker are
to be avoided. Amrit, as a nine year-old, may choose to draw or
paint rather than play with sand, or he may feel able to answer
some of the questions developed by Herbert (1991); see p. 153
above.

Step 4—Identifying a positive profile

With careful enquiry, a depressed child's strengths and positive
qualities can usually be brought to light. A perceptive teacher
has noticed that Amrit has written a story or poem of great

sensitivity; another is aware that he is particularly responsive to the natural world, while a third remembers how he 'came alive' when talking about animals. So soon Amrit's positive profile can be set out:

1. He always responds to his teacher's greeting.
2. He takes great care of the family pet, brushing it and preparing its food.
3. Since he learned to make a cup of tea, he brings his mother a cup every morning without fail.

Step 5—Identifying target behaviours

Smita says that there are several patterns of behaviour which she would like Amrit to show:

1. To attend football and sport sessions each once a week—as before.
2. To speak to her friends when they visit the house—and not to hide away.
3. To spend at least two hours weekly out of the house with a friend or group.

Amrit seems frightened when asked what patterns of behaviour he would like to change in his own life but with help is able to say that he wants to eat fewer snacks and he would like to play football again.

Step 6—Arriving at a formulation

This formulation of the difficulties shown in Box 6.8, might need discussion, for while the predisposing and organic factors may be clear to Smita and Amrit, it will probably be difficult for them to understand that by offering attractive alternatives to activities with children of his own age, Smita may be making it *more* likely, in the long term, that Amrit will become depressed.

Step 7—Collecting details of behaviour

Sanita and Amrit agree to collect a record of how Amrit spends his time for one week.

Box 6.8:   Preliminary assessment of/rationale for Amrit's difficulties

1. *Predisposing life events for this child and members of this family:*
   (a) Amrit has never known much about his Dad: Mum never talks about him but Amrit seems to wonder a lot about him.
   (b) Amrit is a boy of dual heritage. This is important to him and he needs help in valuing the many aspects of himself, the two cultures to which he belongs and his dual ancestry.

2. *Organic factors, or those intrinsic to the child, e.g. developmental stage, disability:*
   Amrit is beginning to be fat for his age: he hates this.

3. *Immediate variables: interactions within the family (A–B–C)*:*
   Some of these could be analysed in the following way:

Antecedent	**B**ehaviour	**C**onsequences
(a) Amrit is feeling miserable.	He stays in his bedroom.	His mother takes him food on a tray.
(b) A teacher suggests Amrit should play football.	Amrit refuses.	His mother takes him to Macdonald's to cheer him up.
(c) Amrit's class is going on an outing to a farm.	Amrit says he will not go.	His mother takes him to the pictures instead.

   * Parents may not understand this concept, but it is useful to introduce it at this stage.

Step 8—Planning

It is likely to be possible to help Amrit and Smita by a plan with a number of steps:

1. To help Smita herself by listening supportively to her story.
2. To ask what she thinks would help Amrit: for example:
   (a) Talking with Amrit about his Dad.
   (b) Enabling Amrit to meet his Dad regularly—even though this is hard for her.
   (c) Going to places with Amrit: the library, museum, but not as an alternative to activities with his school.

(d) Helping him take up his interest in sport again: swimming, football.
(e) Inviting someone Amrit suggests home to play after school.
(f) Helping Amrit lose weight—keeping a chart.

Involving the child in the planning

Amrit must be involved in clarifying the ideas about how his depression has developed and in exploring plans for the future; in each case, his wishes are incorporated where possible. Amrit may well reveal that while he knows his mother has ceased visiting his Dad in prison and seems to want to break all contact with him, he, Amrit, does not want to break contact; in fact, he very much wants to strengthen it but fears to tell his mother. He may also say that he is afraid of Roy, who shouts at him.

Three further components of the plan to help Amrit may then emerge:

(g) The worker will talk with Smita about Amrit's wish to see his father.
(h) The practitioner will discuss with Smita how to improve Roy's and Amrit's relationship.
(i) The worker will talk with Smita about how to enable Amrit to learn more of both aspects of his heritage.

Step 9—Implementation of the plan

This takes place over the next few weeks, with records to show first the initial states of affairs and then the impact of agreed changes: these might relate to:

- The number of times Amrit has visited his father and how much time they have spent together.
- Diary of Amrit's developing interest in his Indian and his British heritage.
- Amount of time spent by Amrit taking part in activities, as distinct from in his bedroom.
- Time spent by Amrit in swimming, football and other sport.
- Weight change as Amrit begins to reduce his intake of food and to take exercise.

- Measures of Amrit's depression pre- and post-intervention.
- The impact of the worker's gentle questioning of Amrit's asser-
  tion, 'I am no good'; what is the evidence for this statement? This
  is a cognitive therapy approach. The aim is to help children and
  adults recognise that they are themselves diminishing their
  sense of worth by rehearsing such statements. Instead they are
  helped to work out positive, self-encouraging statements. This
  approach is known to reduce depression in young people
  (Kendall, 1991).

This is the stage at which to return to the original goals set out in
Step 5 and to highlight any progress which has been made towards
them. They may need amending but there is likely to be some
progress. There will be setbacks, but it is the areas of improvement
which should be highlighted and reinforced.

Step 10—Review and Evaluation

These are based upon the evidence of the impact of the plan—
reviewed at agreed intervals and adapted as necessary. The
worker acts as facilitator and trouble-shooter and gives encouragement to all concerned. The intervention would be finally evaluated
at the end of an agreed period of intervention and booster
meetings arranged.

7

HELPING FAMILIES
WITH CHILDREN'S
SLEEPING PROBLEMS

Broken sleep causes great stress for families. Anyone who has paced the floor with a screaming baby in the small hours knows how desperate one can feel for something, *anything*, that will stop the crying. So sleeping difficulties are included within this book because, although they are of a rather different order from others, there is much help that can be given by appropriately trained staff. Improving sleeping patterns often contributes to the well-being of all concerned and to the reduction of other difficulties attributable to fatigue and stress.

DEFINITION OF SLEEPING DISORDER

To say that a child has a 'sleeping problem' requires clarification. This term is used to distinguish children who depart from statistical norms, in that they display sleeping patterns which are markedly different from most of their contemporaries, and which affects the child's well-being as well as that of family members. Let us examine the research on sleeping difficulties in the light of these concepts.

Skuse (1994) identifies three main areas for the study of sleep disorder:

1. Children who fail to settle at night—bedtime difficulties.
2. Children who wake in the night and do not readily return to sleep.
3. Disorders of sleep: sleepwalking, nightmares and night terrors.

Each will be considered here, although the main focus will be on the first two areas.

THE PREVALENCE OF SLEEPING/WAKING DIFFICULTIES

Epidemiological Studies

In respect of very young children, it is difficult to distinguish between bedtime problems and waking problems, so the two fields will be considered together. Many practitioners, moreover, regard a 'sleeping problem' as being a culturally invented 'disorder', pointing out that to place very young children to sleep alone is a Western practice considered by many other cultures as little short of barbarism. Yet the fact remains that many families do expect their infants to sleep alone, although a recommendation has been made by Scragg et al (1996), on the basis of their research in New Zealand, that to reduce the risk of sudden infant death syndrome infants should sleep in the same bedroom as their parents until they are at least six months old.

Richman, Stevenson and Graham (1982) found that 11–14% of two and three year-old children were waking frequently at night and 8% were continuing to do so when they were aged four, while Butler and Golding (1986) found that no less than 46% of children who had sleep problems as infants continued to have them at age five. Douglas (1989) suggested that the more serious the sleeping problem in young children, the more likely it is to persist.

In respect of waking difficulties, there is an unfortunate assumption that unless a baby settles readily and 'sleeps through the night' from a very early stage, there is something wrong. This is inaccurate. Reporting a major study, Skuse (1994) writes:

> Whether or not night waking is regarded as a problem by parents will depend on what they believe to be normal. Few think that

infants less than three to four months of age can be expected to sleep through the night without interruption. Even after four months there is considerable variation in their expectation. Scott and Richards (1990a) recently conducted a survey on this matter. They found that about one in four infants, at one year of age, were waking five or more nights a week. Ten per cent of their mothers did not regard that as a problem. However, 37% of those whose babies woke less often did regard their sleep pattern as a problem. These findings have implications for studies that rely solely on parental reports for their identification of children with sleep disorders.

There is thus great variability in the age at which infants and young children 'sleep through the night'. It seems that the first year of life is one in which immature infants have to make huge adjustments from living in the womb to living in the world, to sensations of hunger and satiety, to changing sequences of light and dark and that, as with all other areas, each infant with its own genetic endowment will adjust to its environment in different ways.

Concerning the third area, disorders of sleep, Vela-Bueno and colleagues (1985) who examined 900 children aged from six to 12 years, found that 20% reported nightmares. Skuse (1994) indicates that these, which are dreams occurring during the REM stage of sleep (see below), are best understood as a form of post-traumatic stress response, as the child or adult attempts by reprocessing the frightening events to assimilate them into consciousness. Night terrors are much less frequently reported, occurring in only 3% of children (Klackenberg, 1987); they appear to take place during the non-REM sleep cycle and are not fully understood. For some children, both nightmares and night terrors seem to be responses to very stressful experiences, such as viewing horror films on television. Sleepwalking seems to occur very occasionally in about 30% of children but is common in only 2.5% (Klackenberg, 1987); the peak age for this disorder is between five and seven years and its frequency diminishes after nine years. There appears to be some genetic underpinning to the difficulty, as monozygotic twins are much more likely to be concordant for sleepwalking than dizygotic twins.

RESEARCH INTO THE ORIGINS OF BEDTIME AND WAKING PROBLEMS

Studies of Affected Children

Extensive research has taken place concerning possible associations between sleeping difficulties and specific variables: Richman (1985) concluded that first- or second-born children were more likely than later children to have sleeping difficulties, but Skuse (1994) suggests that an alternative interpretation is that later children experience less parental anxiety about whether they will sleep or not as their parents become more experienced. There is no greater tendency for one gender to be more prone to sleeping problems than the other (Thoman and Whitney, 1989).

Several studies, such as Wright (1987), have shown that breast-fed babies tend to wake more frequently during the night than bottle-fed infants, but Skuse (1994) cautions that infants who wake at night are not necessarily hungry: it may fall to the health visitor to advise anxious parents as to whether nutrition is likely to be a factor for a given age of child.

An association not commonly known is that between maternal depression and children's sleeping problems. Richman (1985), for example, showed that the mothers of toddlers with these difficulties were far more likely to be depressed, to be coping with family stress and to lack a confiding relationship than were those of toddlers in a control group. It is hard to distinguish which comes first, maternal depression or toddler behaviour difficulties. In my own work (Sutton, 1995), the level of maternal depression fell significantly when the sleep and behaviour problems of their young children improved, so it seems likely that maternal depression and sleeplessness in young children interact, forming a vicious circle which is hard to break.

Underpinning Physiological Processes

The human body experiences rhythmic changes which prepare it for cycles of activity, interspersed with cycles of quiescence, which

prepare it for sleep and restorative rest. These physiological processes are powerful, so sleep does eventually take over, but they
are not so powerful that they cannot be disrupted or thrown out of
phase with the cycles of the rest of the world. Nurses do adjust to
night duty, but often with discomfort and physiological distress;
similarly, infants do eventually develop a sleeping pattern, but it
may not be the conventional, rhythmic one for which their caregivers long. There are, however, steps we can take to encourage
the usual 'day for activity: night for sleep' routine.

The pineal gland, deep within the brain, responds to light and
dark and the changes associated with this gland trigger the sleep
process. It is therefore helpful if, right from birth, babies come to
associate darkness with the sleeping response. Babies *can* sleep in
bright and noisy rooms but it is often helpful if they learn the same
patterns as the rest of the world as they grow older. It is also
helpful if they can learn to sleep through the sounds of most
households, doorbells or telephones ringing or television in a
neighbouring room, rather than waking at the slightest sound. The
young child's body responds to a calm and soothing environment

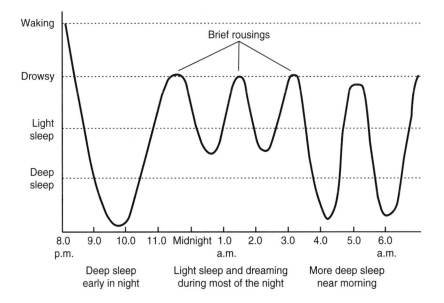

Figure 7.1: Typical progression of the stages of sleep (after Ferber, 1986)

by reducing physiological arousal and by lowering blood flow and muscle tone in preparation for sleep; so parents can take advantage of this naturally occurring cycle by ensuring that the hour or so before they wish the child to go to sleep is one of relative calm, without stimulating interactions and involving quiet activity only.

As is commonly known, patterns of sleep are of two main kinds, rapid eye movement (REM) sleep, accompanied by dreaming and increasingly known as *active sleep* (Ferber, 1986), and non-rapid eye movement (non-REM) sleep, known as *quiet* sleep. The function of REM sleep seems to be linked with the processing of emotional material, while that of non-REM sleep seems to be largely restorative. These two types of sleep follow each other cyclically through the night, as shown in Figure 7.1 (Ferber, 1986).

Bedtime Problems

These are addressed first because they happen earlier in the night than typical waking problems, but the two are of course intimately linked. Some problems may have arisen because a child has been ill and has needed much attention at bedtime or in the night, but often bedtime difficulties arise from not establishing a routine at the time of evening when the family wish the child to sleep. Often parents appear not to take advantage of the child's readiness to fall into quieter activities as night approaches and the physiological level of arousal begins to fall. In some families, this time of early evening is accompanied by the return of one parent from work and understandably he or she wishes to spend enjoyable and sometimes very stimulating time with the child. Thus, at the time when the children would, given a little encouragement, cooperate in preparing for sleep, demands are being made upon them to wake up and play lively games. I recall one father who used to tuck his two year-old son under his arm and rush around with him as though he were a rugby football, to the delight of the little one but to the despair of his mother, who then had to try to get a wildly excited child ready for sleep.

In other families a child has been put to bed at a reasonable time for his or her age but has objected loudly; new parents, lacking strong role models and the confidence that comes from experience, allow the toddler to rejoin their more stimulating interactions and to eat their snacks. In no time at all, the toddler stays up until the parents go to bed, while they feel powerless to do anything about it. I recall one family with a delightful little daughter, aged two and a half, who charmed her loving mother and her giant of a father for several hours first one evening and then every evening—only for them to find themselves quite unable ever to insist that she stay in bed and allow them some time alone. She stayed up until midnight, sitting on her Daddy's lap, demanding and receiving stories, television and snacks until *they* fell asleep, exhausted. The little one was still ready for more!

Other children repeatedly come downstairs, plaintively claiming that they are afraid but with broad smiles upon their faces. In my experience, they are often allowed to sit in a corrner of the sofa and told that they can stay as long as they are quiet. It then becomes increasingly difficult for families to invite friends in for the evening or to go out themselves; visiting adults are likely to be less tolerant of a toddler at 9.30 p.m. if their own children have already been asleep for two hours.

I am aware, of course, that children's bedtime and sleeping routines are culturally influenced and that each family will have its own expectations about both. Let me state that I am not trying to be prescriptive: rather, I am drawing upon research findings to support those families who ask for help with what *they perceive* to be a bedtime or sleeping difficulty in their child. They set the goals, not me.

Waking Problems

We see from Table 7.1 that it is natural for children to experience both *active* and *quiet* sleep, to rouse frequently and briefly and to go back to sleep again. As Ferber (1986) puts it:

> What most parents don't realize is that what they view as abnormal wakings in the night are actually quite normal. And what they do to try to treat the 'abnormal' wakings—namely going in to help their child go back to sleep—is actually *causing* the disturbance (p. 55).

What seems to happen is that when children rouse briefly, as they pass through the cycles of the sleeping sequence, they momentarily

Table 7.1: Summary of the stages of sleep in children (after Ferber, 1986)

Part of night	Approximate times	Type of sleep	Pattern of sleep
Early	8.00–11.00 p.m.	Deep non-REM	Several brief wakings
Middle	11.00–5.00 a.m.	REM	Several brief wakings
Later	5.00–6.00 a.m.	Deep non-REM	Brief wakings

check their environment for familiarity and security (see Figure 7.1). If they have become accustomed to a specific sets of 'sleep cues' or 'sleep accessories', a blanket, a Teddy, a bottle and even a Mummy all to hand for security, when they rouse they check that these accessories are all more or less in place. If they are, they readily fall back to sleep: but if they are not—and the more accessories the more long-drawn-out the checking may have to be— instead of falling back to sleep they become more wakeful and distressed. Sometimes this sequence can occur five or six times a night as the sleep patterns cycle through. Thus, the waking is not abnormal: what is problematic is the difficulty the child is having in going back to sleep again.

Relevance of Cognitive-behavioural Theory

Despite many short and readable books for parents, such as *My Child Won't Sleep* by Douglas and Richman (1984), the relevant principles are not yet common knowledge. For sleep, although a pattern of behaviour with clear biological underpinnings, is also an environmentally influenced phenomenon. Children can be trained to wake or to stay awake or to sleep longer by means of certain prompts, stimuli or rewards. These principles are in operation whether we are aware of it or not or whether we approve of them or not. As professional people it is our duty to be aware of how the principles operate, so that we can ensure that they are employed ethically and to meet the needs of the families seeking help.

For example, the principles of encurging certain patterns of behaviour and discouraging others can be employed to help families whose children often have major difficulties: those with disabilities. Lyn Quine (1996), in her excellent book *Solving Children's Sleep Problems*, has shown how, with a careful assessment and a structured intervention, it is often possible to give much help to families whose children have learning disabilities and who experience great difficulties in helping them settle to sleep.

RESEARCH INTO THE MANAGEMENT OF BEDTIME AND SLEEP PROBLEMS

Many studies show how a range of professionals can help families with sleeping difficulties. What used to be regarded as a specialist field of skill, the province of paediatricians and psychologists, now rightly features in the repertoire of skills of many health visitors, social workers, school nurses and community psychiatric nurses.

Helping Families Get Off to a Good Start: the Usefulness of Routines

There is increasing evidence of the usefulness of helping babies and young children develop flexible routines (Ferber, 1986; Kerr, Jowett and Smith, 1997). As the young infant grows, cycles of

---

Box 7.1:   One possible bedtime routine (Sutton, 1996)

1. Quiet activities for an hour before bed—or as quiet as possible!
2. Child is told 10 minutes before bedtime, 'Bedtime's in 10 minutes/ very soon, so start to put your toys away'.
3. Help a young child to put toys away.
4. Carry or lead a young child to the bathroom.
5. Child uses toilet.
6. Bath or wash and brush teeth.
7. Into bed (we suggest the child should not come downstairs again).
8. Short, calm story or look at picture book together (five minutes).
9. Tuck child up, give a kiss and say something like, 'Sleep well; see you in the morning'.

waking, feeding and sleeping become established and Ferber has shown how these mesh with and become part of the child's developing circadian rhythms. Reasonable regularity is thus beneficial; indeed, Ferber claims that in households where there is little structure children do not receive these regular cues and it may therefore be more difficult for them to develop patterns of sound sleep. A routine can be valuable in preparing the child for sleep. Box 7.1 shows one possible routine, which I have published elsewhere (Sutton, 1996).

Using Principles of Cognitive-behavioural Theory

This body of theory has been found to be central in dealing with children's sleeping difficulties. It is being taught to health visitors and other practitioners all over the country and they in turn are now running successful sleep clinics (Roberts, 1993).

Graded desensitisation: the gradual approach

Desensitisation, which we encountered in Chapter 6, is a procedure whereby a child or adult is helped to overcome a fear or anxiety by being exposed very gradually to gradations of the feared situation. At each step, the practitioner ascertains that the person is entirely relaxed and comfortable before slowly introducing the next. This is the procedure which helps many children who have acquired a fear of being alone at bedtime. The steps of the 'gradual approach', which have been found to be very helpful to a child, are shown in Box 7.2.

Avoiding rewarding waking: the direct approach

The above procedure is obviously time-consuming and some parents, after trying it, say they can't be doing with such a long-drawn-out approach! They want a speedy solution, and for them, assuming the practitioner has undertaken a careful assessment, and has screened out other possible explanations for the difficulty, a direct approach may be more fitting. This may be so particularly

---

Box 7.2: The steps of a desentising process for an anxious child: the 'gradual' approach

1. The child should be naturally tired at bedtime.
2. The parent should explain to the child that there has been a lot of upset for everyone at bedtime, so in future Mummy will do things a bit differently. The aim will be that eventually the child can go to sleep happily by herself.
3. The child is put to bed in a calm, matter-of-fact way. If the parent is upset, the child will pick this up and behave anxiously in response.
4. If the parent has previously had to lie on the bed, she should decline to do this but should sit by the bed. She should insist that the child stays in bed, making it a condition of having a story. She should stay until the child falls asleep if absolutely necessary.
5. After three or four nights, she should move a few feet nearer the door, but again she must be prepared to wait until the child falls asleep. Over the next week or so, again, move the chair a little nearer to the door, leaving toys or books for the child if he is not sleepy, but insisting on looking at her own book rather than watching him. She shouldn't even glance at him, but instead concentrate on her own book.
6. Over time, her chair should be moved towards and in due course out of the door. She should keep completely calm, but be ready to return the child to his bed if he comes searching for her. Parents should not be afraid to be very firm, but calm, in requiring the child to stay in bed.
7. If this approach is used, it must not be rushed. School holidays, or at least a weekend, is a good time to make a start.
8. If another caregiver can be encouraged to take part in the bedtime or waking routine, this enables the child to become less dependent upon the mother.

---

if it appears that the child is 'trying it on'. It must be the parents' choice. The steps of the 'direct' approach are shown in Box 7.3.

HELPING FAMILIES WHOSE CHILDREN HAVE BEDTIME/WAKING PROBLEMS

Parents whose children settle or sleep poorly are often very stressed, as the shortage of sleep affects the functioning of the

Box 7.3:   The steps of managing bedtime or waking: the 'direct' approach

1. The child should be naturally tired at bedtime.
2. The parent should explain calmly but firmly to the child that there has been a lot of upset for everyone at bedtime, so in future Mummy will be managing things differently. She will check that the child is all right, but she will not bring him downstairs again however much he calls out. He can have story books if he wants them. Soon he will be able to go to sleep happily by himself.
3. As in the other example, the child is put to bed in a calm, matter-of-fact way. If the parent is upset, the child will pick this up and exploit her distress.
4. The parent says 'Goodnight' and then leaves the room, leaving the door open or closed as usual.
5. If the child does scream, the parent waits 1 minute and then does as she said she would. She stands at the door, out of sight, and says in a very firm voice, 'It's sleep time, Johnny. I'm here, but I have my work to do. Goodnight'. Then leaves.
6. If the child goes on screaming, she waits 3 minutes, then goes in and says the same. If the child goes on screaming, she waits 5 minutes, then goes in and says the same. If the child goes on screaming she waits 7 minutes, then goes in and says the same and so on. She increases the interval by 2 minutes each time and sounds very firm, but calm, each time she has to go in.
7. If the child gets out of bed, she makes sure he cannot leave the room; she fixes the door, perhaps with a stair-gate but *never* locks the door. If the child goes to sleep on the floor, she lets him; he can be lifted into bed later on.
8. If the child wants the door left open, she makes this a condition of staying in bed. He can choose: either he stays in bed and the door can be open, or he keeps getting out of bed and the door must be closed.
9. If the child makes himself sick, he will have to be cleaned up, but this should be done without comment, and he should be put straight back to bed. The same routine can also be used in the middle of the night. There should be no speech and no eye contact. The parent should remain as calm as is humanly possible.
10. The point of dealing with the child in this way is that it reassures him, but does not reward him with attention for the waking behaviour.
11. It is essential to keep records when dealing with a bedtime or waking problem. They will show if things are getting better or worse (see Appendix 12).

whole family throughout the day. The steps of the ASPIRE process (see Chapter 4) lend themselves to assessing and reducing this stress. The first contact is crucial; it is an opportunity to allow people to release pent-up tension and frustration, to show empathy and understanding to them and, by means of patient and careful listening, to gather crucial information which will assist in relieving or resolving the sleeping difficulty. This is **Step 1** of the process.

Assessment

Step 2—Gather information

Holistic assessment of the child's sleeping difficulty within the overall family is essential. Completing the assessment instrument (see Appendix 1) or another of a similar kind with the service user will elicit much information of which key details can be entered on Table 4.1 (Appendix 4). This will include information concerning predisposing variables, such as hospital admissions, separations or other distressing events which may be, or may have come to be, associated with bedtime; it will also include relevant developmental or organic factors such as a tendency to asthma on the part of the child.

The example of Sebastian, aged four: Let us consider Sebastian, a 'precious child', in that he was longed-for for many years before he was conceived. He is an only child of older parents and one who has learned, because of inexperience on the part of his parents, that if he keeps demanding long enough and often enough they give way. His mother, Felicity, is deeply unhappy; she gave up her work as a financial consultant in her delight at conceiving and told her friends of her intention to become 'a perfect mother with a perfect child'. Her husband, Hamish, is as disappointed as his wife and the two parents alternate between issuing harsh threats, never carried through, and indulging the child's whims. If Sebastian does not get his way, he resorts to screaming, tantrums and hitting and kicking his mother.

Step 3—Identify problem behaviours

Unless it is already apparent that many of the child's difficulties are exclusively attributable to an organic difficulty or to an event in the child's life, such as abuse, it is appropriate to ask the parents to identify their difficulty in terms of exactly what the child *does* which constitutes the bedtime or sleeping problem. So, in the case of Sebastian:

1. Sebastian keeps coming downstairs after he has been put to bed; he does not eventually settle in bed until his parents go to bed at 11.00 p.m.
2. Once downstairs, he gets out all his toys and spreads them all over the floor.
3. If reprimanded, he calls his mother horrible names and kicks her.

Here it will be apparent that Sebastian is being rewarded, unintentionally but systematically, by the consequences of his behaviour. This makes it highly likely that the behaviour will happen again— and again and again.

Step 4—Identify positive behaviours

When requested to identify the positive features of their child's behaviour, both parents identify distinctive and pleasing characteristics. For Sebastian:

1. Once asleep, he stays asleep; he sleeps soundly until roused next morning.
2. When asked to help lay the table or wash up, he complies readily.
3. He helps his Dad in the garden, sweeping leaves and digging weeds.

Step 5—Clarifying realistic goals

So far we have identified the main 'problems' and 'positives' in Sebastian's behaviour. Now, briefly, we need to establish what the parents really want. We need to help them cast their minds forward to identify the key areas of their child's behaviour where they long for improvement. Here we have to help them strike a balance between requiring perfection ('He must go to bed and fall asleep right away') and not setting the standards high enough. Here our experience and judgement will help us to negotiate three specific goals which our experience tells us are likely to be attainable—and to rank these in order of their attainability. For we, too, need success; we need the encouragement which comes from people saying, 'We've had the best night's sleep in years!' So we should use the same theoretical ideas to structure success for families and for ourselves. For Sebastian, the three goals might be:

1. That Sebastian will stay in his room once put to bed.
2. That he will speak calmly and quietly to his mother.
3. That when told 'No', he cannot have something, he will accept this calmly and quietly.

Step 6—Problem formulation shared with parents

When the practitioner has gathered as much relevant information as possible, then, drawing upon material offered by the parent(s)

Box 7.4: Preliminary assessment of/rationale for Sebastian's difficulties

1. *Predisposing life events for this child and members of this family*
   (a) Sebastian is a 'precious child'; his parents waited many years before he was conceived.
   (b) His mother gave up a satisfying professional life to give him full-time care. She now regrets this deeply.
   (c) His parents had had little to do with babies or children before Sebastian was born; when the extent of the baby's impact on their lives was apparent, they lost confidence.
   (d) Sebastian's mother is understandably depressed: she feels totally powerless over bedtimes.
2. *Organic factors, or those intrinsic to the child, e.g. developmental stage, disability*
   Sebastian has always been a very lively little boy, apparently needing less sleep than many children of his age.
3. *Immediate variables: interactions within the family (A–B–C)**
   Unwittingly, his parents seem to have been rewarding the very behaviour they want to stop by allowing Sebastian to stay downstairs—while at the same time complaining about this behaviour.

*Parents may not understand this concept, but it is useful to introduce it at this stage.

Table 7.2: Base-line information for the number of times Sebastian comes downstairs during one week (see Appendix 12)

SLEEP CHART   Name: Sebastian (4)   Date: 14 March

Shade in the times of sleep, and mark with small crosses any periods of prolonged crying. Mark instances of coming downstairs with a D.

	7 a.m.	8	9	10	11	noon	1 p.m.	2	3	4	5	6	7	8	9	10	11	12	1 a.m.	2	3	4	5	6	Total for week
Sunday													D	DDD	DD	D	D	█	█	█	█	█	█	█	
Monday														DD	D	DD		█	█	█	█	█	█	█	
Tuesday														D	D			█	█	█	█	█	█	█	
Wednesday														D	D	D	D	█	█	█	█	█	█	█	
Thursday														D	D	D	D	█	█	█	█	█	█	█	
Friday														D	D			█	█	█	█	█	█	█	
Saturday														D				█	█	█	█	█	█	█	25

Example:

	7 a.m.	8	9	10	11	noon	1 p.m.	2	3	4	5	6	7	8	9	10	11	12	1 a.m.	2	3	4	5	6	Total for week
Sunday	█	█				█	█						█	█		xxxxx									
Monday	█					█	█						█	█											

and, as appropriate, by the child him or herself, it should be possible to *explore with the family* some preliminary rationale for/formulation of the child's difficulties. If the child is old enough to contribute to this formulation then, of course, this information must be incorporated. The overall formulation might be as shown in Box 7.4. Exact information concerning the timing and extent of the difficulty is desirable. Appendix 12 can be photocopied to permit accurate data concerning either bedtime or sleeping problems to be gathered (see Table 7.2). Often the information which becomes available is of no less interest to the parent(s) than to the practitioner. Sometimes the child comes downstairs or wakes less often than is thought; sometimes other patterns, such as the way the children respond differently to their mothers and to their fathers, become apparent—thus opening the way to a discussion of how parents are responding differently to the child.

Step 7—Gathering base-line data as an aid to assessment

Accurate information is needed now concerning the extent of Sebastian's negative behaviour, his 'coming downstairs' after bedtime and one of his positive behaviours, say, his 'helping in the house', such as laying the table. This information could be collected on the chart shown as Appendix 8.

Let us assume that the records for the first (base-line) week show that Sebastian came downstairs 25 times (see Table 7.2) and was helpful only three times.

Step 8—Planning with the Parents

The practitioner and parent are partners in a shared endeavour to help the whole family. It is vital that we offer both support for the individuals concerned as well as confidence that we have a strategy for helping them. At this stage the practitioner discusses with the parent(s) how they may test out the ideas above. The following plans may be developed concerning Sebastian:

1. Sebastian's Mummy will explore with her former employer the possibility of doing some part-time work.
2. The worker will telephone three times weekly to offer support.

3. Sebastian's Mummy and Daddy will explain to him that, come what may, he will not be allowed to come downstairs once he has been put to bed. Each time he comes down, he will be taken *straight* back to bed.
4. Each evening Sebastian stays in bed quietly; however, he will win an animal sticker to put on a chart. His Daddy will help him make the chart. Any week when he achieves five or more stickers out of seven, his Daddy will take him swimming on Saturday morning.
5. If he does come downstairs, there will be no snacks and no toys will be permitted. His Mummy and Daddy will not talk to him or even look at him. He will be taken straight back to bed.
6. His Daddy will arrange to be at home at bedtime on Friday, Saturday and Sunday evenings so that both Mummy and Daddy can follow the plan in the same way.

Step 9—Implementation of the Plan

At all stages, the safety of the child is paramount, so the practitioner should familiarise herself with the layout of the house and sleeping area and check the environment for safety. Then, on the agreed day, the plan is put into action.

Ordinarily, practitioners would expect to make no more than once-weekly visits or contacts, but in serious situations, where parents are desperate for support, a brief visit or telephone call after two nights or even after one night is usually very welcome. One would not expect any change at this stage: on the contrary, things are likely to be beginning to be worse at this point—as the child realises that limits are being set to his behaviour. The role of the practitioner is to 'trouble-shoot'—to be sufficiently familiar with and confident in the use of the theoretical framework to encourage parents not to give up once their child becomes more difficult as a prelude to his adapting to the new routine. We must recognise the demands this places on parents and give much encouragement for their efforts to follow the plan.

Over the next six weeks at least, the parents are asked to keep careful records of Sebastian's patterns of bedtime behaviour. This

SHOWING THE INCREASE OR DECREASE WEEK BY WEEK

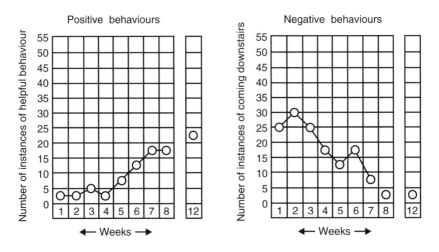

Figure 7.2: Sebastian's positive and negative behaviours over eight weeks and at one month follow-up

will not be easy for them, but from this data arises information as to whether things are getting better or worse, when difficulties happen and the relationship between events in the child's life and their impact upon behaviour. Typically, things are likely to be considerably improved by one month but sometimes it takes longer for the child to respond to the new methods of management. Figure 7.2 shows a very typical course of events, as the child receives fewer and fewer rewards for coming downstairs and more and more attention and praise for his pro-social behaviour.

As there is improvement towards one goal, so a further pair of behaviours, one negative and one positive, can be identified and targets set. The newly learned strategies for managing the first pair need to be consolidated, but the links between aspects of improvement in the child's behaviour and the new ways in which the parents are handling him/her are probably by now becoming apparent. Unless there is absolutely no change in the child's behaviour, parents should be asked to persist in their efforts. If there is absolutely no such evidence, then different explanations may need to be considered and tested in a similar way.

Step 10—Review and Evaluation

Through all the weeks of attempting to put the theoretical principles into practice it is essential to learn from the parents' experience. For example, as I write, I am in touch with the family of a five year-old boy who repeatedly hit and punched his mother when she tried to send him back upstairs when he came down after being put to bed. She tells me that she learned that she had to sit on the stairs outside his bedroom and the instant that the child showed his nose outside, she stood, gave him a hard stare, and ordered him back to bed. It gave her great satisfaction to give her child an 'order' and see it obeyed—after realising that for many months she had been carrying out *his* orders! She found the approach extremely effective and it was necessary to sit at the top of the stairs for only a few evenings before her child learned that Mummy was now in charge!

ANOTHER EXAMPLE: RAJITA, AGED 15 MONTHS

Assessment

During Steps 1–2 the practitioner builds supportive relationships with Rajita's parents and gathers relevant information. Rajita is the daughter of Poonam and Vickram. She is a delightful little girl, but her parents are desperate because of shortage of sleep. Rajita had always been put to bed by Poonam, but as Poonam has had to take an evening job, Vickram now has to put Rajita to bed.

Step 3—Identifying problem behaviours

1. Rajita wakes up five or six times during each night.
2. She insists that her mother lie beside her to get her to go to sleep.
3. Each time she screams until she is given a bottle of milk.

Here it seems probable that Rajita, who is having to adjust to a new routine, has learned to expect both to being settled to sleep during the night by her mother and to have a bottle feed as well! Thus, she is being rewarded for waking up by two very gratifying rewards. It is most unlikely that she will change this routine of her own accord.

Step 4—Identifying positive profile

1. She goes to bed readily: there is never any problem at that time.
2. She is a very loving little girl: she comes to kiss her Mummy and Daddy.
3. She 'helps' her Mummy prepare meals in the kitchen.

Step 5—Identifying desired outcomes

The parents are not expecting that there will never be broken nights. They understand that Rajita is still a tiny child who is taking time to move to a consistent pattern of sleeping. They hope, however, that within two months they will experience only two broken nights each week.

Step 6—Formulation of Rajita's poor sleeping patterns

The overall formulation might be as shown in Box 7.5.

Box 7.5: Preliminary assessment of/rationale for Rajita's difficulties

1. *Predisposing life events for this child and members of this family:*
   (a) Rajita, aged 15 months, is not used to sleeping alone.
   (b) Her mother, Poonam, has had to take up evening employment; her father, Vickram, now puts the toddler to bed.
2. *Organic factors, or those intrinsic to the child, e.g. developmental stage, disability:*
   (a) Rajita is eating well during the day; night feeds are not necessary.
   (b) She is warmly dressed; she does not seem to be waking because of heat or cold.
3. *Immediate variables: interactions within the family (A–B–C)*:*
   (a) Rajita wakes repeatedly during the night from 10.00 p.m. Each time her mother goes and gives her a bottle. Each one takes about 15 minutes.
   (b) The number of wakings is increasing—from about three to about five nightly.
   (c) Unintentionally, Poonam may be 'teaching' Rajita to wake, by giving her a bottle and cuddling her each time she does so.

*Parents may not understand this concept, but it is useful to introduce it at this stage.

Step 7—Data gathering

Data are collected just as for Sebastian, but since this is a tiny child, with the approval of the General Practitioner, records must be kept to see how frequently Rajita is waking for unnecessary attention during the night. Appendix 12 is likely to be useful here.

Steps 8 and 9—Planning and Implementing the Plan

When the baseline information is available, the following plan is likely to help Rajita's parents, in discussion with the family health visitor:

1. Rajita is too young to be involved in the plan, but her parents agree to work together.
2. The existing routine should be maintained, but in future Rajita's mother will make a point of spending at least 20 minutes playing with the little girl each afternoon.
3. At night, she will put first water and milk and then water only in the bottle, when initially she continues to go to her.
4. She will choose which of the two strategies described above (pp. 187 and 188), the gradual or the direct approach, is more acceptable to her.
5. Both parents will continue to keep records and to encourage each other.
6. The worker will telephone three times a week to offer support.

It is very likely that, given a consistent response night by night to Rajita's waking, she will gradually relinquish her pattern of waking and sleep for longer and longer periods. If Poonam has to go to her, she will avoid talking to her or looking at her. With the worker's support the family's goal of only two nights' broken sleep each week is likely to be achieved by the end of two months.

Step 10—Review and Evaluation

It will be essential to offer 'booster' contacts to both these sets of parents after the main intervention has finished. This is to reinforce practices of managing the child, which are very newly learned by the parents and which, as we should expect from our understanding of cognitive-behavioural principles, may all too swiftly fade away. Both Sebastian's and Rajita's parents need repeated re-inforcement and encouragement for their efforts to change their ways of managing their child. *We should use the theory to maintain the effectiveness of every intervention.*

8

HELPING FAMILIES WITH CHILDREN WITH EATING PROBLEMS

It is difficult to understand that such an intense and primary need as that for food and drink can become so subverted that young children not only take insufficient nourishment to meet their growth needs but actively turn away from food so frequently that they lose weight. This often causes acute anxiety to parents, who may believe that their child will starve to death and, in their distress, may get into frequent confrontations with the child—who becomes ever more reluctant to eat. How common are these difficulties and how can we help families who experience them?

PROBLEMS OF DEFINITION

It is not easy to establish a clear definition of what constitutes an eating problem because of differing criteria used by different researchers. For some, it has been sufficient for the mother to report that there is a problem for this to be accepted; for others, the problem must have been of a particular duration, and for yet others (Dahl and Kristiansson, 1987) certain strict criteria, such as those below, must be met:

1. The mother and health visiting nurse must agree that a problem is present.

2. It must have persisted without interruption for at least one month.
3. Simple advice on management provided by the nurse must have been insufficient to resolve the problem.

As infants develop, a clearer means of delineating a feeding difficulty becomes available: the measured loss of weight according to centile charts (Tanner and Whitehouse, 1959). Children typically gain weight according to 'centiles' which represent norms; for a child to 'fall off' his or her typical centile gives grounds for concern, while falling below the third centile gives major grounds for concern. This means that where a child falls within the lowest 3% of children in respect of weight, such a situation requires very careful monitoring.

PREVALENCE OF FEEDING/EATING PROBLEMS

Birth to twelve months

With such variability, it is not surprising that there is little agreement over the prevalence of feeding difficulties. The Swedish study, referred to above, by Dahl and Kristiansson (1987), who screened babies between four and seven months, found that only 1.4% of the infants met their tight criteria for an established feeding difficulty. Another Swedish study by Lindberg, Bohlin and Hagekull (1991), however, of infants between six and twelve months, found that about 25% had feeding problems, while an American study by Forsyth (1989) of babies between birth and four months reported that about 33% of mothers indicated that they had a moderate or severe feeding problem. While criteria for what constituted a 'problem' clearly differed greatly, nevertheless it is of great interest that the mothers' conclusion that they had a problem was so very much stronger than the views of the independent researchers who set stringent but impersonal criteria. In view of the movement to empower parents and to view situations empathically rather than clinically, services are required to meet the perceived needs of the *parents*, rather than those of researchers.

Pre-school Children

There are more studies of the prevalence of eating problems in pre-school children, and the major report by Minde and Minde (1986) concluded that 12–34% of children were affected. Other studies suggest an even higher figure. Workers in the Child Support Project in Swindon, UK, found that parents reported that many difficulties began at the time of weaning, but that some stemmed from the period of about 15 months, when babies are typically beginning to develop a sense of independence. Skuse (1994) suggests that, while for a proportion of these children there may be a genuine persistence of difficulties from the earlier months of life, for many the difficulty has arisen through a conditioning process (see Chapter 2 and below).

RESEARCH INTO THE ORIGINS OF FEEDING/EATING PROBLEMS

There are several major fields of research in this area: we have space only to consider three:

1. Circumstances which seem to be linked with feeding or eating difficulties.
2. Some features of so-called 'failure to thrive'.
3. The relevance of principles of cognitive-behavioural theory in helping families.

Circumstances Linked with Feeding Problems

Several sets of circumstances may combine so that feeding gets off to a poor start. The first is the rare circumstance of inadequate milk on the part of mothers who are breastfeeding their babies, which may contribute to the infants' restlessness and fretfulness. This circumstance is more likely to be imaginary than real and more temporary than permanent, but many mothers, hearing their babies crying, assume that they are hungry and, swiftly losing confidence in their ability to breastfeed, cease trying to do so. With encouragement and information from supportive and experienced midwives, health visitors or other professionals, however, many mothers can produce a sufficient supply of milk for their babies.

The second set of circumstances which may pose difficulties is the introduction of weaning, that is, the supplementation of breast milk by solid foods. Skuse (1994) makes a strong case for abandoning the term 'weaning' and using instead the expression 'mixed feeding'—a practice I shall adopt in this book. He reports:

> The present-day recommendation in the UK is that solid food shall be introduced into an infant's diet between the ages of about four and six months (Department of Health and Social Security, 1988).

This period seems to accord with the possibility of there being a 'sensitive period' when solid foods are more readily acceptable than at other times. Skuse comments:

> If children are not exposed to solids that require chewing by about 6–7 months of age, they tend to be resistant to accepting these textures in later childhood (Illingworth and Lister, 1964). Feeding problems can then result, with refusal to accept lumpy foods and even vomiting.

A third contributory factor, according to Skuse, is colic, which is associated with the baby's experiencing acute abdominal discomfort, often in the evening. This leads to crying which persists despite every attempt on the part of the caregivers to offer comfort. This seems to affect between 10% and 30% of infants and to persist for about three months. Spasms of pain may interrupt feeding and produce tension in all concerned. As Skuse says, the persistence of difficulties of this kind, particularly in new parents, can seriously undermine their confidence. Other problems may arise either through reflux vomiting or through lack of coordination between the many systems necessary for sucking and swallowing—such as may occur, for instance, in children born with cerebral palsy.

A fourth contributory cause may be the way that parents respond to the first signs of reluctance to eat on the part of the child. Because parents are usually anxious that their child shall eat, not only in order to gain weight appropriately but because eating well is a socially approved behaviour in young children, they often over-encourage eating, regardless of the size of the child's appetite or of what has been eaten since the last meal. Mealtimes all too readily becomes an aversive, rather than an enjoyable, experience for the child and a vicious spiral may be established in which the parents become ever more anxious and the child ever more determined to eat only minimal amounts.

Many readers will be familiar with scenarios in which children are required to eat certain types of food or certain amounts of food at mealtimes—sometimes, in the worst situation, with the same food brought to them again and again. It is extraordinarily difficult to make a child eat who has set his will against doing so—but the anxiety levels of the parents in such circumstances are intense; it is no simple matter to reduce them. The child ultimately always has the upper hand.

Overlap with Field of 'Failure to Thrive'

The research field of eating problems overlaps substantially with that of failure to thrive. Iwaniec, Herbert and McNeish (1985a) highlight studies which attempted to distinguish particular antecedents in the history of children who fail to thrive by comparison with children with non-problematic histories. They quote, for example, Pollitt, Eichler and Chan (1975), who studied the economic, social, family, nutritional and medical circumstances of 38 families in which a child was failing to thrive by comparison with controls. The researchers anticipated that the target group would show higher levels of mental ill-health and more stressful marital histories, but in fact this was not found to be the case. Iwaniec, Herbert and McNeish (1985a) report:

> The largest between-group statistical differences were found in the scores drawn from the mother–child interaction check-list. The mothers in the experimental group showed less frequent verbal and physical contacts, were less positively reinforcing and warm. These differences in verbal interactions were noted on various socialization tasks. Substantial differences were also noted in maternal affection, described as 'inoperant' in many of the index mothers.

Researchers such as Lachenmeyer and Davidovicz (1987) also pinpointed feeding difficulties as key variables leading to the onset of failure to thrive, while factor analytic studies, such as that of Bithoney and Newberger (1987), confirmed that disturbed feeding situations were deeply implicated in the aetiology of the disorder.

Treatment models have not, until fairly recently, been well developed. When children are diagnosed medically as 'failing to thrive' there is real concern for their well-being; many are admitted to hospital and may, when they are fed by hospital staff, readily gain weight—only to lose it again after discharge. This may offer pointers to practitioners seeking to *prevent* these difficulties from becoming entrenched. That is, the feeding problems seem to be person specific.

Iwaniec, Herbert and McNeish published two seminal papers in 1985. The first examined numerous features, demographic, social and individual, of a group of parents whose children failed to thrive and distinguished several sets of specific circumstances that characterised them:

- Most of the mothers demonstrated ambivalent feelings and behaviour to their children.
- Some of the mothers felt indifference and hostility towards their children (but Iwaniec and colleagues note that almost two-thirds felt that their children had first rejected them, in that they had refused 'that very basic symbol of mother care—food').
- The child's poor physical appearance and apathetic behaviour brought much criticism from health visitors and neighbours— which in turn led to tension and further anxiety in the feeding situation.
- A history of feeding problems (inability or reluctance to suck) while the infants were on liquids.
- The majority of mothers dated the onset of really *acute* feeding difficulties from the time when solids were introduced.

Iwaniec et al (1985a) identified a theoretical formulation which seems central to both understanding the development of the feeding problems and suggesting how to relieve them. They reported:

All parents in the non-organic index group reported specific feeding difficulties with their children . . . the majority dated the onset of really acute feeding difficulties from the time when solids were introduced . . . *the possibility that the child has learned to fear broad aspects of the feeding process is overlooked* (present author's italics).

The second seminal paper published by Iwaniec et al (1985b) concerned the successful testing of a model of intervention based upon principles of social learning/cognitive-behavioural theory applied within a 'systems' framework. It is to this that we now turn.

RESEARCH INTO THE MANAGEMENT OF EATING DIFFICULTIES

The Relevance of Cognitive-behavioural Theory

Iwaniec, Herbert and McNeish (1985b) worked with the parents of 17 children who were failing to thrive, using an innovative model of intervention and comparing the progress of these children with children in two control groups. The parents of the children in the first (focus) group were offered help based upon principles of cognitive-behavioural theory within a 'systems' framework, and since they were able to demonstrate that the children gained weight to an extent which brought them within the normal ranges which characterised the controls, their seminal work is being widely disseminated as a model of *preventive intervention* (Hampton, 1996).

There were two main stages in the approach. First, help was made available via the many systems of which the family were a part: this involved the researchers in arranging for parents to be offered occasional places at community resources such as a day nursery; approaching welfare agencies to ensure that parents were receiving all the financial support to which they were entitled; enabling parents to attend a self-help group; and enlisting community volunteers. Second, individually tailored help was given within the framework of cognitive-behavioural theory to do two main things:

(a) To desensitise (where necessary) the mother's tension, anger and anxiety when in the child's company.
(b) To provide her with a set of strategies for learning new responses to the child.

The essential point is that the tension is seen as a *learned* response to the child's difficult feeding behaviour—and thus as one which the parent can, with help, replace with other, more constructive responses, provided she is offered support and encouragement.

The Application of Cognitive-Behavioural Principles

The principles are systematically applied, as set out in Box 8.1. Iwaniec, Herbert and McNeish (1985b) reported:

> There were several 'rejecting' mothers in our sample and they usually found this [nurturing] very difficult and at times distasteful. This aversion gradually lessened when the child began to smile back, seek her presence and in other ways respond to her overtures. This period of therapy requires a lot of support for the mother and the whole family . . . It could take three months of hard work to bring a mother and child closer together and to the point of beginning to enjoy each other.

The evidence from this study was very positive: of the 17 children whose families took part in the study, 11 showed 'satisfactory' improvement (i.e. they improved to the extent that the children resumed growth to the point where height and weight were within normal limits); five achieved 'moderate' improvement with weight gain renewed; for only one was there no improvement.

Building on this work, and in an attempt to avoid admission to hospital and the cycle of weight loss and gain so often noted, interdisciplinary teams in Swindon and Trowbridge, Wiltshire developed a resource for offering families a service in their own homes. The main bodies of theory employed are humanistic psychology, child development theory within a multi-racial and multi-cultural community and cognitive-behavioural theory. The first, associated with the names of Rogers and Maslow, is invoked in that the infants and young children concerned are in danger of not having their most fundamental needs met—the needs for food and drink, together with individual nurturing and care. The second underpins the monitoring of each child's development and takes into account each one's progress according to recognised developmental charts; knowledge of norms for child development is

Box 8.1: Programme for increasing mother–infant nurturing, Stages 1–3 (after Iwaniec, Herbert and McNeish, 1985b)

Stage 1—to reduce tension and anxiety at mealtimes
- A very structured approach is followed.
- Parents are asked never to feed the child when feeling very tense or angry.
- They are asked to avoid screaming, shouting and threatening the child.
- They are helped to develop a quiet and calm atmosphere at mealtimes.
- The parents are coached in talking reassuringly and pleasantly to the child.
- If the child refuses food, the parents are guided to leave him or her for a while, and to avoid getting into a confrontation with him or her. If he/she persists in refusing the food, they are advised not to exert pressure.
- The food is arranged attractively and the child is given very small portions.
- When he or she does take food, the mother is guided to show her pleasure and to encourage the child.

Stage 2—to promote and encourage attachment and bonding
- The objective of developing closer relationships with the child is explained to the parents (the authors report that sometimes a contract to support the approach is devised). The mother is asked:
  - Each day in the first week, to play for 10–15 minutes with her child.
  - Each day in the second and third week, to play for 15–20 minutes with her child.
  - Each day in the fourth and later weeks, to play for 25–30 minutes with her child.
- The parents, who sometimes need help in learning how to play with their child, are supported in this activity by the practitioner.
- Parents are shown how to interact gently with their child, to smile at him or her, to give him or her encouragement and praise and to touch and stroke him/her (for some parents who have never received this nurturing behaviour themselves, this is very difficult. They too need much encouragement and clear examples by the worker which they can copy).
- Fathers are encouraged, wherever possible, to take part in the child's care.
- The earlier feeding strategies are continued and weight is monitored regularly.

Stage 3—to consolidate gains and to promote independence
- The plan for this stage is explained to the parents and their involvement sought.
- The mother is asked to take her child with her almost everywhere she goes, for two weeks of increased mother–child interaction.
- She is asked to smile at the child a lot, to talk to him or her and to cuddle and hug him or her often.
- She tries to engage the child in play with any other children of the family.
- The earlier feeding strategies are continued and weight monitored.
- If improvements are noted and are maintaining, the practitioner gradually withdraws.

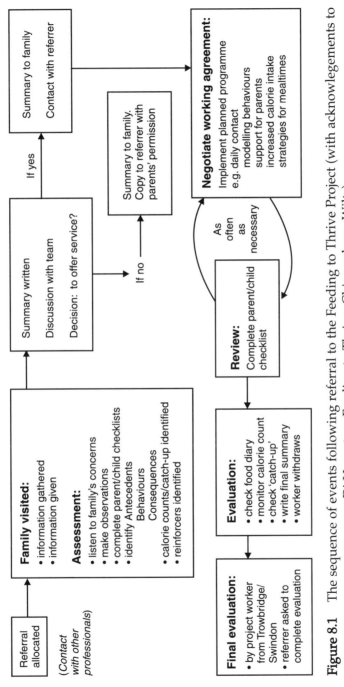

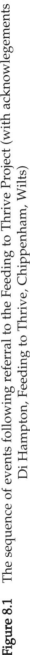

Figure 8.1 The sequence of events following referral to the Feeding to Thrive Project (with acknowlegements to Di Hampton, Feeding to Thrive, Chippenham, Wilts)

central to the effective work of the project. The progress of children from ethnic minority groups is considered carefully in order that norms which apply to white children should not be used inappropriately. The third main body of theory employs cognitive-behavioural principles, and Figure 8.1 is a flow chart showing the sequence of events which follows referral to the project. My own evaluation of the Infant Support Project (Hampton, 1996) reported that 73 of the 108 children showed satisfactory gain as measured by either weight or height gain, or both.

HELPING FAMILIES WITH CHILDREN WITH EATING DIFFICULTIES

Here I am not considering children who have reached the stage of failing to thrive but those who may be displaying the patterns of eating difficulty which *might* lead to failure to thrive. For example, the innovative work by Hampton and colleagues required videoing mealtimes of children who were eating poorly, and while that is undoubtedly often revealing, I seek here to avoid that necessity.

Assessment

Step 1—Introducing oneself

In tense situations, the practitioner may have to work hard to overcome resentment and hostility. Parents tend to locate the problem *in* the child and are likely to be bewildered and unable to grasp any other explanation. In such circumstances the quality of the relationship developed between the family and the practitioner is crucial; it must be seen by the family members as supportive, friendly and non-critical—otherwise one will join the ranks of the many other people dismissed as having nothing to offer.

Step 2—Information gathering

Many children will have been screened for conditions predisposing to eating difficulties, such as allergies. Great tact will be necessary to help families accept situations where no such factors are found as well as the inevitable conclusion that there are difficulties intrinsic to the feeding situation which are contributing to the child's difficulties. However, there may well have been medical factors which interacted with the feeding problems, so it is important to elicit the events of that history. The practitioner will use discretion about how much detail is required. Have there always been difficulties, or did things become markedly worse at a certain stage of development, such as at the introduction of mixed feeding? Do all family members experience difficulty in getting the child to feed, or, deepest humiliation of all for the mother, is it only her food which is rejected, while husband and grandmother experience no problems? The practitioner is likely to be drawing upon counselling skills of empathic listening, showing positive regard and demonstrating personal warmth if this kind of story unfolds.

The example of Lisa: Let us consider the situation of Clare and Keith, parents of Lisa, a little girl of just over 3 born with a cleft palate. She has had extensive surgery which has repaired the palate, leaving only a slight scar on her upper lip, but this has contributed to much tension around feeding. Clare, in particular, is becoming increasingly anxious and there is some concern that Lisa is beginning to fall off her weight centile.

Step 3—Identifying the problem behaviours

It will probably be beneficial for some emotionally uninvolved person to be present during at least one meal to observe in a supportive way the interactions of the child and her parents. This might be the practitioner or some 'friend of the family' who wishes to be supportive to them all and who will be empathic with the mother in her distress. It may then be possible to identify eating or mealtime behaviours which are causing difficulties. For example:

1. Lisa screams if her mother, Clare, tries to get her to eat. She turns away from her.

2. If they are placed in front of her, she will eat a very limited range of foods: bananas, yoghurt and baked beans.
3. She will eat a little more if her Daddy (Keith) or her granny sits with her.

Step 4—Identifying positive profile

It is next necessary to identify features of the child's behaviour which parents already enjoy and would like to see happening more frequently. These positive behaviours can be in areas quite removed from the eating situation. This serves to reassure parents who are losing confidence that there are features of their parenting which are entirely successful. For example, family members will be reassured to hear the worker's appreciation of some aspect of their parenting: the child's friendliness, her ability to find things or her smile. Such parents are usually very demoralised; they have had difficulties in a field of great significance: that of nurturing their child. They need *much* empathic support. We are trying to foster positive, warm, nurturing interactions between parent and child, as these serve to reduce anxiety and tension—so reducing angry, rejecting interactions. Thus, Clare and Keith might identify:

1. Lisa's outgoingness; she is friendly to people who come to the house.
2. Lisa's kindness to other toddlers; if one cries, she tries to give comfort.

Step 5—Discover desired outcome

Most parents whose children have eating difficulties have few unreasonable expectations. They generally want their child to eat a reasonably balanced diet and to maintain his/her weight and growth. In precise terms, this might be stated as follows:

Target 1 That within eight weeks, Lisa will be eating a diet comprising protein, carbohydrates, fats, etc. during each week (precise figures to be devised by a dietician).

Target 2 That Lisa will maintain this diet over the subsequent 12 weeks.

Step 6—Summarising key information and offering a rationale

A matter-of-fact approach, which emphasises that feeding problems are common and that the practitioner is particularly interested in them, often acts to reassure parents. Enabling them to talk to other parents who have had a successful outcome to their child's difficulty may be an effective strategy. If this is not possible, then another good strategy is to show letters from 'satisfied customers', that is, a number of pro formas, kept in a loose-leaf file, in which

---

Box 8.2: Preliminary assessment of/rationale for the difficulties of Lisa, aged 39 months

1. *Predisposing 'life events' for this child and members of this family*
   (a) Lisa, aged three, is the first child of Clare and Keith. She was born with a cleft palate.
   (b) Clare feels helpless and inadequate because of the feeding difficulties. Lisa is her first child, and her medical needs cause Clare much anxiety.
   (c) Clare's mother-in-law, Lisa's grandmother, tries to help but Clare feels criticised by her.
   (d) Clare worries about whether she might have harmed Lisa during her pregnancy.
   (e) Keith is self-employed. He has tried to adjust his work so that he can come home to help feed Lisa, but this is straining his and Clare's relationship.

2. *Organic factors, or those intrinsic to the child: e.g. developmental stage, disability*
   (a) Lisa's cleft palate has required substantial surgery, upsetting to all concerned.
   (b) Feeding has been difficult from the start, apparently sometimes initially associated with pain.
   (c) Lisa is beginning to lose weight; she is on the point of falling below her centile.

3. *Immediate variables: interactions within the family (A–B–C)**
   (a) When Lisa refuses food Clare has provided, Clare feels *very* tense and angry.
   (b) Clare acknowledges that she has tried to force-feed Lisa, who screamed and screamed.

* Parents may not understand this concept, but it is useful to introduce it at this stage.

parents who have had successful outcomes have written brief notes about their child's eating problems and how they felt about them before and after they received help.

The overall formulation of the difficulty, offered supportively to the parents, might be as shown in Box 8.2.

Step 8—Planning

The practitioner and parents are now partners in a joint endeavour to help Lisa. It is crucial to explain to the parents that she seems to have a *fear* of eating in her mother's presence: she is not just being naughty. No-one is to blame for this, but everyone can work together to improve matters. It will probably be appropriate to explain what is known about desensitisation from the standpoint of cognitive-behavioural theory. The practitioner can make a number of points which will vary according to the age and circumstances of the child. In respect of Lisa, these might be:

1. Lisa's fear of her mother going into the kitchen will diminish if Clare keeps going in but comes out again without any food in her hands and without looking at Lisa.
2. Lisa's tensions about food, arising from the necessary medical treatment, will subside if mealtimes can become relaxed and casual times.
3. Lisa will be less fearful of eating if Clare explains to her that although she had tried to force her to eat in the past, she will never do so again.
4. Lisa will gradually become used to having her mother present at mealtimes if her mother and her Daddy together sit to eat with her, behaving in a very relaxed and casual way about what Lisa eats.
5. Lisa will gradually become used to eating if, when her Daddy provides her with food, her mother also, casually, puts some of Lisa's favourite finger foods, such as yoghurt-covered sultanas, near her plate—but takes no interest initially in whether she eats them or not.
6. Lisa will gradually respond to eating a wider variety of food if she is told in a calm and casual way, 'Well done, Lisa' at the end of a meal.

   Keith and Clare have already begun to realise that they must reward Lisa's occasional willingness to extend the range of her foods, and a simple explanation of the A–B–C formulation is likely to be acceptable to them. It will be helpful to give them a means of recording Lisa's intake of food and drink, via a simple chart showing the days of the week and the times of day when anything is eaten or drunk. Guidance should be given about, for example, the type of milk or cheese she should be offered so that although her diet is small it is nutritious.

   Clare will need much help in accepting, at least temporarily, Lisa's rejection of her but may be reassured by the worker's confidence that her little girl is likely to regain her affection for her. Clare will certainly need the practitioner to model how to remain calm in her interactions with Lisa, particularly when the food she has prepared is rejected. Because of her anxieties that she may have harmed Lisa in some way during her pregnancy, she may agree to referral to a counsellor, if the current practitioner has not received appropriate training in counselling. Clare will probably know who or what would help her most: perhaps a medical explanation from a specialist health visitor or perhaps a talk with the paediatrician who first helped care for Lisa. She may need several forms of support.

   Some elements of the plan might therefore be:

1. Initially there will be no change in the plan of caring for Lisa.
2. Gradually, Clare should resume caring for Lisa in all other respects except feeding. She can play with her, read her stories, bath her, help her dress and so on.
3. Keith should continue to give Lisa her meals as far as his work permits; Clare should eat her own meals in Lisa's sight, but offer her nothing.
4. As Clare feels calmer and more relaxed, she should place some finger food near Lisa, saying nothing to her and not even looking at her.
5. If ever Lisa does eat it, again, for the time being, Clare should say nothing—although if this pattern becomes established, she should say casually, 'That's nice; well done'.
6. If Lisa gets messy or sticky, Clare should clean her up without comment.

7. The parents should keep a record of Lisa's intake on a daily basis.
8. Clare should make her interactions with Lisa as relaxed and calm as she can during the rest of the day.

These strategies are put forward as a range of ways of first, making the eating situation far more relaxed, and second, desensitising Lisa and her mother to the learned fears associated with eating. These fears have been learned over many months; it is likely that gaining confidence about eating will also take many months. The plan must not be hurried.

Involving the child in the plan

Lisa, too, can be involved as fully as her understanding permits— so that it can be explained to her that Mummy understands that she seems frightened to eat. Mummy did once try to make her eat, but she will not do that again. Everyone hopes she will come to enjoy eating like most people do, but for the time being they're not going to pay much attention to it.

Step 9—Implementation of the Plan

The next step will be for Clare, Keith and Lisa's Granny to attempt to put the plan into effect. There are bound to be disappointments and set-backs as Lisa tests out the new 'management' and as her mother has further experiences of rejection; if the plan is followed carefully, and as the practitioner gains experience in the use of cognitive-behavioural principles, he or she is likely to be able to 'trouble-shoot' the difficulties which will inevitably arise. It will be important for Keith to cooperate with the plan and for the worker to enlist the support of Lisa's Granny, who may be tempted, because of her own anxiety and impatience with her daughter-in-law, to try to hurry the plan forward. On some occasions it is necessary to ask the various participants to develop an agreement (see Chapter 12, p. 299) with the worker which effectively engages their cooperation with the plan and prevents their taking things into their own hands.

Step 10—Review and Evaluation

The main measure of the effectiveness of the plan will, of course, be Lisa's weight gain. She should be weighed at regular intervals; this will be a reliable indicator of whether there is or is not evidence to support the various hypotheses. If, for example, it seems that the hypothesis that Lisa has learned to fear the feeding situation is not supported, then another must be systematically tried. Cognitive-behavioural approaches offer a wide range of theoretical principles to help families deal with feeding and eating difficulties. The principles can be discerned at any meal, whether they be the satisfaction and rewards which people typically gain from eating or the difficulties which arise when eating ceases to be enjoyable.

9

HELPING FAMILIES WITH CHILDREN WITH SERIOUS BEHAVIOUR PROBLEMS

DIFFICULTIES OF ARRIVING AT DEFINITIONS

There have been many attempts to tease out differences between types of misbehaviour in young children; the hope of clarifying, for example, whether any have an organic basis, whether patterns of early onset give more grounds for concern than do those of later onset, and whether there are innate predispositions towards aggressiveness. While there is still much disagreement between researchers, some progress has been made. For example, there is increasing consensus that a pattern of behaviour marked by extremely restless and impulsive behaviour, named attention deficit/hyperactivity disorder (AD/HD), is sufficiently different from, say, a general tendency to aggressive behaviour, for it to be accepted as a distinct syndrome; accordingly, this chapter will address severe behaviour problems/anti-social behaviour and the next will focus upon AD/HD.

Children with severe behaviour problems are described as 'conduct-disordered' according to the two major systems of classification: the *Diagnostic and Statistical Manual*, 4th edn (DSM-IV) (American Psychiatric Association, 1994) and the *International*

Classification of Disorders, 10th edition (ICD-10) (World Health Organization, 1992). The term is not customarily used for pre-school children. Both systems of classification require the presence of at least three of the features shown in Box 9.1, and while this has been devised with older children in mind, it is included to indicate the types of behaviour that may give grounds for concern, especially if exhibited in more than one setting, for example at home as well as at playgroup or nursery. The precursors in young children of the terms in Box 9.1 are destructiveness, disruptiveness, defiance and physical and verbal aggressiveness.

Box 9.1: Features of children's behaviour which may lead to an assessment of conduct disorder (data from American Psychiatric Association, 1994)

Lies	Initiates fights	Uses weapons
Is destructive	Is cruel to animals	Is cruel to people
Stays out late	Sets fires	Steals
Runs away	Engages in robbery/mugging	Forces sex
Bullies	Burgles	

PREVALENCE OF AND CONTINUITIES IN CONDUCT DISORDERS

Because of the increasing evidence of the link between early anti-social behaviour and subsequent aggressive and offending behaviour (Robins, 1966, 1981), serious misbehaviour has been the focus of extensive research, both in the UK and in the USA. A broad consensus is emerging upon a number of issues.

Prevalence

Studies undertaken in different countries and in different parts of those countries all indicate a much higher rate of serious misbehaviour for boys than for girls (Earls and Jung, 1987; Offord, Boyle and Racine, 1991) and all show a higher rate in urban environments than in rural ones (Rutter and colleagues, 1975a, b). In the UK, prevalence rates range from 6.2% to 10.8% of 10 year-old children, with the lower figure found in rural populations (Department of Health, 1995).

Longitudinal studies also show a worrying picture. The British National Child Development Study (Davie, Butler and Goldstein, 1972) followed the development of some 15 000 children born in one week in 1958. Assessments by teachers when the children were seven indicated that 14% were considered to present serious problems and a further 8% were showing some signs of disturbed behaviour; again, boys were more highly represented than girls. A more recent study by the Thomas Coram Research Unit (Tizard et al, 1988) of children aged four to seven in Inner London infant schools reported 16% as having definite behaviour problems in the eyes of their teachers and a further 17% as having mild behaviour problems. The teachers' views were confirmed by independent observers in the classroom.

Woodhead (1995), however, urges caution in reading too much into these figures, pointing out the differences in ways of assessing the behaviour difficulties in the various studies, in where they were assessed and by whom. Nevertheless, there must be grounds for serious concern, particularly in relation to the study by Tizard et al (1988), in that it is relatively recent that teachers' perceptions were confirmed by direct observation, and that almost one-third of the total number of children were reported as having some behaviour problems.

Continuities from Early Childhood into Adolescence and Adulthood

There have been many attempts to follow up children seen as having behaviour disorder in childhood into later life. The seminal study by Robins (1966) found that nearly half the children with this diagnosis in her large sample of children in a US town went on to develop anti-social personality disorder as adults. Some of the children who did not become anti-social showed other forms of disturbance, including alcoholism or schizophrenia. Olweus (1979) reviewed a number of studies on this topic, some of which followed up subjects for long periods, in some instances as long as 20 years. He concluded that the degree of stability in the area of aggression was substantial; moreover, he found that 'marked individual differences in habitual aggression level manifest themselves early in life, certainly by the age of 3'. Further, the major study by Zoccolillo et al (1992) in a longitudinal study of adults who had spent much of their childhood in foster care, showed that the great majority experienced a variety of social problems in adult life.

Other studies give further grounds for concern. Robins and Price (1991), in their longitudinal study of young people with conduct disorders, found, as reported by Earls (1994), that, 'Conduct disorder may predict adult substance abuse about as efficiently as it predicts antisocial behaviour . . .'. There was a difference, however, between young men and young women; Earls reports, 'For females, conduct disorder predicted depression and anxiety disorders more strongly than it did antisocial behaviour and substance abuse'.

Many researchers, such as Loeber (1990), have found a relationship between early age of onset and more serious forms of disturbance. It is increasingly accepted that the more serious and the earlier the onset of behaviour disturbance, the greater the probability of its continuing into adolescence and beyond.

In summarising this area of research, Webster-Stratton and Herbert (1994) have concluded that certain risk factors contribute to the continuation of disorders:

- Early age of onset (pre-school years) of oppositional–defiant disorder (ODD) and conduct disorder (CD). Those children with conduct symptoms prior to age six are at greater risk for developing anti-social behaviour as adults than those whose problems start during adolescence.
- Breadth of deviance (across multiple settings, such as home and school). Those children most at risk of continuing anti-social behaviour as adults had conduct problems which occurred not only in the home but also at school and in other settings.
- Frequency and intensity of anti-social behaviour. The likelihood of becoming an anti-social adult increases in direct proportion to the number of different behaviour problems evidenced as a child.

- Diversity of anti-social behaviour (several versus few) and covert behaviours at early ages (stealing, lying, firesetting). The greater the variety of both covert and overt behaviour problems, the greater is the likelihood of becoming an anti-social adult, although aggressive behaviour is probably the most stable over time.
- Family and parent characteristics (Kazdin, 1987). Children whose biological parent has an anti-social personality are at greater risk.

RESEARCH INTO THE ORIGINS OF CONDUCT DISORDERS

The evidence suggests that a multi-factorial model encompassing many contributory factors is necessary to understand conduct disorders. The Frontispiece shows the major contributory variables which, research suggests, contribute to the development of problem behaviours. Earls (1994) has suggested five main contributory sets of variables which pose risk for the development of such behaviour: community factors, family environment, poor mental health of the parents, psychosocial factors in the child and factors intrinsic to the child. Each will be considered briefly below.

Community Variables: Socio-economic and Structural Factors

Many studies have shown the association between children's behaviour problems and parental poverty, poor quality of housing in inner city areas, unemployment and general disadvantage (Rutter et al, 1975a, b; Rutter, 1978). Many explanations for these high associations have been put forward: among the most persuasive are those of, for example, Dunning, Maguire, Murphy and Williams (1982), who have suggested that some boys from deprived areas, with poor educational records and excluded from the employment and other opportunities available to their more privileged counterparts, find status and release from boredom by involving themselves in delinquency and football hooliganism. There is substantial evidence in support of this argument.

Family Variables

Extensive research is available in this area. Bandura and Walters (1959), in an early comparative study, compared 26 aggressive youths aged 14–17 with 26 non-aggressive youths matched for age, IQ, socio-economic status and social background, focusing particularly upon the parenting practices of each group. They noted that the parents of the aggressive young people were more likely to:

- Use physical punishment.
- Disagree with each other.
- Be cold and rejecting to their sons.

Bandura further reported:

> Parents of non-aggressive adolescents rarely reinforced their sons for resorting to physical aggression in response to provocation. Parents of aggressive delinquents, on the other hand, tolerated no aggressive displays whatsoever in the home, but condoned, actively encouraged and reinforced provocative and aggressive actions towards others in the community.

West and Farrington (1973, 1977) conducted a major, longitudinal study of 411 London boys. Data was gathered roughly annually from parents during the six years when the boys were aged eight to 14. Teachers completed questionnaires on the boys at ages eight, 10, 12 and 14; and 95% of the group were themselves interviewed at ages 14, 16 and 18. Concerning aggressiveness, they reported:

> 36.44% of the 44 boys rated aggressive by their teachers at age 8 were among the 76 boys highest on self-reported aggression at age 18.

Herbert (1978) has focused upon the stresses experienced by parents and, writing from the standpoint of cognitive-behavioural theory, has highlighted the difficulties which parents, often isolated and distressed, encounter in providing firm and consistent management for active and challenging children. In a study comparing Asian and English children, all aged between nine and 12, Kallarackal and Herbert (1976) found the Asian children more stable and less unruly than their English counterparts, and they attributed this in part to the way in which the Asian parents managed their children. They wrote:

> We do think that the quality of Indian family life may positively help to reduce the risk of developing deviant behaviour in Indian children . . . Indian parents were found to be insistent on close supervision of children and firm discipline at home.

A further very important enquiry, the Newcastle Thousand Family Study (Kolvin, Miller, Fleeting and Kolvin, 1988), examined family environment and parental characteristics when the target young children were pre-schoolers and followed them up over a 30-year period. Those children who subsequently became offenders were far more likely to come from lower socio-economic groups and to have experienced neglectful or poor parenting. Other associated circumstances were large family size, parental mental illness and troubled relationships between parents.

There has been much interest in the impact of abuse in childhood upon those children's subsequent lives. Studies by Lane and Davis (1987) and Widom (1989) showed that about a quarter of children who had been physically abused or neglected in childhood became offenders. Research continues upon the specific variables which lead to some children following a route into offending but by far the greater number avoiding it.

The impact of violence on television has been much under scrutiny. The evidence in this field is inconclusive, but Rutter and Cox (1985) concluded from their overview that:

> It seems reasonable to infer that films and television may have some impact on attitudes and behaviour and hence that they may play a small part in the predisposition to violent behaviour . . . the effect seems likely to be greatest in young children, in those already showing psychosocial problems, and in situations where the influence of the media is consonant with other influences in the home.

Parental Mental Ill-health

A number of studies have investigated the impact of the mental health of parents upon their children's behaviour. Earls (1994) cites the work of Stewart and colleagues (1979) and of Lahey and colleagues (1988), who both showed an association between alcohol-related difficulties and anti-social personality in the father, low socio-economic status and conduct disorder in the children. It is extremely difficult, however, to pinpoint the precise causal factors. Lahey et al (1989) went on to examine aspects of mental health in mothers and found that maternal anti-social personality has a direct effect on child conduct disorders. Earls (1994) comments (p. 316):

> How to interpret this relationship in causal terms is open to question. Is it through the production of a disorganized rearing environment, as suggested by the Kolvin et al (1988) study, or are both the mother's and the child's deviant personality genetically mediated?

It is my own view that the 'disorganized rearing environment' contributes more to the total variance than the genetic factors, although inherited temperamental factors, such as a tendency to hyperactivity, may well contribute in some children. I have arrived at this conclusion because, as already indicated, in one of my own studies (Sutton, 1995) I found that the pre-intervention mean score of the mothers on the Beck Depression Inventory bordered on 15, the cut-off score indicating clinical depression, but that this fell dramatically over the course of eight weeks to within normal limits as the mothers learned skills of managing their aggressive and disruptive children. If these tendencies to behave very aggressively had been innate, it would have been unlikely that they could have been so easily overridden by a short parenting programme.

Behavioural and Cognitive Variables

Important contributions have been made by many researchers, for example Hollin (1991) and Kendall (1991), in drawing attention to factors arising from a cognitive-behavioural analysis of serious misbehaviour. They stress how inconsistency on the part of parents may lead to the very patterns of behaviour of which the parents frequently complain, namely aggressiveness and disruptiveness. Parents do not typically understand that this misbehaviour is often unwittingly reinforced by their attention, in the form of repeated reprimands to their children, but which are, however, not followed through, and by their neglect of their children's positive and desirable behaviours. This analysis has already been discussed in some detail in Chapter 2.

Within this same cognitive-behavioural framework, Dodge and Frame (1982) have shown how aggressive children perceive people and events differently from non-aggressive children. Lochman, White and Wayland (1991) have summarised this growing body of research as follows:

> . . . aggressive children have been found to encode and retrieve significantly more cues that convey hostile connotations than do non-aggressive children . . . aggressive children are hypervigilant in scanning their social environment, attending to more immediate cues, especially hostile cues, than do non-aggressive children . . .
>
> In the milliseconds after cues are perceived, aggressive children form inferences about others' intentions, and these efforts to decipher the meaning of others' behaviour have been found to be significantly influenced by their higher rate of detection of hostile cues and by their prior expectations that others would be hostile towards them . . . As a result, aggressive boys have been found to be 50% more likely than non-aggressive boys to infer that antagonists in hypothetical provocations acted with hostile rather than neutral or benign intent (Dodge, 1980).

RESEARCH INTO INTERVENTION IN CONDUCT DISORDERS

There is still a shortage of sound research concerning effective ways of intervening in conduct disorders: rather, there are a few small-scale studies, with isolated and specific groups of children and young people, which have not been extensively followed up. We saw in Chapter 1 that a number of strategies have been evaluated by Kazdin (1995) who, on the basis of his review of the evidence of effectiveness, distinguished interventions which he described as 'highly promising', namely cognitive problem-solving skills training and parent management training.

Cognitive Problem-solving Skills Training

This is an approach which focuses upon the thinking processes of the young people involved. Kazdin reports that although several different models have been developed, there are several features common to all:

1. The emphasis is on *how* children approach situations—that is, what are the beliefs, thoughts and judgements which provide the context for their decisions, such as whether to assault an elderly person or not.
2. Children are taught to engage in a step-by-step approach to solve interpersonal problems.
3. The strategy is very structured, with games, stories and role-plays all used to broaden the young person's repertoire of perceptions for handling life challenges. Over time, the skills are increasingly applied to real-life situations.
4. Therapists usually play an active role in the intervention, modelling the cognitive processes by making verbal self-statements, coaching the participants in using the strategies and providing feedback and encouragement.
5. The approach involves several different procedures, including modelling, practice, role-play and use of reinforcements.

The evidence is that children with conduct disorders do respond to these approaches, but that they tend to be older and less disadvantaged in socio-economic terms. Positive results have been shown to be maintained for up to one year. Since this book is focusing upon preventive work with young children, this approach will not be discussed further here.

Parent Management Training

Kazdin explains this as follows:

> Parent Management Training refers to procedures in which parents are trained to alter their child's behaviour in the home. The parents meet with a therapist or trainer who teaches them to use specific procedures to alter interactions with their child, to promote pro-social behaviour and to decrease deviant behaviour. Training is

based on the general view that conduct problem behaviour is in-advertently developed and sustained in the home by maladaptive parent–child interactions.

Here, too, Kazdin reports a number of characteristic steps:

1. The parents meets with a therapist/trainer who teaches them specific procedures to use in managing their child.
2. Parents are trained to identify, define and observe problem be-haviours carefully. This is the A-B-C analysis.
3. The sessions cover principles of social learning theory: positive reinforcement, mild punishment (e.g. loss of privileges) and contingency contracting.
4. The sessions provide opportunities for parents to discuss how their attempts to practise the techniques are or are not proving effective and for the trainer to offer guidance and encourage-ment to continue.

Researchers are very positive about parent management training because there is much evidence for a number of favourable outcomes:

1. Children's behaviour improves in ways which can be measured both quantitatively and qualitatively (Patterson, Dishion and Chamberlain, 1993; Kazdin, 1993).
2. Mothers' levels of depression fall to within normal limits (Sut-ton, 1995).
3. Siblings of referred children also improve, as parents practise the strategies with them as well.
4. In pre-school children, the capacity for attachment behaviours—cuddling, kissing, saying affectionate things—re-emerges (Sutton, unpublished data).
5. There is maintenance of improved behaviour for 1–3 years after training (Kazdin, 1995; Sutton, 1992). One study reported main-tenance of gains 10–14 years later (Long et al, 1994).

Particular strategies taught in parent management training

1. Targeting specific behaviours: negative and positive.
2. Tracking and recording these behaviours.
3. Identifying Antecedents to and Consequences of the behaviours.
4. Giving clear messages to children: praise and encouragement (see Box 9.2).

5. Giving clear sanctions and penalties: Time Out as a last resort.
6. Using the principles for a range of behaviours: aggressiveness and disruptiveness, but also wetting, eating difficulties and shyness.

Coaching parents in the use of Time Out/Calm Down: I found in my research that while many parents found it difficult to praise their children, some found it even more difficult to use Time Out. Indeed, I found that those parents who either did not use Time Out when it was appropriate or used it inconsistently were unlikely to be successful in learning to manage their children effectively. Box 9.3 therefore shows the principles for using Time Out.

Box 9.2: Parenting positively. Some guidelines for parents

PARENTING POSITIVELY
Helping parents improve children's behaviour

Parenting Positively: Some Notes for Parents

1. Work out some house or family guidelines: for example, 'All toys must be put away before bedtime'. Everyone helps each other to carry out the guidelines.
2. Find three behaviours each day which you can praise a child for. Catch them being good!
3. Reward behaviour you want to encourage, by attending to it and showing how pleased you are with it.
4. Ignore small misbehaviours: whining, pestering, tantrums. Turn your back on the child.
5. Try to be consistent. If you promise or threaten something, you must carry out the promise or threat.
6. Speak directly and firmly to your child when giving instructions.
7. Encourage others who care for the child to use these same guidelines.
8. Take a day at a time.
9. You'll have some bad days. Try to commend yourself for what you have already achieved.
10. Try to find someone you can confide in when it all seems to be falling apart. Don't give up.

Box 9.3:   Principles for using Time Out/Calm Down
Reproduced by permission of De Montfort University

1. If you decide to use Time Out, give one warning only before carry-ing it out.
2. Never threaten to use Time Out and then fail to follow through.
3. You *must* be consistent. The child cannot learn the rules about how you want him/her to behave unless you are consistent.
4. Never use a frightening place for Time Out, but do use a place that is *safe, unrewarding and dull*: the foot of the stairs, standing or sitting in a corner facing the wall, an empty room, a hallway.
5. Always check for safety.
6. *Never* lock a child in a room. Just keep returning him or her to the Time Out place, insisting that the child stays, until the penny drops with the child that you really mean it.
7. A useful rule of thumb for how long that a child should remain in Time Out is the number of minutes corresponding to the child's age. For example:
   - a 2 or 3 year-old remains 2 minutes on each occasion
   - a 4–9 year-old remains 4 minutes on each occasion
   - a 10 year-old remains 10 minutes on each occasion, and so on . . .
8. There is no point in making the Time Out interval very long. We are trying to help the child learn a new association between misbehav-ing and the inevitability of the penalty. He/she will learn this asso-ciation better from each instance of misbehaving being followed every single time by a brief Time Out than from misbehaving being followed occasionally by Time Out for an arbitrary period of time.
9. If the child who has been placed in Time Out repeats the same misbehaviour the moment he/she comes out of Time Out, then return the child to the Time Out place immediately. If need be, repeat this as many as 10 (or more) times a day, so that a new association is learned between the misbehaviour and the inevitable penalty which will follow.
10. The person who puts the child in Time Out takes him out.
11. Do persevere! Even if you think you are getting nowhere, carry on in the way we have suggested.
12. Keep a simple record of how often you have had to use Time Out day by day. This will show whether instances of the misbehaviour are increasing or reducing.
13. *Things may get worse before they get better*. This is important. Having been the centre of attention for so long, the child will work hard and play up all the more in order to keep his dominant and controlling position. If you persist, however, the message will eventually get through: *you* are in charge now.

HELPING PARENTS WITH CHILDREN WITH SERIOUS BEHAVIOUR PROBLEMS

Because the focus of this book is upon prevention, the intervention which will be emphasised here is that of Parent Management Training—the second of the approaches which Kazdin considers to be 'highly promising'. Moreover, this approach has also won the approval of a Committee of the House of Commons upon *Child and Adolescent Mental Health Services* (House of Commons Health Committee, 1997) in whose report it is noted that, on the basis of the evidence heard by the Committee:

> We were impressed by what we heard of Parent Management Training, and recommend that the Department of Health should support this and similar techniques, while at the same time ensuring that they receive systematic evaluation and monitoring as to their effectiveness and cost-effectiveness.

To recapitulate, Parent Management Training is:

> . . . designed to alter the pattern of interchanges between parent and child so that prosocial rather than coercive behavior is directly reinforced and supported within the family (Kazdin, 1987).

We turn now to exploring how we can introduce Parent Management Training using the steps of the ASPIRE process.

Step 1—Building Supportive and Empathic Relationships

Families with children having serious misbehaviour problems are often very agitated about their circumstances. They have often tried everything that they can think of in an attempt to manage their children, following advice from grandparents, neighbours and friends for a few days at a time, only to abandon each strategy when the child's behaviour fails to improve. They are often deeply demoralised (Webster-Stratton and Herbert, 1994) and need a great deal of support before being willing yet again to attempt to improve deeply stressful situations. Some researchers, for example Puckering et al (1994), have shown that offering psychotherapy for mothers both helped the mothers and facilitated their acquiring skills in managing their children. Of the 12 children on the Child Protection Register, 10 were able to have their names removed—which compared favourably with the rate for a control group. Such therapy for mothers is obviously desirable, but since there are so many thousands of children whose parents are asking for help with their difficult behaviour, this is unlikely to be available. I am taking it for granted, however, that practitioners consistently offer parents the warmth, genuineness and unconditional positive regard which Carl Rogers (1951) insisted upon as central to his 'client-centred' therapy, and which Truax and Carkhuff (1967) showed to be essential components of effective counselling and psychotherapy; I also take it for granted that, where resources are available, parents are offered supportive counselling. This relationship-building is **Step 1** of the process.

Assessment

Step 2—Gathering information

Parents of children with serious misbehaviours are likely, perhaps more than some other groups of parents, such as those whose children are anxious or withdrawn, to need time to unburden themselves of their embarrassment and distress, as their children's conduct can be publicly humiliating. Listening to these accounts can be very time-consuming but it is time well spent, since if parents are too tense they will be unable to attend to what is being said or to understand what they are being asked.

It is essential to seek information about the development of the child's difficult behaviour from birth onwards. Again, we are seeking an answer to the question, 'How, together, can we understand how this situation has come about?'. Once the parent(s) are calm enough we can ask them to tell us when they first noticed that their child was very active or reluctant to comply with requests; and it is likely that the period of two to three or three and a half years will be worthy of particular attention. Did anything intensify the child's difficult behaviour? If so, these circumstances should be written down, in chronological order. Sometimes parents can pinpoint a date or a period which they think contributed significantly to the child's difficulties: an episode of post-natal depression, an accident, an admission to hospital, or a separation of the child's parents.

Completing Appendix 1 with the parents may provide invaluable additional information concerning the aetiology of the child's difficulties, while the 'Strengths and Difficulties Questionnaire' (Goodman, 1997) (see Appendix 6) will help parents clarify the nature of their child's behaviour difficulty, provide a score on a standardised tool of assessment and also highlight the child's strengths; this is likely to be a helpful counterbalance to focusing upon his or her shortcomings. This Questionnaire can also be completed by the child's teachers—so giving a more rounded picture of the child— and older children could complete it themselves.

Ensuring that children receive clear instructions: Parents with challenging children often do not give them clear instructions. Like all of us, they tend to shout from one room to another, to call up the stairs or to give no warning that it is necessary, say, to bring a game to an end because it is time to go out. Challenging children need very clear messages, delivered in a firm, I-expect-you-to-do-as-I-say voice. Box 9.4 shows some useful steps relevant to young children.

Box 9.4: Giving a child a clear instruction

1. If possible, give a few minutes' warning of a change in activity; a meal, going out.
2. Go to the child and say his name.
3. Put your hands on his shoulders.
4. Gain eye contact.
5. Say firmly, 'John, we have to go out. Please find your shoes'.
6. As he begins to comply, say, 'Well done; thank you'.
7. If he does not begin to comply within, say, one minute, repeat the above.
8. If he still does not comply, explain that a penalty will come into effect; for example no television that day. Try to keep calm and 'matter of fact'.

AN EXAMPLE: SIMON, AGED SIX. Let us consider the example of Simon, who has never been an easy child but whose behaviour became more difficult when his father left the household. Simon's dad has 'access' but does not always keep to the agreement that Simon will spend Saturdays with him. Simon is told to expect him, only to find that he does not turn up. Simon then, understandably, becomes impossible to manage for the whole weekend.

Step 3—Identifying problem behaviours

Having gathered relevant background information and identified major predisposing variables and organic or developmental factors intrinsic to the child, we can move to asking parents to identify specific problems in the child's behaviour. For Simon, these might be,

1. Simon is aggressive: he often kicks and hits his mother, Donna.
2. He is deliberately disruptive: he overturns furniture and throws it about.
3. He damages things deliberately—toys, household tools, electrical equipment—but not his own belongings.

The arrival of Clancy, Donna's new partner, is exacerbating the situation. Simon's behaviour is getting worse. It is also apparent that Simon is being repeatedly rewarded for his disruptiveness and rudeness by Donna's and Clancy's attention to his misbehaviour in the form of reprimands, rows and complaints.

Step 4—Identifying a positive profile

When asked if Simon shows any positive forms of behaviour, Donna winces and says that he used to be very loving—but this seldom shows itself now. However, she is able to think of three behaviours which Simon still occasionally displays.

1. He brings Donna the newspaper to read every morning before she gets up.
2. However awful his behaviour, he still says, 'Sorry, Mum' when he goes to bed.
3. He looks after Toffee, the family dog, very well.

It will of course be essential to meet with Simon and to gain his view of the situation. He may wish to meet with an educational welfare officer if one is available. There may well be early events or other predisposing factors which are contributing to his disruptive and aggressive behaviour, of which Donna and Clancy are unaware. It may be that Simon is being subjected to bullying which he has not told Donna about. If this is so and if, with Simon's permission, the practitioner is able to tell Donna about this, she is likely to be very concerned for her child.

Step 5—Clarifying what Donna really wants

Since Donna has parental responsibility and Clancy's future in the household is uncertain, it will be Donna who says what she really wants in respect of Simon's behaviour, but it will probably be necessary to try to involve Clancy in the plan. Donna is likely to understand, since it emerged in the assessment that Simon is missing his own Dad badly and she knows already that it is his Dad's failure to turn up to collect Simon which acts as the Antecedent or trigger to Simon's worst behaviour. In respect of Simon's day-to-day behaviour, however, she may well be able to specify the following goals:

1. That when she has to refuse Simon money or deny him something at any other time, he will accept this.
2. That even if he is feeling angry, he will speak calmly and quietly to Clancy.
3. When he is angry, he will go and kick a football about outside.

Step 6—Arriving at a formulation: key ideas shared with parents

At this stage there are likely to be two tasks confronting the worker:

1. To provide the parents with a rationale of why the problems developed in the first place, taking into account the life events of the parents, the extended family and the child. This can be seen as a formulation of the problem.

2. To teach the parents some basic strategies for managing Simon
   when his behaviour becomes troublesome. These are based on
   common sense but it will be necessary for all those who care for
   the child to work together. We can assure them with confidence
   that there is excellent research evidence for the effectiveness of
   the strategies, which we can teach them.

I have found it useful to describe the problems, both the predisposing ones and the immediate ones, in terms of 'stresses'
which the various family members are coping with. This term is
usually acceptable; everyone experiences stress and it is a non-
stigmatising word. So we can reframe what we have heard of their
'life events' in terms of the stresses they have caused. In this case
we can convey our empathy for Donna and Clancy in their difficult
position, but then we can show our concern for Simon; he is likely
to be deeply distressed by the changed relationship with his Dad
and to idealise him in his absence, while he also has to adjust to the
arrival of Clancy as his mother's new companion.

The overall formulation might be as shown in Box 9.5.

Box 9.5: Preliminary assessment of/rationale for the difficulties of
Simon, aged six

1. *Predisposing life events for this child and members of this family*
   (a) Simon's Dad left when Simon was four. He seems to be missing
       him very deeply.
   (b) Simon may be being bullied or otherwise unhappy at school.
   (c) Clancy joined the family eight months ago. Simon resents him.
2. *Organic factors, such as developmental stage or any disability or
   relevant illness*
   (a) Simon is still quite small for his age; this embarrasses him.
   (b) Simon seems to be a lonely child; he has no friends.
3. *Immediate variables: interactions within the family (A–B–C)**
   (a) The antecedent (cue) to the worst misbehaviour is Simon's Dad's
       failure to collect him on a Saturday morning.
   (b) Unintentionally, Donna and Clancy have been rewarding the
       very behaviour they complain of in Simon, by inconsistent reac-
       tions to it.

* Donna and Clancy may not understand this concept, but it is useful to
introduce it at this stage.

Table 9.1: Number of instances of Simon's positive and negative behaviours over one week

CHARTING BEHAVIOURS				Name: Simon		Week beginning: 14 May		
Behaviour	*Sunday*	*Monday*	*Tuesday*	*Wednesday*	*Thursday*	*Friday*	*Saturday*	*Total*
Behaviours to encourage and praise								
Morning	✓✓	✓	✓	✓	✓	✓	✓	
Afternoon	✓						✓	
Evening	✓				✓		✓	12
Behaviours to discourage								
Morning	✓✓						✓✓✓	
Afternoon	✓✓		✓✓	✓✓✓✓		✓✓✓✓	✓✓✓	
Evening	✓✓	✓	✓✓		✓		✓✓	24

Step 7—Data gathering as an aid to assessment

Donna has identified three positive and three negative behaviours whose frequency can be recorded. It will be wise to start with the least complex of the three behaviours—since the practitioner herself needs to experience success in her efforts to help parents before tackling deeply entrenched and longstanding difficulties. Thus, starting with damaging toys or tools would probably be the wisest course, or another not-too-deeply-entrenched behaviour from the Strengths and Difficulties Questionnaire.

It is a mistake to embark upon a plan of intervention without gaining a 'baseline' against which to measure improvement or deterioration. In this first week Donna should continue to handle Simon just as she has before, not attempting to do anything differently. She should, however, gather the 'baseline' counts of both the negative, the destructive behaviour and the positive, the helpful behaviour. The chart (see Appendix 8) used to collect the data is likely to look something like Table 9.1.

Parents often ask whether they should hide the record sheets while they are gathering the baseline and other data. My view is that they should be matter-of-fact about them: they should have them available to record information, make no attempt to hide them and if questioned about them by their son or daughter, give a truthful but non-committal answer—something along the lines of, 'Oh, I'm just keeping a count of how many times you kick me—or swear at me—and how many times you do something I ask you to do'.

Step 8—Planning

Donna, the practitioner and Clancy, if this seems fitting, are now participants in a shared effort to help Simon. As a six year-old, he too can be involved in the plan. As indicated, one way forward is the method of testing hypotheses. We may or may not use this terminology with the parents, but we ourselves should be clear about what hypotheses we are testing. In respect of Simon, the ideas being tested might be:

1. Simon's aggressive behaviours will decrease if it is possible to explain to Paul, his Dad, how much his little boy is missing him;

he needs his reliable support and encouragement (an agreement might be one way forward). See Chapter 12.

2. Simon's destructive behaviours will decrease:
   (a) As he experiences more attention for his positive behaviours.
   (b) If there are clear sanctions for his damaging things.
3. Simon's non-compliance (disobedience) will reduce as he experiences more consistent responses to his demands.

In order to test out these ideas, it will be necessary to use the baseline measures of Simon's positive and negative behaviours as benchmarks against which to assess progress or deterioration (see Table 9.1). This baseline information is likely to offer Donna some surprises. Typical reactions on the parts of parents are:

- The 'good'/'bad' behaviour is much more frequent than had been expected.
- The 'good'/'bad' behaviour is much less frequent than had been expected.
- The 'good'/'bad' behaviour occurs at specific times of day/days of the week.
- The 'good'/'bad' behaviour occurs in association with certain people, etc. etc.

When the new information arising from these records has been discussed and its implications explored, we can guide Donna in a systematic attempt to improve Simon's behaviour:

Reward/reinforce positive features of Simon's behaviour. Donna should pay clear, direct attention to the positive aspects of Simon's behaviour: his bringing her a morning cup of tea or his saying 'Sorry' after each outburst. We should ask Donna to tell Simon clearly and directly after each instance of the positive behaviour that when he behaves in this way she is very pleased with him. This praise may open the way to some renewed communication between Donna and Simon. At this stage, when they are trying to rebuild their relationship, Donna should have Simon's needs to the fore and she should avoid talk of Clancy.

Penalise instances of negative behaviour. There are three main strategies for dealing with these, as we saw in Chapter 2.

(a) *Ignore petty, demanding behaviours* so that they fade away because they are not reinforced with attention. Whining, pestering, grumbling and fault-finding can all usually be successfully dealt with in this way.

(b) *Give a mild punishment*, e.g. the loss of television time or a pocket money fine.

(c) *Time Out/Calm Down time* (Webster-Stratton and Herbert, 1994). This involves removing the child from the rewards of being in the centre of things to a place where he can be totally ignored. For details of using Time Out/Calm Down, see Box 9.3.

Helping Donna explain the plan to Simon

If a child is to be dealt with in a different way, with his positive behaviours attended to and commended and the negative behaviours ignored or mildly punished, then it is only sensible to explain the intended changes to him; otherwise there will be an unnecessary confusion for the child while he is trying to 'work out the new rules'. We should therefore advise Donna to set aside a few minutes to explain the new way in which she will respond to Simon, and if this will be difficult, we can go through the necessary steps by means of a simple role-play. Some families find it helpful to write down the precise steps which they should take in some specific circumstances—for example, turn your back on petty, irritating behaviours and attend to the ones you would like to see happen again. The plan to help Donna and Simon might look something like that in Box 9.6.

Step 9—Implementing the Plan

Over the next few days, it will be important for the worker to be in touch with Donna as she attempts to put the plan into effect. Sometimes a weekly contact is sufficient, but in line with cognitive-behavioural theory it may well be appropriate to offer more immediate contact—say within two or three days of her embarking on the new regime. This is to reinforce Donna's efforts to alter her patterns of responding to Simon. She should be encouraged to follow the agreed plan and to continue to keep records (Figure 9.1) to see if the problem behaviour gets worse or better.

Box 9.6: Plan devised by Donna, Simon and Melanie (social worker)

PARENTING POSITIVELY
Helping parents improve children's behaviour

Planning with parents

Name of child: Simon   Date of birth: 10 October 1992

Things talked about

The following factors may be contributing to the child's difficulties:

1. Simon is missing his Dad badly and wants regular contact with him.
2. He is being called horrible names at school and is sometimes being bullied.
3. He is finding it hard to get used to Clancy being about and taking Donna's attention.

Target behaviours for this week:

Positive: Simon's bringing Donna a cup of tea or newspaper.
Negative: Simon's damaging toys or household items.

Action plan agreed with parent(s)

In order to try to help Simon, Donna has agreed to the following points:

1. Concerning the predisposing factors
   (a) To contact Simon's Dad and agree to cooperating fully over Access arrangements.
   (b) Go to Simon's school and report that Simon is being bullied.
2. Rewards and penalties in Simon's day-to-day life
   (a) To find three things for which to praise Simon each day: for example, bringing her a cup of tea, coming straight home from school and taking his plate and cutlery to the sink after a meal.
   (b) To tell Simon that she knows it is hard for him to say 'Sorry' after one of his outbursts, and although she would rather not have the breakages, she is glad he says 'Sorry'.
   (c) Each school day, Donna will spend 10 minutes listening to anything Simon would like to tell her about what he has done at school. She will show interest and not tell him off about anything.
   (d) If Simon damages toys or household items, she will give him one warning. If he continues, she will send him to spend four minutes Calm Down time in the hallway, where he will be completely ignored. If he does damage there, he will stay a further four minutes. Damaged items will not be replaced.

This will be reviewed on . . . .

Signed . . . .   Signed . . . .   Date . . . .

SHOWING THE INCREASE OR DECREASE WEEK BY WEEK

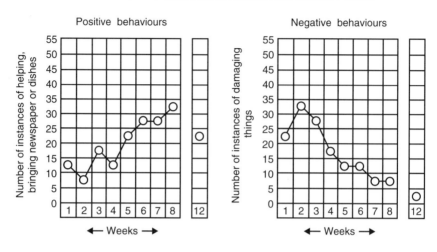

Figure 9.1: Simon's positive and negative behaviour over eight weeks and at one month follow up

Step 10—Reviewing and Evaluating the Intervention

To review the intervention is to monitor it on a regular basis—usually weekly or twice weekly to see how far it is being successful. It will require the practitioner to be in touch with Donna frequently, particularly at the beginning of the intervention, for three purposes:

1. To commend and reinforce Donna's efforts to manage Simon by positive methods.
2. To consider the quantitative data—that is, the counts of positive and negative behaviour which Donna is recording on the charts and to encourage Donna to persist in her efforts to attend to Simon's positive behaviour rather than the negative.
3. To consider the qualitative information—that is, Donna's accounts of her experiences in trying to respond differently to Simon's troublesome behaviour.

Donna has some questions to ask:

Question 1: What should she do if Simon misbehaves at someone else's house, if, for example, they are visiting friends or relatives?

Answer: Donna should express confidence in Simon before they leave home and say that she is looking forward to going visiting with him. She should say this as if she meant it, even if she has her worries.

Question 2: What should she do if Simon nevertheless misbehaves at her friend's house?

Answer: Donna should say to her friend that Simon does sometimes misbehave. Is there a safe, dull and boring place where, as at home, Simon could be required to spend four minutes alone? In other words, Simon should be dealt with as far as possible in exactly the same way as if they were all at home.

Question 3: What should Donna do if Simon behaves badly when out shopping?

Answer: If at all possible, they should go home at once, and Simon should be required to spend four minutes in Time Out as soon as they go through the front door. If this is impossible, then Simon should be told calmly that he will lose so many minutes of his permitted television time that day or the next, or he should be told that he will lose so much of his weekly pocket money. This should be put into effect as soon as possible in a calm, matter-of-fact way. Donna should *not* argue with Simon, but she must do as she has said she will.

Evaluation takes place at the end of the intervention. It is the systematic comparison of the state of affairs at the beginning, in respect of both Donna's feelings of depression and Simon's difficult behaviour, with the state of affairs at the end. If any scales have been employed to measure any of these circumstances, for example the Beck Depression Inventory or the Strengths and Difficulties Questionnaire, then these can be completed again and the start and end scores compared.

There are bound to be difficulties in attempting to help parents change patterns of behaviour which have been established over many months and years of a child's life. If the assessment has been carried out accurately, however, and the parents are actually attempting to carry out the principles which have been discussed and incorporated into the plan, then it is highly likely that the child's behaviour difficulties will begin to subside and more positive behaviours to increase.

10

HELPING FAMILIES WITH CHILDREN WITH ATTENTION DEFICIT/ HYPERACTIVITY DISORDER

DIFFICULTIES OF ARRIVING AT DEFINITIONS AND DIAGNOSES

As explained in Chapter 9, there is increasing consensus that a distinct syndrome, with organic underpinnings, has been distinguished from the over-arching category of conduct disorder. This syndrome has been variously named. At the time of writing the World Health Organization in its *International Classification of Diseases*, 10th edn (ICD-10), published in 1992, uses the term 'hyperkinetic disorder' and this has in the past been used in the UK. However, it is fast being overtaken by the American term, 'attention deficit/hyperactivity disorder' (AD/HD) which is included in the *Diagnostic and Statistical Manual of Psychiatric Disorders*, 4th edn (DSM-IV) published by the American Psychiatric Association in 1994. The term 'attention deficit disorder' (ADD) is sometimes used to describe the same condition.

Descriptions of AD/HD

There is increasing consensus that the syndrome of AD/HD includes three main characteristic behaviours: attention deficit (short attention span), overactivity and impulsiveness. These are also features of most children's behaviour, but where they are severe and continuing and where they are manifested in many different settings, a diagnosis of AD/HD may be considered. Taylor (1994) gives the following descriptions:

- *Attention deficit.*   The behaviours involved are those of orientating only briefly to tasks imposed by adults, changing activities rapidly when spontaneous choice is allowed, orientating towards irrelevant aspects of the environment, and playing for brief periods only.
- *Overactivity.*   Overactivity means an excess of movements. While the idea is simple, there is a wide range of activity in the normal population, and no very clear point at which activity level becomes excessive. Overactivity can refer to an increased tempo of normal activities, an increase in purposeless, minor movements that are irrelevant to the task in hand (fidgeting), or an amount of movement of the whole body that is excessive for the situation (restlessness). The excess of movements is there even when hyperactive children are in bed and asleep (Porrino et al, 1983), so it is unlikely to be secondary to attention deficit.
- *Impulsiveness.*   This means acting without reflection. In different contexts this may imply getting into dangerous situations because of recklessness, thoughtless rule breaking or impetuously acting out of turn when with other children.

Taylor goes on to remind us that:

> All these styles of behaviour are present to some degree in many normal children . . . Clinical definition of an affected individual therefore needs to be based upon a firm idea of what is expected of children at that age and of that developmental level . . .

Differences between Diagnosing Hyperkinetic Disorder and AD/HD

Lyon (1996) notes that it is more difficult for children to meet the criteria for hyperkinetic disorder than for AD/HD and that this is for two main reasons:

1. In order to be classified as suffering from hyperkinetic disorder, the professional making the diagnosis must witness the behaviours at first hand, i.e. not simply take the word of parents and teachers.
2. In order to be classified as suffering from hyperkinetic disorder, a child must meet the criteria for both inattentiveness and hyperactivity/impulsiveness. A child who is only inattentive, or only hyperactive, will not receive this diagnosis, whereas using DSM-IV he or she could.

Additionally, many diagnosticians require that because some very active children show situation-specific behaviour, for example they are constantly moving and on the go at home with mother or father, but are models of quiet behaviour with Gran, who 'won't put up with all this jigging-about behaviour', their hyperactivity shall be assessed independently in at least two settings, typically home and school.

Conduct disorders and AD/HD overlap substantially and some researchers consider that they are the same disorder from different perspectives. Taylor (1994), however, considers that the indications that AD/HD is often associated with developmental delays in motor, language and cognitive skills, while conduct disorders are not, suggest a different aetiology. Further, children who were found to be both hyperactive and conduct-disordered when referred at age seven or eight continued to be at risk of conduct disorder when followed up: by contrast, those with conduct disorder at age seven did not become hyperactive when followed up (Taylor et al, 1991). This author concludes that 'hyperactivity is one of the routes into conduct disorder' (see Rutter, Taylor and Hersov, 1994, p. 289).

Features of Children with Attention Deficit Disorder

Green (1995) has distinguished a number of features of AD/HD. He suggests that attention deficit disorder:

- Is a real condition which mildly affects up to 10% of all children, 2% of children being severely disadvantaged.
- Is mostly a 'boy problem'. Boys are six times more likely to be referred than girls.
- Is caused by a minor dysfunction in the normal brain.
- Refers to a reasonably consistent cluster of behaviours that include inattention, impulsivity, overactivity, insatiability, disorganisation and social clumsiness.
- Is usually a hereditary condition. Most ADD children have a close relative (usually male) affected to some degree by the same problem.
- Is a chronic problem which affects learning and behaviour as the child matures.
- Over half the children who present with ADD are also troubled by specific learning disabilities, for example dyslexia, language disorder or a weakness with mathematics.
- Lack of attention (inattention) causes school children to underfunction. They find it hard to complete work unless they are stood over and given one-to-one supervision.
- Playground behaviour is frequently a problem. At school the ADD child is often known by all, but liked by few.
- ADD children generate great stress for those around them through the intensity of their nagging and interrogation.

PREVALENCE OF ATTENTION DEFICIT/ HYPERACTIVITY DISORDER

Because of the looseness of definition of the term, several researchers have found, unsurprisingly, different patterns of prevalence. A working party of the British Psychological Society (1996) reported that in the USA, where AD/HD is an inclusive psychiatric category, rates of 2–10% have been reported. As explained, European diagnostic practice is more stringent and reports suggest a prevalence rate of 0.5–1.0% of the total child population, but as many as 1.5% of seven year-old children living in the inner cities (British Psychological Society, 1996).

Patterns of response to AD/HD in the USA and the UK vary widely: Bosco and Robin (1980) found that one child in every 100 was receiving medication for the condition in the US but in the UK only one in 2000 received such medication. This pattern may change, however, as paediatricians claim increased evidence of under-diagnosis of this syndrome in the UK (Bushby, 1996).

RESEARCH INTO AD/HD

Research into Origins

The evidence suggests that a multi-factorial model encompassing many contributory factors is necessary to understand AD/HD. Some of the major ones are considered below:

Genetic and organic influences

Goodman and Stevenson (1989) undertook an analysis of data from teacher and parent questionnaires on a large sample of twins from the general population, and concluded that the greater frequency with which hyperactivity is found in monozygotic rather than in dizygotic twins indicates a genetic contribution to the disorder. Other researchers, such as Green (1995), go further and attribute a greater part of the aetiology to inheritance and there is now a general consensus that genetic factors are implicated in the disorder.

Socio-economic and structural factors

As indicated, there is a higher prevalence of children who appear to exhibit the behaviours characteristic of AD/HD in the inner cities than elsewhere. This suggests that features accompanying the disadvantage that often characterises families living in the inner city, such as high levels of stress for parents and reduced play opportunities, may be contributing to the manifestation of the syndrome, and this is supported by other studies.

Factors highlighted by a cognitive-behavioural analysis

The unwitting and unintentional rewarding of demanding and restless behaviour in children and inconsistent management by isolated and exhausted parents almost certainly make a major contribution to the persistence of very active behaviour (Barkley, 1995; Sutton, 1995).

What Affects the Prognosis for an AD/HD Child?

As indicated, longitudinal studies have shown that there are many continuities in patterns of behaviour between infants as they grow into children, adolescents and adults. The studies of Olweus (1979), for example, drew attention to the fact: 'The degree of stability in the area of aggression was found to be quite substantial; it was in fact not much lower than the stability typically found in the domain of intelligence testing'—although it is important to point out that children with AD/HD are not exceptionally aggressive.

Lyon (1996), in a detailed analysis of a multi-factorial model, has reported:

> The prognosis of an AD/HD child depends upon how nature and nurture interact with one another. It is when a high level of hyperactivity . . . combines with other risk factors that a negative outcome becomes likely. Conversely, decreasing the number of risk factors greatly increases the likelihood of a good outcome. The risk factors are as follows:

- Depressive or mental illness in mother.
- Anti-social father.
- Previous failed marriages.
- Lack of mutual support within marriage.
- High level of negative expressed emotion in family.
- Parents who are overly directive, issuing many commands to their child.
- Parents who initiate fewer interactions.
- A high level of hyperactivity when the child is young.
- Low self-esteem (created by failure in other areas).
- Poor social skills (as a result of social ineptness, and/or because of language difficulties).
- Aggression.
- Conduct disorder.
- Social, academic or learning difficulties at school.

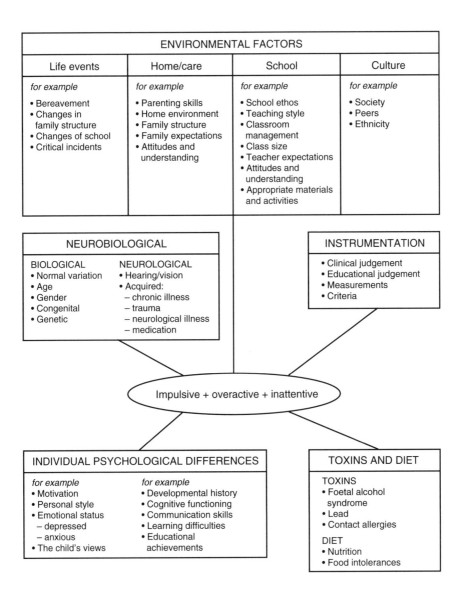

Figure 10.1: Areas of information to be considered in assessment of AD/HD (reproduced with permission from British Psychological Society, 1996)

RESEARCH CONCERNING THE MANAGEMENT OF AD/HD

A Multi-factorial Model

There is common agreement that, just as there is no single model of the aetiology of AD/HD, so there is no single model of effective intervention. The British Psychological Society (1996) has concluded that a multi-dimensional conceptualisation of both causation and intervention is necessary (Figure 10.1). While acknowledging this multi-dimensionality, we can still distinguish some common approaches in trying to help parents of affected children, their teachers and the children themselves. Four major approaches will be examined: adjusting the diet of the individual child, cognitive-behavioural strategies, problem-solving approaches and adapting the environment to the child.

Research Focusing upon Dietary Factors

The Working Party mentioned above also notes the links which have been made between AD/HD and substances in the diet of the affected child. It reports two well-designed studies (Egger et al, 1985; Carter et al, 1993) which found associations between certain specific substances in the child's diet and subsequent behaviour difficulties. These were children with 'multiple food intolerances' and parents had already noted the tendency for their children's behaviour to deteriorate when they had eaten specific allergens, including chocolate and certain food additives. In these circumstances, the advice of a nutritional expert is essential. The Working Party regarded the field of the impact of diet upon children's difficult behaviour as 'under-researched and controversial'. In view of the difficulty of designing studies which control for the impact of increased parental interest in the outcome of studies of dietary treatment, it does not recommend that dietary control should be an appropriate intervention for all children with these behaviour difficulties.

Research Focusing upon Cognitive-behavioural Approaches

The same Working Party reviewed the evidence for a range of ways of managing affected children. It cited the review by Fiore, Becker and Nero (1993), who considered 150 studies of intervention most of which were based upon cognitive-behavioural principles. The authors identified seven strategies of intervention, four of the most successful of which are paraphrased as follows:

1. *Positive reinforcement or token reinforcement.* These strategies appeared to result in reduced activity, increased 'time on task' and improved academic performance. The methods were seen as cost-effective, could be applied fairly easily to individuals or groups and were relatively familiar to most educators.
2. *Behaviour reduction strategies.* Mildly aversive short and immediate procedures (reprimands or redirection) seemed effective with primary age children, especially when combined with positive reinforcement.
3. *Response cost.* A combination of positive and negative reinforcement procedures through the use of tokens was seen as promising for teachers. This would represent the next step if positive reinforcement did not result in sufficient effects.
4. *Parent or family training.* Some studies demonstrated effectiveness in reducing activity level and conflict intensity with an increase in 'on task' behaviour and compliance. Parents reported reduced stress and better interaction and communication with their children. Medication formed part of most treatment strategies.

Research Focusing upon a Problem-solving Approach

The essence of this approach has been described in Chapter 2. It has been found particularly relevant to the management of AD/HD because of the multiplicity of complex situations which a child with AD/HD generates and because of their impact upon other people. To recap, the essence of the approach as suggested by

Falloon, Laporta, Fadden and Graham-Hole (1993) is that one goes through the following steps:

1. Pinpoint the problem or goal.
2. List all possible solutions.
3. Highlight likely consequences of each course of action.
4. Agree on 'best' strategy.
5. Plan and implement this stategy.
6. Review results.

This approach has been found effective, by comparison with other approaches for handling a range of complex situations, and is certainly of relevance for the management of children with AD/HD. It could only be employed, however, with children with a level of cognitive development adequate to understanding the steps of the approach.

Research Focusing upon Organisational Strategies

Burcham, Carlson and Milich (1993) in their review of studies in the USA, which address the management of children with AD/HD from the perspective of how to structure and organise the experiences from which children can best benefit, found that settings which proved helpful to children and their families were those in which there were 'positive attitudes and understandings of AD/HD arising from staff development, support at authority policy level and provision of coordinated intervention through teams of professional workers'. In other words, money and resources have to be made available to develop individualised care and educational programmes for children and to see that they are faithfully monitored and evaluated.

Barkley (1995), an American psychologist who has specialised in the field of AD/HD and who has written a particularly helpful book for parents, *Taking Charge of AD/HD*, has concluded that the two most effective strategies for managing children with this difficulty are Time Out/Calm Down time (see page 230) and response cost (see page 72). Jenny Lyon (1996), a British educational psychologist who has specialised in this area, while agreeing with Barkley, favours three additional strategies:

1. *Helping the child to learn to relax.* A simple tape can be used for this, and all family members can enjoy resting together. The child may need quiet, soothing encouragement to rest calmly until a ringer sounds, and can earn some simple but satisfying reward for this. This time can gradually be extended from, say, two minutes to five or ten.
2. *Managing the environment.* Arranging the house or classroom to minimise upset and damage which can arise from restless and impulsive behaviour.
3. *Problem-solving.* As children grow older, involving them in the task of how to manage the difficulty, much as one would if a child had diabetes or was enuretic. This essentially identifies times or situations which cause stress for the child and his or her caregivers and draws upon the child's creativity, experience and thoughtfulness as a means of solving the problems created by restlessness and over-activity.

HELPING PARENTS WITH CHILDREN WITH FEATURES OF AD/HD

At present in the UK it is usually necessary for a diagnosis of AD/HD to be made by a paediatrician or senior medical officer. General practitioners are not usually in a position to make this diagnosis and to prescribe medication. As indicated, it is desirable that the child's behaviour shall be observed in each of the main settings where the child spends time: certainly independent measures in the home and school environment are called for. When such a diagnosis of AD/HD *has* been made and if medication *is* prescribed, then there is the necessity for close liaison among those who have responsibility for the child. By contrast with medical approaches, I shall here be focusing upon the psychological support and management of the child and his family. The same steps as the ASPIRE process, Assessment, Planning, Implementation, Review and Evaluation, are followed.

Parents of a child who exhibits features of AD/HD are likely to be exhausted. Their restless, impulsive child may have worn them out by sheer liveliness, demandingness and inability to settle to any sustained period of playing, reading or writing alone. Further, they are likely to have few friends and relations willing to invite the child to their house or to babysit. Many seek a medical diagnosis in order to give a respectable explanation for their child's difficult behaviour. It is crucial to allow parents to give voice to their frustration, anger and exasperation and to their distress as they see their child getting into social and educational difficulties. This relationship building constitutes **Step 1** of the approach.

Assessment

Step 2—Gathering information

Where there is concern about whether a child is displaying features of AD/HD, a medical examination is essential. As services for this group of children improve, so there are likely to be improved screening and diagnostic tools available for both parents and teachers. The authors of the BPS Working Party Report (British Psychological Society, 1996) identify two of the most commonly used scales. They note:

1. The Child Behaviour Checklist for Parents (Achenbach, 1991) and the Teacher's Report Form (Achenbach and Edelbrock, 1986), which together give three scales dealing with social competence (activities, social behaviour and school behaviour) and nine scales dealing with specific childhood diagnostic categories. The inventory is regarded as one of the most comprehensive and has been subjected to psychometric standardisation in many languages.
2. The Conners Parent and Teacher Rating Scales (Conners, 1973; Goyette, Conners and Ulrich, 1978) have become widely used inventories. They include a 48-item scale for parents with five factors: impulsive-hyperactive, learning problems, conduct problems, psychosomatic factors and anxiety. The 39-item Teacher Rating Scale collects complementary information from the school setting.

It may be difficult for health visitors, social workers and school nurses to gain access to these scales. I hope this situation will change and that appropriate training will be made available for those of these professional groups whose work brings them into contact with children thought to be displaying AD/HD. In any case, in the interests of the child an effort should be made for an inter-disciplinary team to develop first a coordinated assessment and then a coordinated care plan for the child.

Ideally, one person should become key worker to child and family. While working towards such a plan, the following basic information can be gathered:

- The child's developmental history, including physical and neurological conditions. Appendix 1 may provide a suitable pro forma, or may be adapted.
- Information from the child's parents and, according to age, from the child also.
- Psychological assessment:
  - Measurements of intellectual ability.
  - Reports of levels of attainment.
  - Tests of attention and impulsiveness.
  - Social adjustment.
- Information from the child's teacher(s) about classroom behaviour/performance.
- Information from rating scales completed by both parents and teachers.

The example of Sandra, aged five: identified problem behaviours: Consider Sandra, an African-Caribbean child aged five. She is an exceptionally active child, who slept poorly from birth and whose parents, Valerie and Michael, are desperate for help. They had thought that things would improve when Sandra went to school, but the opposite has happened: the teachers at two schools have complained about Sandra, and so they have removed her and persuaded another school to take her. Both parents are beginning actively to dislike their child and they say they are tempted to tell her so. No-one will invite her to play with their children and no-one will babysit. As a result the parents have lost all their friends. They have sought help from their GP, but he has told them there is nothing he can do: the child is not ill. Sandra says, 'I try to keep still, but my body won't let me'.

Step 3—Identify problem behaviours

Having gathered relevant background information and identified major predisposing variables and organic or developmental factors intrinsic to the child, we move to asking Valerie and Michael to identify specific problems in the child's behaviour. The following behaviour difficulties can be identified:

1. Sandra is extremely restless: she runs everywhere and finds it hard to sit still.
2. She is very impulsive: she seldom seems to think ahead or plan and only has to hear of an activity to rush to undertake it.
3. She has a very short attention span, moving quickly from one activity to another.

Whatever Sandra's inherited tendencies, her behaviour has become unacceptable to both her parents and to her teachers. Similarly, whether or not a formal diagnosis of AD/HD is made, there needs to be a concerted effort on the part of her parents and teachers to help her calm and control her behaviour.

Step 4—Identifying a positive profile

When asked if Sandra shows any positive forms of behaviour, her parents initially say 'No', but then acknowledge that she still shows a few behaviours which they like very much:

1. She is very affectionate. The only time she does sit still is when she is sitting on her Mum's or Dad's lap. This can last for five minutes or more.
2. She will sit quietly for a few minutes if doing a jigsaw or watching television.
3. While sitting on someone's lap, she will look at story books for up to five minutes.

When we talk to Sandra, she says she hates being 'so jumpy' but 'she can't help it'. When asked about sitting on her parents' laps, she smiles and says that that is 'lovely'. She doesn't feel so jumpy then.

Step 5—Clarifying what Sandra's parents really want

Sandra's parents are quite clear what they want: they want Sandra to 'calm down'. They have been to see their GP repeatedly and he has finally agreed to refer Sandra to the local paediatrician. There is, however, a lengthy waiting list. Meanwhile they are begging for help from anyone who has clear suggestions about what to do. They pinpoint the following goals:

1. That Sandra will learn to sit quietly for three periods of 15 minutes daily at home.
2. That Sandra will learn to sit quietly for three periods of 15 minutes daily at school.
3. That when Sandra feels 'jumpy' she will tell a grown-up and talk about how to deal with the 'jumpiness'.

Step 6—Arriving at a formulation: key ideas shared with parents

When the practitioner has gathered as much relevant information as possible from parents, teachers and the child him or herself, it may be possible to offer a provisional rationale for the child's difficulties. This is likely to incorporate both medical and environmental factors. Parents who have been seeking a primarily medical formulation may find it difficult to accept that circumstances within the environment even make a contribution, but as there appear to be few children for whom an exclusively medical diagnosis is made, it is probably wise to attempt to incorporate the contribution to the child's difficulties of both medical and environmental factors.

As stated in Chapter 9, we have several main responsibilities to those who seek our help:

1. To provide the parents with a rationale for why the problems may have developed in the first place, taking into account all the available evidence. As already indicated, it is often helpful to describe the family's life in terms of 'stresses' with which the family is having to cope.
2. According to our role and the decisions made concerning the use of medication, we may need to clarify that we shall be liaising with medical and other personnel.
3. To teach the parents some basic strategies for managing Sandra to complement the effects of any medication which may be prescribed.

We can convey empathy for the parents who are finding their lives increasingly centring around Sandra. We can also show concern for Sandra herself, who is likely to be an unhappy little girl, with no friends at school and little affection at home. Moreover, she is unable to find her own way out of her predicament. Even though medication, if prescribed, is likely to calm Sandra's behaviour down somewhat, it is unlikely to relieve the problem of her over-active behaviour permanently and it certainly will not provide her with ready-made friends. Liaison among all concerned is essential. The paediatrician may or may not consider medication appropriate, but in any case there is increasing evidence (Herbert, 1997) that a coordinated strategy of offering a brief period of medication, supplemented by support for the parents by teaching and training them in cognitive-behavioural strategies, provides the most constructive response to AD/HD.

The overall formulation might be as shown in Box 10.1.

Box 10.1: Preliminary assessment of/rationale for Sandra's difficulties

1. *In terms of predisposing factors*
   (a) Sandra has already had two changes of school.
2. *In terms of organic and developmental factors*
   (a) It seems at least likely that a medical diagnosis of AD/HD will be made.
   (b) She *is* very active and may have inherited a predisposition to this, as Valerie has a sister who has great difficulty in concentrating.
3. *In terms of immediate variables (A–B–C)*
   Just in order to cope with Sandra, her parents have reacted to her as situations arose. They have had no structure or plan for managing her, so have probably been unintentionally rewarding the very behaviour they find so difficult. For example, when Sandra's Grandma brought a box of chocolates for the family, Sandra grabbed it, shouted, 'I don't like plain chocolates!' and shoved it back at her Grandma. Valerie tried to ignore the incident, but Michael was furious and shouted, 'You're a spoiled brat!'. He had a huge row with Valerie about Sandra. Sandra seemed quite pleased to have got everyone so worked up. Grandma left in tears.

Table 10.1: Number of three-minute periods of Sandra's very restless and very calm behaviour in two sample daily hours over one week

CHARTING BEHAVIOURS   Name: Sandra   Week beginning:

Behaviour	Sunday	Monday	Tuesday	Wednesday	Thursday	Friday	Saturday	Total
Behaviours to encourage and praise								
Morning 7.00–8.00 a.m.				✓✓	✓✓			
Afternoon				✓				
Evening 6.00–7.00 p.m.		✓						6
Behaviours to discourage								
Morning 7.00–8.00 a.m.	✓✓✓	✓✓✓ ✓✓	✓✓	✓✓✓	✓✓✓✓	✓✓	✓✓	
Afternoon								
Evening 6.00–7.00 p.m.	✓✓✓	✓✓	✓✓	✓✓✓✓	✓✓	✓✓	✓✓	36

Step 7—Data gathering as an aid to assessment

Sandra's parents have identified three positive and three negative behaviours whose frequency can be recorded. As in the case of Donna (p. 234), it will be wise to start with the least complex of the three behaviours—since the practitioner herself needs to experience success in her efforts to help parents before tackling deeply entrenched and longstanding difficulties. Thus, starting with trying to extend Sandra's time of calm behaviour would probably be most appropriate.

In this first week Sandra's parents should gather 'baseline' counts of both the negative, restless, roaming-about behaviour and of positive, calm, settled behaviour. An instance of calm behaviour is to be defined as:

> Sandra is provided with story books, bricks and Lego and is encouraged to settle to play with them. She plays with them for a period of three minutes.

An instance of restless behaviour is to be defined as:

> Sandra is provided with story books, bricks and Lego and is encouraged to settle to play with them. She ignores them and roams or runs about restlessly for a period of three minutes.

Because of the impossibility of observing her behaviour all day, the observation periods might take place for one hour in the morning and one hour in the evening, say, 7.00–8.00 a.m. and 6.00–7.00 p.m. Her parents should continue to handle her just as before, not attempting to do anything differently. Appendix 8 would provide a suitable chart on which to collect the data and the completed charts for one week might look something like Table 10.1.

Step 8—Planning

The parents and ourselves together are now partners in a shared effort to help Sandra. She too can be involved as fully as her understanding permits, and her 'jumpiness' discussed with her—as one might discuss the management of diabetes or epilepsy with another child. The baseline information in itself is likely to offer Valerie some surprises. When this has been discussed and its implications explored, we can guide Valerie and Michael in a systematic attempt to pay clear and explicit attention to the positive aspects of Sandra's behaviour, especially the few brief intervals when she is calm and settled. We should ask them to tell her clearly and directly after each instance of settled behaviour that when she behaves in this way they are very pleased with her—putting an arm round her shoulders or giving her a quick cuddle.

We have learned that Sandra loves cuddles, so these may be a good means of extending her attention span. Intervals of drawing, using playdough, playing with bricks or copying shapes could be rewarded by a short interval of sitting on her Mummy's or Daddy's knee to look at a story book together. A chart would helpfully show Sandra's extending capacity to settle to a quiet activity as the rewards take effect.

In respect of the negative or misbehaviour, there are two main strategies for dealing with these, as we saw in Chapter 2. The first is to ignore the irritating, demanding behaviour so that by avoiding reinforcing it with attention it gradually extinguishes, or dies away. If this is insufficient to reduce misbehaviour, then it may be necessary to practise Time Out or Calm Down, that is, removing the child from the satisfactions of being in the centre of things. It will be difficult to ignore Sandra, but the principle *must* be observed in some way or there is no opportunity for her to learn the necessity of inhibiting her restless behaviour.

Some children may be seen by paediatricians or child psychiatrists as suffering from so serious a form of AD/HD as to require medication. This has the effect of stimulating the inhibitory systems within the brain and may benefit certain children. Increasingly, however, medication is being supplemented by training parents in cognitive-behavioural methods, which may include periods of active play so that they have strategies in place to manage the child if medication is reduced or withdrawn.

As with most families with a child displaying AD/HD, Sandra has almost certainly received a great deal of intermittent and occasional attention, with the effect that some of her behaviours have been arbitrarily reinforced—often not the ones her parents and teachers would wish. Valerie and Michael will probably need help in learning how deliberately to ignore certain patterns of behaviour, and a five year-old child can be helped to understand that however much she throws herself about or interrupts her mother, she will be ignored. They may be very interested in the possibility of all family members learning to relax and to extend the relaxing period little by little; they may think that to round this off by a family story time in which Sandra is rewarded for her relaxing practice by sitting on her Daddy's lap for a story would be of benefit to everyone!

Helping the parents explain the plan to Sandra

We should therefore advise Sandra's parents to set aside a few minutes to explain the new strategy to her in a confident, non-apologetic way and, if necessary, go through the necessary steps in a practice session. If Sandra can be helped to see her difficulty not as 'naughtiness' but as a problem to be managed, much as some children have to manage being hearing or visually impaired, then a plan can be developed which avoids connotations of blame in favour of a focus upon *management*.

Some families find it helpful to write down the specific steps which they should take in specific circumstances, for example ignore petty, irritating behaviours and attend to the ones you would like to see happen again. Appendix 10 can be used for this: a plan for helping Sandra is shown in Box 10.2.

Helping the parents explain the plan to Sandra's teachers

It is apparent that an essential part of the intervention to help Sandra will be to inform her teachers and to seek their cooperation. They are likely to be interested in the written plan and, since most teachers seek the well-being of their pupils, will probably cooperate so long as this does not make too many demands upon them and does not interfere with the well-being of other pupils. A simple version of the plan, involving a brief note to be sent home each evening highlighting Sanda's *achievements*, rather than her shortcomings, may be very helpful.

Box 10.2: Plan devised by Mr and Mrs Green, Sandra and the practitioner

PARENTING POSITIVELY

Helping parents improve children's behaviour

Planning with Mr and Mrs Green

Name of child: Sandra   Age: Five years

To help improve patterns of behaviour, we have agreed to focus on the following behaviours:

Positive: Sitting quietly doing a jigsaw or playing with dough.
Negative: Demanding, over-active behaviour; making constant requests.

Action plan agreed with parent(s)

Now that there is a record of Sandra's patterns of behaviour for one week, it is agreed:

1. To encourage positive behaviour:
   (a) When Sandra has sat quietly for three minutes doing a jigsaw, her mother will come and sit by her and together help fit in some more pieces. Then Sandra plays alone.
   (b) When Sandra has looked at a story book quietly for three minutes, her mother or father will come and sit by her and they will look at it together for a further three minutes. Then Sandra reads alone again.
2. To discourage negative behaviour:
   (a) If Sandra is making too many demands, she will be given one warning and then placed in Time Out/Calm Down for four minutes.
   (b) Each time Sandra runs inside the house, she will lose one of the 5p pieces which she has been given out of the total of ten for the week (response cost).
3. In addition, either Valerie or Michael will relax on the floor or sofa with Sandra for a few minutes (five minutes the first week, six the second, up to a maximum of half an hour). They will use a relaxing tape provided by the social worker/health visitor. If Sandra can achieve this, she will earn the right to watch 15 minutes of a suitable children's video.

This will be reviewed on . . . .

Signed . . . .   Signed . . . .   Date . . . .

SHOWING THE INCREASE OR DECREASE WEEK BY WEEK

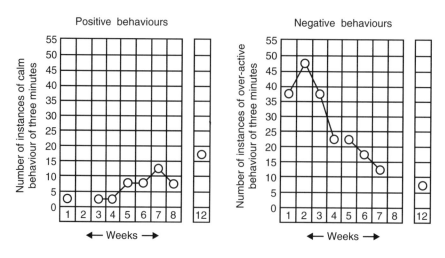

Figure 10.2: Sandra's calm and over-active behaviour during two sampled hours over eight weeks and at one month follow-up

Step 9—Implementing the Plan

Over the next few days, it will be important for the worker to be in touch with Sandra's parents as they begin to put the plan into effect. Sometimes a weekly contact is sufficient but, in line with cognitive-behavioural theory, it may well be appropriate to offer more immediate contact—say within two or three days of embarking on the new regime. This is to reinforce the parents' efforts to alter their patterns of responding to Sandra. They will have been warned that her restless behaviour is likely to get worse before it gets better and they should be encouraged to follow the guidelines devised with her of how to respond to their daughter's difficult behaviour; they should also continue to keep records (Figure 10.2) to see if the behaviour gets worse or better.

Step 10—Reviewing and Evaluating the Intervention

To review the intervention is to monitor it on a regular basis—usually weekly or twice weekly to see how far it is being successful. It has two main purposes:

1. To consider the quantitative data—that is, the counts of positive and negative behaviours which Valerie and Michael are recording on the charts.
2. To consider the qualitative information—that is, their accounts of their experiences in trying to respond differently to Sandra's troublesome behaviour. They are likely to have some questions for which they will be seeking answers.

Evaluation takes place at the end of an intervention. It is the systematic comparison of the state of affairs at the beginning, in respect of both the parents' moods and Sandra's difficult behaviour, with the state of affairs at the end. If any scales have been employed to measure any of these circumstances, for example the Beck Depression Inventory or the Strengths and Difficulties Questionnaire, then these can be completed again and the pre- and post-scores compared.

11

HELPING FAMILIES WHOSE CHILDREN WET OR SOIL

ENURESIS/BED-WETTING: DEFINITION AND PREVALENCE

This first part of this chapter will focus mainly upon nocturnal enuresis, of which one definition is:

> Repeated involuntary passage of urine during sleep in the absence of any identified physical abnormality in children aged above five years (Shaffer, 1994).

Primary enuresis refers to bed-wetting when a child has never been dry; secondary enuresis is bed-wetting when a child has achieved dryness but lost it again.

Prevalence of Enuresis

Differences in definition have led to discrepancies in statistics. However, Morgan (1992) has devised a graph, shown as Figure 11.1, which indicates the extent of nocturnal enuresis and accords with data from international studies. Several studies, for example Essen and Peckham (1976), have shown that bed-wetting is equally

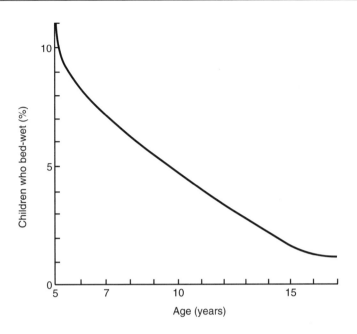

Figure 11.1: The frequency of bed-wetting (reproduced with permission from Morgan, 1992)

common in both boys and girls until age five. Thereafter, boys predominate and by age 11 they are twice as likely to be wet as girls. Boys seem less likely than girls to become dry spontaneously as they get older. The reasons for this variability are not understood.

In respect of daytime wetting, 2–4% of children aged five to seven wet at least once a week during the day and a further 8% are wet at least once a month. Daytime wetting is more common in boys than girls and about half those children who wet during the day are also wet at night.

RESEARCH CONCERNING THE ORIGINS OF BED-WETTING

It is clear that as with so many children's difficulties, enuresis is the outcome of many interacting variables. Reference will now be made to some of the major contributory factors, as shown by a range of studies, but other variables may be implicated in the future.

Socio-economic Variables

In an early study, Miller et al (1960), who studied 750 children in Newcastle for a period of several years, noted that children who wet the bed were more likely to:

- Come from large families.
- Be second children.
- Come from socio-economic classes 4 and 5.
- Be subject to over-crowding in the home.

Psychological Factors: the Association with Stress

It is important to distinguish between primary enuresis, when the child has never been dry, and secondary enuresis, when the child has been dry but has lapsed. It is usually appropriate to look for stress factors contributing to secondary enuresis. From the National Children's Bureau longitudinal study (Douglas, 1973) of over 4300 children, there seems to be some association between the number of stressful events in the first four years of the children's lives and patterns of enuresis. There were correlations/associations between bed-wetting and the following life events:

- Break-up of the family through death, divorce or separation.
- Temporary separation from the mother.
- The birth of a younger brother or sister.
- Moving house or home.
- Admission to hospital.
- Accidents.

The implication of these findings is that stressful situations affect some, but by no means all, children. Those most likely to be affected by stress may be those who already have a genetic vulnerability.

The Contribution of Genetic Factors

There have been a number of efforts to establish whether genetic variables make a contribution to noctural enuresis. Bakwin (1973) examined 338 pairs of same-sex twins and found that bed-wetting was equally common in identical and non-identical twins and that identical twins were *both* found to be bed-wetters more often than were non-identical twins.

Researchers such as Zaleski, Gerrard and Shokeir (1973) considered the issue of small bladder capacity. They compared 75 children between four and 14 with enuresis and 223 children without enuresis and confirmed that children who wet the bed:

- Have smaller bladder capacities than non-wetters.
- Pass urine more frequently than non-wetters.
- Have bladders that are functionally, but not structurally, small.

There are indications that about 16% of children with a urinary tract infection will present as bed-wetters and that successfully treating the infection will stop the enuresis in about 30%. All these variables point to the necessity of conducting a careful assessment of a child who wets the bed, examining many possible hypotheses as to aetiology.

Summary of the Research Findings

In their review of the evidence of how children become dry, MacKeith, Meadow and Turner (1973) reported:

> We conclude that children become dry at night in the following way. At birth some partial mechanisms are already present. In the next four years, maturation takes place in the central nervous system, making the behaviour of nocturnal bladder control possible. This behaviour is not dependent on training or learning. It is destined to emerge during the first four years, providing nothing acts at the time of maturation to inhibit its emergence. Such negative factors may be transient or continuing stresses, amongst which unsuitable toilet training is probably important. The emergence of nocturnal bladder control cannot be accelerated, but it can be retarded. A few children become dry at night by the age of one year, a large proportion in the second and third years . . . In children under the age of five, but not in older children, delayed maturation is one of the factors leading to the delayed appearance of nocturnal dryness . . . Genetic factors probably play a part by affecting either the age of maturation of necessary mechanisms or the development of nocturnal bladder capacity.

RESEARCH CONCERNING THE MANAGEMENT OF BED-WETTING

There have been many studies investigating various forms of intervention in terms of their short- and long-term effectiveness. McGonaghy (1969) compared five forms: prescription of imipramine; prescription of amphetamine; prescription of placebo; random waking (to control for the giving of attention); and behavioural training, using the bell and pad. The last approach was found to be the most effective, followed by the prescription of imipramine; the behavioural approach was also found to be superior at one year follow-up. Other studies have investigated the impact of psychotherapy, but this has not been found to be helpful in reducing bed-wetting.

Turner (1973) reviewed 17 studies of behavioural treatment for enuresis, involving 1067 children, where the criterion for success was seven consecutive dry nights. He found success rates of 64.8–100%. All children were followed up for periods ranging from one to 63 months, and while there was an average relapse rate of 27% across the studies, many of these relapsed children, some of whom had wet only once in seven months, reponded to a second intervention with bell and pad. Morgan (1992) reported the use of the enuresis alarm to be the most effective generally available treatment for bed-wetting. This is typically offered when the child has reached the age of seven years and when other approaches have been tried but not found helpful.

HELP FOR FAMILIES WITH CHILDREN WHO WET THE BED

Since there is evidence that a number of children wet the bed in response to stress (see above), or because of an infection, it is appropriate when trying to help a family with this difficulty to undertake a thorough assessment. A medical examination of the child is called for in order to eliminate a range of contributory factors.

Assessment

As has been discussed in previous chapters, parents will need time, empathy and understanding to enable them to say just how many difficulties the child's enuresis causes, both for the child and for other family members. Not least, wetting is very expensive, because of the cost of washing and drying bedclothes and night-wear, so if information and support can be given concerning any services available, this will be important. This is **Step 1**.

Step 2—Information gathering

A wide range of information will be sought concerning the child's earliest years and about the patterns of becoming dry at night of siblings and both parents, if this is available. It will be important to know what efforts the parents have already made to help the child become dry and something of the parents' attitudes to the wetting: for example, whether the issue is a cause of great stress or whether, say, because she herself was not dry until she was 10, the mother may be *expecting* her daughter to wet the bed until then. In summary, it is *how the parents respond to the child's wetting* which is the particular focus of interest: does their response cause more stress for the child, or less?

An area which should always be checked is, how easy is it for the child to reach the bathroom in the middle of the night? Is the light switch easy to reach and is he or she confident about using the toilet? For children who wet during the daytime, what is the state of the school lavatories? Are they well supplied with toilet paper? Do they offer privacy?

A further area which anecdotal evidence suggests is important is the timing of the child's intake of fluids. If it is difficult to obtain plenty to drink at school, children may be drinking the greater part of their fluid intake in the early evening—so placing a strain upon their bladders. This is an important issue, well worth exploring, if necessary, with the school governors.

Aids to assessment

It is essential when a child wets the bed that he or she is examined by a doctor or another appropriately trained person so that a range of medical factors, such as urinary infections, can be eliminated. It may be embarrassing for a child, particularly an older child, to have to be seen by a doctor for bed-wetting, but the problem is so common and help so generally accessible that parents should be encouraged to take their child to the doctor just as they would for an injection or a chest infection. In other words, bed-wetting is a normal and common occurrence and there is help available for most who seek it.

An example: Andrew, a six year-old who has never been dry at night: This little boy seems healthy. He is settled at school, but is upset that he cannot go and visit his cousins because he wets the bed. His Mummy is at home and his Daddy goes to sea for long spells. Andrew always goes to sleep in his own bed but often if he wets, while his Daddy is away, his Mummy lets him come to sleep in her bed. This is not allowed when his Daddy is home from sea. There is a lot of tension between Andrew and his Daddy, who thinks that Andrew is becoming too 'soft' and who thinks a good spanking might cure the wetting. He was smacked whenever he wet the bed and it 'did him no harm'. Both parents wet the bed until they were in their primary school years, and they think he may well have inherited this pattern from them. Andrew has a sister, Jane, aged four, who is already dry at night.

Step 3—Identify problem profile

1. Andrew, aged six, wets the bed most nights.
2. He occasionally wets during the day—when he is anxious.
3. When his Daddy is home, he hides wet pyjamas as he is afraid he will be told off.

Step 4—Identify positive profile

Upon being asked about Andrew's strengths and positive behaviours, his parents are able to agree that there are several:

1. He is a cheerful and friendly little boy, who shares his toys readily with other children, although not so well with Jane.
2. He can already read several short stories.
3. He can concentrate for long periods—building high and complicated structures with wooden or plastic bricks.

Step 5—What are the goals for Andrew?

When asked gently what he would like to happen, Andrew says, 'I just want not to wet the bed'. His Mummy agrees that that would be nice but says that she would be satisfied if she could be re-assured that Andrew would eventually become dry and if only he would not hide his wet pyjamas.

Step 6—Arriving at a formulation

The overall formulation might be as shown in Box 11.1. Points which may arise in the discussion of this preliminary formulation include:

1. Andrew is *not* being naughty: he would be dry if he could. He is, however, sometimes being placed in a situation which does not make it any easier for him to become dry at night, as he is often 'rewarded' for being wet by being allowed to come into his Mummy's bed—only to be rejected when his Daddy returns. This conflict is hard for a six year-old.
2. He is genuinely afraid of his Daddy's threats. These are serving to make him more anxious and more likely to wet. It will help him if his Daddy ceases to show his crossness to Andrew.

Box 11.1: Preliminary assessment of/rationale for Andrew's bed-wetting

1. *In terms of predisposing variables*
   (a) Andrew has had to cope with the arrival of a younger sister and one who is now already dry.
   (b) While many children have to cope with a Daddy who is at home only occasionally, it places extra stress upon them, as they have to adjust and readjust.
2. *In terms of organic factors*
   Andrew may well have inherited a genetic tendency to bed-wetting, as both parents have a similar history.
3. *In terms of immediate variables (A–B–C)*
   (a) Unintentionally, his mother has been rewarding Andrew for wetting the bed, as when her husband is away she allows him to come into her bed after putting on dry pyjamas.
   (b) When Andrew's Daddy returns, Andrew is not allowed to sleep in his parents' bed.

---

3. Andrew has had a urine test and there is no evidence of a
   medical problem.

Clearly these points are shared tactfully and tentatively with the
parents, and their contributions and reactions are taken directly
into account. The formulation is provisional but provides some
working hypotheses.

It is now the turn of the practitioner, having gathered information, to give information—that bed-wetting is a very common
phenomenon among young children, that many children are upset
and worried by it, that it is not in their power to stop it by will-
power and that cognitive-behavioural theory has much to offer.
This, of course, may not be the language chosen, but nevertheless it
is important to convey to parents that there is a substantial body of
knowledge about bed-wetting which has proved helpful to many
children and families and that the practitioner is knowledgeable in
this field. It is helpful to instil confidence that we know what we
are doing!

Step 7—Gathering baseline data

Andrew's cooperation should be sought in gathering counts of one
positive and one negative behaviour. Since his Daddy clearly approves of his construction skills, this might be the positive one to
focus upon, while wetting might be the appropriate undesirable
one. Two charts could be completed (see Appendix 8) for one full
week to provide baseline information. A useful anecdotal suggestion is that only a child's behaviour in the desired direction should
be recorded—for example, a wet night should be left blank upon
the chart, but dry nights or parts of nights could feature a star, an
animal sticker or something chosen by the child. The whole thrust
is towards instilling more confidence, a greater sense of achievement and more positive attention from parents into the child's life.

Step 8—Planning

The following plans, or similar ones, should be explored with the
parents and Andrew:

1. As it is not fair to Andrew that he should sometimes be allowed to sleep in his Mummy's bed and sometimes not, it would be best if he got used to sleeping in his own bed all the time (in this way, there will be no reward for his wetting the bed).
2. His Mummy and Daddy are going to notice all the things Andrew does well, such as his building with blocks and his readiness to share toys. They will tell him how pleased they are when he behaves in these positive ways.
3. They will encourage him to be dry during the night and Andrew should decide if he wants Mummy to wake him at, say, 10.30 p.m. when she goes to bed. If he has been able to be dry up to that point, he will gain a sticker and much praise.
4. For his part, Andrew promises to tell his Mummy if he wets the bed and to put his wet pyjama bottoms into the laundry basket.
5. Daddy promises that when he comes home from sea, he will not tell Andrew off.
6. Mummy will take him out, swimming/to the harbour/ birdwatching for two hours on either Saturday or Sunday, regardless of whether he has been able to be dry or not.

Step 9—Implementation of the Plan

After due discussion and adjustment of the above plan, it will be put into effect. The *whole* approach must be kept positive, with real appreciation of any progress Andrew is able to make towards being dry and minimal attention to any accidents. Any dry nights, or parts of nights, should be commended, and the whole matter should be dealt with in as positive a way as possible. As suggested, only successes, whether for a full night or for the hours before Andrew is woken at his parents' bed-time, should be entered on the chart; these records will demonstrate whether progress is being made.

If at the end of an agreed period, say eight weeks, there is no indication of progress, then it may be appropriate to leave off attempts to help Andrew become dry at night until he is seven and then consider using the *waking alarm*. This works so that the child is conditioned to wake, first to the sound of a buzzer or bell which rings when he begins to pass urine and then to the changes in the sphincter muscles of the bladder.

It is necessary to introduce the waking alarm in such a way that all those involved see and understand it. As its uses become more widely publicised, some parents are likely to know other families where it has been used successfully. The alarm must be introduced with confidence—preferably by someone very familiar with it.

One of the most recent designs is particularly helpful, in that the device which wakes the child can be placed discreetly in the child's pyjama pocket. Both parents and child should receive a careful demonstration and Andrew can experiment with a doll so that he becomes familiar with the device. The routine which will be followed at night should be gone through at least twice, so that everyone knows what will happen and what to do. Dry night clothes and bed clothes should be made available. If the device can first be used on a Friday or Saturday night, or during the holidays, this reduces any anxiety which a child may feel. The worker should be in touch the morning after the first occasion it is used to give support and to see how the family fared. Whatever has happened, the approach should be of anticipation of gradual improvement as the process of learning to wake at signals from the sphincter muscles takes effect.

Step 10—Review and Evaluation

This review or monitoring will be based upon the evidence gathered; progress is unlikely to be smooth, as events of the day are likely to interact with the effects of the alarm. For example, if Andrew has a difficult day at school and feels he cannot cope with his new reading book, this anxiety might affect his waking at night in response to the alarm. The process will take longer for some children than for others but parents should remain positive, encouraging and optimistic that the child will become dry in due course.

The evidence is extremely encouraging that effective treatment using the waking alarm brings about a number of additional beneficial side-effects for the children. Shaffer (1994) reports that many studies (e.g. Moffatt, Kato and Pless, 1987) have shown that children who have been successfully helped by the alarm become 'more assertive, independent and happy and that they gain in self-confidence'. If this intervention with bed-wetting is successful, it is highly likely that Andrew's daytime wetting will also improve. The greater sensitivity to the bladder which a child develops when undergoing training with the alarm seems to carry over into daytime situations, so that the child becomes more sensitive to the signals of a full bladder. A spare pair of pants and trousers should be available in Andrew's school bag for the occasions when the inevitable accident occurs.

ENCOPRESIS/SOILING

A Definition/Description and Prevalence

It is reported by Hersov (1994) that:

> The term 'faecal soiling' is used to describe disorders of bowel function and control, excluding constipation without soiling, occurring in children over a certain age in the absence of any structural abnormality or disease.

He continues that the age at which faecal incontinence is considered abnormal varies and that Whiting and Child (1953) reported much variation in the age at which control is achieved by children in different cultures. While in the UK almost all the children in the groups studied had achieved bowel control by night and by day by the age of two and a half, Hersov suggests that four years is a more realistic minimum age for diagnosing abnormality of bowel control.

As to prevalence, the study by Bellman (1966), in which the parents of 8863 children aged seven years were asked about this particular difficulty, showed that among children of seven and eight years the frequency was 1.5%, with over three times as many boys affected as girls. This figure has been confirmed by other studies, for example Rutter et al (1975a) in the Isle of Wight studies. Several studies have also found a close association between soiling and enuresis.

RESEARCH INTO THE ORIGINS OF SOILING

A Classification

Several researchers have attempted to devise a scheme of classification for soiling: that which will be followed here is by Herbert
(1991), who distinguishes four types:

1. *Primary encopresis*, where there is a genuine failure to gain bowel
   control. Here the failure to gain control is associated with the child
   having learning disabilities or, more probably, with inconsistent or
   inadequate help in enabling the child to gain control. As in teaching any new skill, it is important to take a positive approach to
   helping children to recognise the signs that they need to use the
   toilet or potty, to commend them when they are successful and to
   minimise the importance of the inevitable accidents.
2. *Secondary encopresis*, where the child has acquired control in
   toileting but has then lost it or failed to exercise it. Many such
   instances arise in which control has been adequately established
   but breaks down under stressful circumstances, such as the
   birth of a sibling or starting school, or a traumatic event, such as
   an accident. If parents can handle this situation sensitively, the
   child usually regains control within weeks or months. Punitive
   responses are particularly unhelpful and are likely to make
   matters rather worse. Smearing faeces is often an indication of
   considerable distress on the part of a child, and again it is
   counter-productive to respond with heavy punishments.
3. *Retentive encopresis*, marked by retention of faecal matter, accompanied by soiling due to leakage of fluid from around the
   faeces. Here the faeces are abnormal in appearance and may be
   associated with a medical disorder, such as ulcerative colitis.
   Sometimes children become severely constipated and the over-
   flow is of associated fluid. These circumstances seem to arise
   from anxiety on the part of the child because of a previous very
   painful episode of passing a motion, or sometimes from an intense conflict which has arisen between parent and child about
   the use of the toilet. This reluctance may be associated with just
   one person or it may have generalised into an unwillingness to
   use the potty or toilet at all.

4. *Non-retentive encopresis*, refers to the involuntary voiding of faeces resulting in soiling. This is best understood as a difficulty on the part of the child in recogising the cues offered by the sphincters and in taking action thereon.

The Timing of Training

The study by Sears, Maccoby and Levin (1957) showed that too early training can be less effective than training which begins later. They found that mothers who began training before the child was five months needed an average of 10 months before cleanliness was established, whereas mothers who began at 20 months or older required only five months. There seems to be increasing consensus that the optimum time to start is when the child is about two years old.

Constipation and Retention

Gabel (1981) found that constipation and retention of faeces are features of most forms of encopresis. They both render the ordinary signals of the need to pass a motion ineffective and typically cause fear and avoidance in the child. Constipation can be a factor in any of the four major types of soiling and must be dealt with as part of the total intervention strategy.

RESEARCH INTO THE MANAGEMENT OF SOILING

It is important that all children who are soiling should be medically examined, ideally by a paediatrician, in order to establish the form of encopresis and also to screen for medical conditions which may be contributing to the overall difficulty. The possibility of anal fissures will probably be considered. If these can be eliminated, then a carefully planned approach in order to enable the child to excrete the hardened stools is likely to be suggested; this may involve laxatives or, occasionally, enemas. In all cases it will be necessary to monitor the child's diet in order to ensure that he/she is receiving sufficient fibrous material and sufficient fluid as part of a balanced intake.

Doleys (1978), in a review of the treatment of children who soil, reported that 93% of cases were successfully helped by the use of behavioural methods. After careful assessment, a wide range of strategies based on the principles of cognitive-behavioural theory were selectively employed to help children who were soiling, and a combination of positive and negative reinforcement, integrated with an approach involving dietary monitoring, seemed to be particularly helpful.

HELP FOR FAMILIES WITH CHILDREN WHO SOIL

Assessment

If parents of children who suffer from enuresis need support, how much greater is the support needed by those whose children soil! Encopresis is not a disorder which attracts a lot of concern and understanding. It is known that children who soil are often the butt of unpleasant comment from other children or adults and their self-esteem is likely to be fragile. Support for the whole family is **Step 1**.

Step 2—Information gathering

The assessment will attempt to explore many systems pertaining to the child's soiling. First, information is needed concerning the child's developmental history in respect of overall toilet training, what age it was begun and what happened as it progressed. Are the current soiling episodes primary or secondary? It is unlikely that the informant's memory will be wholly accurate, but it is of course vital to hear what they think happened. If the child is old enough, his/her view of the difficulty must also be explored. As with enuresis, the parents' own histories should be sought. The assessment should include information about the toileting patterns of other children of the family and also about the child's relationships with all family members. Why do the parents think the child soils? How do they feel about the soiling? How have they tried to cope with it?

Aids to assessment: An older child, say above the age of five, may be able to give some pointers as to why, say, secondary encopresis is occurring. For example, a child who has established control, but who loses it on the birth of a new sibling, may be able either to say or to draw something of how he or she feels about the arrival of the 'intruder'. The aim is to enable the child to accept his or her own feelings, to have these feelings accepted by an understanding and caring adult and to be able to talk without condemnation of, say, jealousy of the new arrival.

An example: Colin, aged five: This is an unhappy little boy. He was toilet trained by the time he was three, but then began to soil when his Mum began a series of admissions to hospital because of mental health problems. His Daddy died from AIDS 18 months ago and Colin still asks for him. He will go to the toilet when told to, but then soils immediately he leaves the bathroom. He has plenty of clean clothes to put on, but hides dirty pants all over the house. He lives with his Nana, his mother's mother, and sees his mother two evenings a week, but she finds the soiling a great strain. She tends to talk with Colin about how hard her life has been and how hard it is now that her daughter has been diagnosed as suffering from schizophrenia. Colin does not like these talks.

Step 3—Identify problem profile

There are many problems to choose from, but his Nana has no doubt about which are the most urgent:

1. Colin frequently soils.
2. He smears faeces on the walls of his bedroom.
3. He hides dirty pants all over the house.

Step 4—Identify positive profile

Upon being asked about Colin's strengths and positive behaviours, his Nana says that apart from this one thing, his soiling, he is a child who 'tugs at your heart strings':

1. He is very affectionate: he comes and sits on her lap, wanting cuddles.
2. He is helpful to her in the house: fetches things and finds things that are lost.
3. He helps her clean up the messes he makes—seems to enjoy doing so.

Step 5—What are the goals for Colin?

When asked gently what he would like to happen, Colin says, 'I want my Daddy; I want my Mummy'. His Nana gets very upset and says she can see why Colin is upset, but she can't understand why he has to show his upset by soiling. We have no answer for her. At the very least, she wants him to stop smearing the faeces and to stop hiding dirty pants.

Step 6—Arriving at a formulation

The overall formulation might be as shown in Box 11.2. It is likely to arise in discussing this preliminary assessment that Colin is a very troubled little boy. The soiling and smearing are signs of his

---

Box 11.2: Preliminary assessment of/rationale for Colin's soiling

1. *In terms of predisposing variables*
   (a) Colin has had several major distressing events in his short life:
      - The loss of a much loved Daddy.
      - The frightening changes in his Mummy.
      - Her having to go to hospital when ill.
   (b) He has had to get used to living with his Nana.
2. *In terms of organic factors*
   The medical checks reveal nothing of note, but much retention of hardened faeces.
3. *In terms of immediate variables (A–B–C)*
   (a) Through sheer frustration, his Nana has been shouting at Colin and telling him that he is a very bad and ungrateful child. This gives him a great deal of attention.
   (b) She has threatened to tell Colin's Mummy how bad he has been; this adds to his anxieties.

---

distress: he is *not* just being naughty. His distress arises from a double bereavement: a total one in respect of his Daddy and a partial one, which he cannot understand, concerning his Mummy. There appears to be nothing medically wrong with Colin, but he is under acute stress which is reflected by patterns of soiling and smearing.

Step 7—Gathering baseline data

Colin's Nana indicates that the negative behaviour she wants to target is:

Episodes of smearing faeces.

and the positive behaviour is:

Coming and sitting on her lap and looking at story books with her.

The practitioner then asks Nana to keep a week's records, on charts similar to Appendix 8, of the number and timing of each of these two behaviours. At the end of one week there should be data available concerning both the episodes of smearing and the times Colin has come for a cuddle.

Step 8—Planning

The practitioner can now discuss with Colin's Nana that it seems to her that Colin is not deliberately playing her up at a time when she can least cope, but that the soiling seems to be a reaction to feelings of great insecurity. Skill will be needed to enlist her willingness to go on putting up with the smearing and soiling, but Colin's Nana is more likely to cooperate if she is assured of continuing support.

Involving the child in the plan

Colin will need to be brought into the plan. He will need both understanding and a firm limit set to the extent and consequences

---

Box 11.3:   A possible plan for helping Colin and his Nana

(a) Nana will try to offer two spells daily when Colin and she can look at story books together.

(b) She will try to make no angry comment when Colin smears, but will help him wash the walls and freshen up the room.

(c) She will ask Colin to go to the toilet and sit on it for five minutes with a story book, about 10 minutes after each meal. If he performs, she will show her pleasure; if not she will say nothing.

(d) Colin will be asked to tell his Nana if he does have an accident and soils his pants.

(e) She will provide a bucket of cold water into which Colin agrees to place his pants if he soils.

(f) The practitioner agrees to meet with Colin for half an hour twice weekly to talk about his Mummy and Daddy.

---

of his soiling. He will need help and time from an understanding person to whom he can put questions and talk with about his Mummy and Daddy, but he may well welcome there being someone who is not shocked or disgusted by his behaviour, but instead seems to understand it and know how to manage it. The plan shown in Box 11.3, which incorporates both elements of direct work with Colin and drawing upon cognitive-behavioural principles, might help.

Step 9—Implementation of the Plan

It may be necessary for Colin to receive treatment in the form of laxatives or suppositories to relieve the constipation, for until this is cleared he is likely to soil his clothes through leakage of fluid around the impacted faeces. This is the role of a paediatrician or general practitioner. When the constipation is relieved a diet which will ensure sufficient fibre and fruit will be necessarily prescribed and when that is established Colin will be able to go back to school.

A simple agreement can be devised along the lines discussed in Chapter 12. This might include clauses such as those shown in Box 11.4. The first week provides a baseline against which future progress can be assessed. Thereafter the practitioner remains in touch

Box 11.4:   An alternative three-way agreement for helping Colin and his Nana

Colin's Nana will:	Colin will:	The practitioner will:
1. Provide Colin with clean pants daily, plus a spare pair.	Go to the toilet when he feels an urge to do so.	Arrange to see Colin for half an hour weekly.
2. Talk with Colin about things that are generally positive.	Tell his Granny if he does have an accident.	Explore resources from the Family Fund.
3. When Colin has no accident on a given day she will tell him she is pleased.	Do something they both like with his Nana each week: e.g. swimming.	Meet with Colin and his Nana for 20 minutes weekly to give support.
4. If Colin does have an accident and he has told her, she will not be cross with him.	Keep a simple chart on which to record, calmly, any soiled pants/accidents.	Monitor progress as shown on the chart.
5. If Colin does have an accident and he has not told her, she will not go swimming with him that week.	Amuse himself instead.	Find some story books for Colin.

for as long as the agreement indicates, offering encouragment to Colin and his Nana and taking practical steps to reduce the pressures upon Colin. This may involve being in touch with Colin's school, liaising with the paediatrician and monitoring developments. The course of the intervention is likely to be 'two forward and one back'. It is unlikely to go smoothly.

Step 10—Review and Evaluation

These steps will be grounded upon the evidence which is gathered. The chart will show week by week whether Colin is managing to recognise the muscular prompting that he needs to go to the toilet and whether, in the event of an accident, he can tell his Nana calmly about it. Such a programme is likely to need recasting at least every fortnight, and perhaps weekly. This review or monitoring will also indicate whether events during the day are interacting with the efforts to support Colin.

It is likely that there will be an improvement if the participants are able to keep to the clauses of the agreement, *but it will take time.* Soiling is almost always the mark of a really troubled child, and while there is good evidence that help can be given, it takes time to foster the necessary neurological and muscular developments. Emotional support is vital, but so is a good understanding of theoretical principles. Here the practitioner is essentially a trouble-shooter, someone who, with a good understanding of the general principles of devising agreements, and in liaison with other colleagues can adapt them within the framework of cognitive-behavioural theory to suit the particular circumstances that occur.

12

PARENT EDUCATION AND TRAINING: VALUES AND RESEARCH

This chapter will focus upon a number of fields at the leading edge of research into working with families to prevent children's distress and unhappiness:

1. Ethical issues; the value base of the work.
2. Supporting families within a multi-cultural society.
3. The content of effective programmes of parent training.
4. Methods and structures of parent training.
5. Devising agreements to support practice.
6. Maintaining improvement.

THE VALUE BASE OF THE WORK: ETHICAL ISSUES

The value base of the work

The principles set out in Box 12.1 were devised by a group of social workers who attended a training workshop organised by myself with the support of the Central Council for the Education and Training of Social Workers. They are reproduced with their permission.

Box 12.1:   The value base of helping families with troubled children

1. All children and young people are intrinsically valuable. They are to be cared for and respected.
2. The overall aim of the work is to enable parents to continue to care for their children.
3. Diverse family patterns are to be acknowledged and respected.
4. Cultural diversity is to be acknowledged and respected.
5. Each child is unique, with a unique history and background.
6. Families benefit from being respected and empowered.
7. Parents' existing strengths, knowledge and experience should be built upon.
8. Practice must be actively anti-discriminatory.
9. The involvement of fathers and grandparents as well as mothers in promoting their echildren's well-being is invaluable.
10. Children are the responsibility of the wider society as well as of their families.

Ethical Issues

Any approach which deliberately makes use of principles of cognitive-behavioural theory lays itself open to the charge that it is unethical and manipulative. This accusation must be taken seriously, for we should recall that workers in the so-called 'Pindown' scandal in the UK, where misbehaving children in the care of the local authority were deprived of liberty and basic human rights, also claimed to be using cognitive-behavioural approaches.

There is no doubt that the principles can be used unethically. To avoid this, organisations which seek to publicise the appropriate use of the principles in an ethical way have devised ethical guidelines. The most highly developed of these, that developed by the British Association for Behavioural and Cognitive Psychotherapy, is printed as Appendix 13 in this book. It will be noted that two of the clearest statements are that, 'The aims and goals of assessments/interventions will be discussed with service users at the outset . . .' and 'Assessments/interventions will be planned in such a way that effectiveness can be evaluated'. It is to these ends that I have insisted on: (1) asking service users what are *their* goals for our work together; and (2) asking that records be kept so that these data can be used for monitoring and evaluation of progress towards these goals.

The area of greatest potential abuse lies in using Time Out/Calm Down. This is the brief period of time during which a child is placed in a safe but dull and boring place immediately after misbehaving. It is infinitely more effective than smacking. The sanction lies in the child's being *ignored and bored*. The effectiveness of the approach was well known to our Victorian forebears and is also known to later generations, for when I enquire among the present generation of grandparents as to what punishments were used for naughty children, often the response is, 'I was sent to stand in the corner' or 'I was sent to sit on the stairs'. It is extremely sad that this folk wisdom has been lost to later generations, many of whom have instead resorted to smacking or hitting, both of which are less effective as deterrents and far more dangerous to the child.

Different forms of Time Out or, as it is sometimes known, Calm Down, are explored on page 230. There are a number of dangers.

The first is that parents have such difficulty in praising or appreciating their child that they do not employ this approach at all, but instead resort only to a punitive use of Time Out. To counter such a possibility, I ask people who attend my training sessions actually to be present sufficiently often at the outset of a programme of work with a child for them to *see and hear* the parent praising the child and to give support and coaching in this, if necessary. Further, a number of health visitors with whom I have worked have reported that they have been so concerned about this issue that they have decided against teaching the use of Time Out: they only teach the approach involving praise and appreciation of the child.

A second danger is that parents assume that if a three-minute exclusion is effective, then a 30-minute one will be even more the case. This is not so. Research by Hobbs, Forehand and Murray (1978) found that for most children aged 4–9 years, four minutes was the most effective length of time, repeated each time the target misbehaviour occurred.

A third danger is that parents or childminders will allow a child for whom Time Out is used to be stigmatised or labelled as a 'bad' or 'naughty' child. This is entirely contrary to the spirit of what I am proposing: the intention is that this sanction shall be used firmly but discretely to manage children to prevent the escalation of disruptive or destructive behaviour which infringes the rights of others. Once the Time Out interval is over, the child should be received back warmly into the group: wherever possible, the incident is over and done with.

SUPPORT FOR FAMILIES IN A MULTI-CULTURAL SOCIETY

This issue has close links with the previous one. It is very important for professional people to realise the power their professional role bestows upon them in the eyes of many members of society and the responsibilities which this imposes upon them. While we as practitioners carry statutory responsibility which requires us to protect children against exploitation of any kind, as well as against neglect and abuse, we may be in danger of imposing our own values and viewpoints upon families who seek our help in relation to matters which have nothing to do with child protection but which are in fact culturally determined. Thus, the timing of going to bed, whether one sits at a table to eat or not, what implements, if any, we use to eat food, are all cultural conventions and it is vital that we respect diversity of practice in these matters.

Our society increasingly looks to science as a source of wisdom in understanding our needs, our development and our difficulties, and indeed this book is intended to make a contribution to that perspective—but research has its limitations. For example, there is no clear evidence from research that children should go to bed at a certain time. In many cultures throughout the world, it is natural and normal for children to go to bed at roughly the same time as the adults in their families: it is Western families who statistically are very odd in insisting that their children go to bed at mid-evening.

To consider the needs of families belonging to ethnic and other minorities, there are a number of steps which workers can take to be sensitive and supportive. These have been discussed in relation to the work of Forehand and Kotchik (1996) (see p. 85).

THE CONTENT OF EFFECTIVE PROGRAMMES OF PARENT TRAINING

Much of the research concerning parent training centres upon children who are displaying serious behaviour problems because so many families seek help for this problem; so this will be the main focus considered here. I shall examine, first, the choice of concepts to be taught; second, whether to teach general cognitive-behavioural principles or strategies for managing specific situations; and third, the choice of teaching strategies, such as role-play.

The Choice of Concepts to Be Taught

This, happily, has been broadly agreed by most of the major researchers in the field, although inevitably different trainers have different emphases. Gordon and Davidson (1981), in an early review of the core concepts and skills proposed by a range of practitioners, reported what they found to be the common core of parent education programmes using behavioural approaches (Box 12.2).

Later trainers have tended to include broadly the same content and I myself used a very similar curriculum in my own research (Sutton, 1992, 1995). I also teach this sequence to groups of health visitors and social workers who, in turn, are reporting considerable success in helping parents. Because this is still a relatively new field, however, there is a shortage of well-designed evaluation

---

Box 12.2: The common core of many parenting education programmes (after Gordon and Davidson, 1981)

Session 1 Learning to define and measure behaviour.
Session 2 Graphing (i.e. recording) behaviours.
Session 3 Using consequences to change behaviour.
Session 4 How to apply reinforcement to behaviour.
Session 5 Using good teaching procedures.
Session 6 How to decrease undesired behaviour.
Session 7 What to do regarding specific behaviours.
Session 8 How to maintain improvements.

studies reported by these practitioners. Barlow (1997) has, however, recently undertaken a review of the effectiveness of parent-training programmes in improving behaviour problems in children aged three to ten, and reports that, 'There is still insufficient evidence to show that parent-training curricula are the decisive factor in producing change'. She considers that there is a need for further research comparing parent-training programmes with parent support/discussion groups, in which no parent-training curriculum is implemented. While acknowledging that there is always need for further research, I must disagree with Barlow, on the basis of both the research I have reported in this book and my own research.

Linking Specific Strategies with Behavioural Principles

As McGaw (1997) has clarified, fully grasping and practising a new parenting skill is composed of three separate stages:

1. Understanding the principle being taught: for example, the principle of rewarding desirable behaviour.
2. Putting the principle into practice: that is, knowing how to practise rewarding desirable behaviours.
3. Maintaining the practice of the principle in later day-to-day life; that is, remembering to go on using rewarding desirable behaviours in the future.

My impression is that most researchers and trainers agree that *it is desirable to teach principles* which can then be adapted to a wide variety of different situations. For example:

- In this situation, what is the target behaviour?
- Is this behaviour desirable or undesirable?
- If it is desirable, is it being suitably rewarded?
- If it is undesirable, is it being suitably discouraged or penalised?

However, I also have the impression that there is general recognition that to expect people who are coping under situations of great stress arising from isolation, poverty and frustration to remember a given principle and then to apply it to their difficult and screaming child is totally unrealistic. Once a careful assessment has been undertaken, they may need, at least in the short term, guidance along the lines of:

'When he does that, you should do this'.

In this situation, it may well be that while we need to teach some practical strategies for dealing with difficulties in the short term, we should be *working towards* helping families understand key principles for use as their children become school children and adolescents. To keep discussing 'principles or strategies' seems to me, as I have said on page 121, a sterile debate.

The Choice of Teaching Strategies

This has also been widely investigated. Studies are ongoing upon which particular features of training carry the greatest probability of bringing about change: for example, brief lectures, video-taped programmes, modelling or role-play. There are indications that modelling, that is, *providing parents with an example* of how to respond to a child's difficult behaviour, is particularly effective. This could not be tested in my own research, however, because one of the methods of training parents was by telephone and it was not possible to provide visual models of how to respond to a child.

PRACTICALITIES OF PARENT TRAINING

With increasing attention being paid to issues of effectiveness and cost-effectiveness, some research attention has been directed towards examining the efficacy of different practice methods of working with families. For example, what are the merits of group, as against individual, training and is it possible to train people by 'distance learning'? How many parents can be trained together and still achieve positive results? And what is the most effective structure of training, that is, what is the optimal number and length of sessions?

Methods of Training

These were reviewed by O'Dell (1985), who reported a number of studies exploring the impact of training parents in groups, by comparison with training them on an individual family basis. A range of outcome measures were used. While pointing out that 'group training' can mean anything from working with just two parents to working with 20, and that there are innumerable variations in group structure, O'Dell concluded that the evidence generally suggested that group training was as effective as individualised training.

There are reports of great diversity in size of group. At one end there are many single case studies reporting highly focused work with individuals, while at the other is the approach of Rinn, Vernon and Wise (1975), who reported a training programme which met their criteria for success in that over 1100 parents attended five, once weekly, two-hour sessions at a community mental health centre. The teaching consisted of conveying general principles with minimal attempts to offer individualised guidance. Groups ranged in size from 16 to 90, with a mean of 41! Further, Brightman et al (1982) worked with 66 families having children with physical and learning disabilites, seeking to enable parents to teach their children self-help skills and to manage behaviour problems. The outcomes for three methods of training were compared: group format, individualised format and waiting-list control. All children improved on some measures, but both group and individually trained families did better than controls on other measures and these improvements were equally maintained at six months follow-up.

The majority of studies, however, report work with smaller groups of participants. In my own research, I compared four active models of intervention: group training, home visit training, training by telephone and a waiting-list control, with five to seven participants in the groups. This was as many as I could cope with in order to give individualised attention to all. I found that all three active training methods achieved equally good outcomes by comparison with the waiting-list control, both at the end of training and some 12–18 months later; parents trained by the home visit method were doing very slightly better than those trained by the other two methods.

In the light of these data, it is obviously cost-effective for family members to be trained by methods which require the least investment of trainer time. In my study, the mean time taken per child in the home visit method was 5 hours, 47 minutes; in the group method, 4 hours, 30 minutes; and in the telephone method, 3 hours 9 minutes. It seems likely from this and other studies that group methods will become increasingly popular and also that training by telephone will be developed, particularly in view of the saving of travel costs and time to families who live in distant places.

The Number and Length of Sessions

There are diversities reported concerning these issues. The numbers reported as achieving effective results are very variable, but there seems to be a broadly emerging consensus that for optimum effect parents meeting in groups should have no less than seven to eight training sessions of about two hours each, and that there should also be ongoing booster meetings at about monthly intervals thereafter in order to maintain the improvement. This last is very important, as a number of studies, including my own, have shown that while it is a relatively straightforward matter to help parents manage their behaviour-disordered children more effectively, 'slippage' occurs after the withdrawal of weekly support and the difficult behaviour tends to reappear as parents slip back into old habits of managing their children. This, of course, is exactly what we should expect within the cognitive-behavioural framework: behaviour (that is, parents' newly learned skill of praising their children) which is not rewarded tends to 'extinguish'; to maintain it, practitioners must continue to reinforce it.

DEVISING AGREEMENTS TO SUPPORT PRACTICE

Theoretical Principles for Writing Agreements

As research increases in the field of helping troubled children, it becomes apparent that there are major difficulties in helping parents to alter their patterns of interacting with their children and, indeed, with older children, in helping them keep to undertakings which they have made. In response to these challenges, a number of researchers, such as Herbert (1981) and Hudson and Macdonald (1986), have advocated devising agreements, discussed and signed by all those participants who are old enough to understand, which have the effect of encouraging the signatories to follow through on agreed courses of action.

The evidence for the usefulness of agreements in supporting parents is substantial: Hazel (1980) demonstrated their usefulness in enabling young people to move from residential care to foster care and claimed that the written agreements reduced the level of breakdown of the foster placements, while Sheldon (1980) has made a very strong case with clear examples for the benefits of 'contingency contracts'.

There are three levels of agreement: primary, secondary and tertiary (Box 12.3) and there are a number of important ideas intrinsic to agreements. First, as they are based on the notion of a cost–benefit analysis, that is, that people are motivated to behave in ways that increase their benefits, be they in material terms, in respect of advancing of their values or those of other people important to them. Thus, everybody should be able to anticipate gaining something from the agreement. This is why writing an agreement may take a long time; it is better to ensure that everybody is satisfied at the outset, rather than trying to save time at

---

Box 12.3:   Types and examples of agreement (after Sheldon, 1980)

Level of agreement	Participants	Example
Primary	An offender and a court representative	A probation order made by a court with an offender
Secondary	Two people	A 'service' agreement made between two people, typically a client and a professional
Tertiary	Three or more parties	A 'contingency' contract among a mother, her 10 year-old son and a teacher

the risk of being unclear or of failing to think of what might go wrong. Second, agreements are expressed in positive terms, that is, in terms of what people should do rather than what they should not do. With practice, it becomes possible to express almost anything in a positive form. Third, the agreement should be devised in such a way as to enable participants to advance by way of small successes. Agreements do not typically bring about dramatic overnight changes; they provide a strategy for people to achieve small

---

Box 12.4: Essential steps in devising an agreement (after Sheldon, 1980)

1. Discuss whether using an agreement is socially acceptable to those involved. It may be familiar for business arrangements but not for personal ones. If so, invite people to try the idea out.
2. Focus upon actions or behaviours, rather than attitudes or feelings.
3. Select one or two behaviours initially. Avoid working with too many problems. Start with a simple goal; early success is vital.
4. Describe those behaviours in a very clear way. Vagueness may seem to make the negotiation seem easier, but all the participants then interpret the agreement differently. This can lead to confusion and anger.
5. Write the agreement so that everyone understands it. Make the wording clear, brief and simple, and write in each person's first language.
6. The benefits for each person must be worth the costs as he or she perceives them.
7. The agreement should be written in positive language, specifying things which are to be done, rather than those which are not to be done.
8. Collect records. It is essential to know whether the situation is getting better or worse. Information can be collected on simple daily charts.
9. Renegotiate the agreement. A series of short-term agreements is generally more effective than one long-term one.
10. The artificiality and short-term nature of the agreement should be explained.
11. The penalty for failure to fulfil the agreement on each person's part should be clear.
12. Everyone concerned should sign the agreement, which should be dated.
13. As soon as a stable position has been maintained for several months, begin to phase out the agreement.

A. The agreement

This agreement is drawn up between:

Name: *Tracey Harris* .... Address: *The Cedars Hostel* .... and

Name: *Jenny Cooper* .... worker from (Agency): *Middleshire Soc. Services*

Address: *17 Lay Lane, Middleton* .... Telephone no.: *74682*

B. What we are trying to do together:

Our overall aim is *to increase Tracey's feeling of control over her life*.

Our particular goals or objectives are:

1. To *enable Tracey to feel better in health*.
2. To *ensure she has claimed all her welfare rights entitlements*
3. To *help Tracey manage Kevin's misbehaviour*
4. To *give Tracey info: about parent & child drop-in centres*.

C. In order to work towards these goals, we have made some agreements:

Agreed by *Tracey* (client)   Agreed by *Jenny* (worker)

1. To *go to the GP serving the hostel for a check-up.*

2. To *go to the welfare rights office to check her entitlements.*

3. To *respond to Kevin's misbehaviour in a consistent manner as suggested by Jenny.*

1. To *phone Tracey's health visitor and liaise with her.*

2. To *get a list of parent & child drop-in centres & crèche facilities.*

3. To *visit Tracey for 3 x 30 minutes to suggest practical ways of managing Kevin.*

D. Other points to be noted

1. The above agreement is to be reviewed and updated every *1* weeks

2. The agreement can be changed if both parties agree to this

3. Failure on ....'s part to keep the agreement may result in

Our next meeting is on 24th October.

Signed *Tracey Harris* Signed *Jenny Cooper* Date *17 October*

Figure 12.1: An example of an agreement between two people (reproduced with permission from Sutton, 1994)

gains, which gradually add up to improvement. There are bound to be failures and disappointments, but so long as the general trend is toward improvement, then people's motivation and morale are likely to rise. Finally, it should be emphasised that writing agreements is a skill which may be learned. Sample agreements are discussed later in his chapter and pro formas are shown as Appendices 14 and 15.

When writing agreements, it is essential to go through the stages shown in Box 12.4.

Examples of written agreements

Figure 12.1 illustrates an example of an agreement devised between two people in respect of a mother with a small child for whom she is seeking help; Appendix 14 provides a pro forma for such an agreement. Box 12.5 provides an example of an agreement devised between several people, one of whom is a child of 10, but the same principles could be adapted for a much younger child and his/her extended family. Appendix 15 provides the pro forma for this type of agreement.

Box 12.5: Example of an agreement between several people

Devising Written Agreements

Agreements in Home–School Work: An Example

An agreement between a young person, his family and an Educational Welfare Officer

A. The agreement

This agreement is drawn up between:
1. *David Morrison*   3. *Ronald Henderson (step-father)*
2. *Rosemary Morrison (mother)*   4. *Mr Roberts (form teacher)*
and *Melanie Jones (Educational Welfare Officer)*
Agency: *Northshire Educational Welfare Officers' Dept.*
Address: *Park House, Speedwell Road, Northchester, Northshire*
Telephone no: *Northchester 2345*

continued overleaf

B. What we are trying to do together

1. *To improve the relationship between David and Ronald*
2. *To enable David to attend school on a daily basis*
3. *To ensure that David has enough suitable clothing for school activities*
4. *To enable David to take further his interest in athletics*

C. To work towards these goals

The worker (*Melanie*) agrees:

1. *To meet with David each Tuesday at 5.00 p.m. for half an hour and with the whole family fortnightly at 5.30 p.m. for an hour to highlight successes and to trouble-shoot problems*
2. *To seek funds so that David can buy necessary sports equipment*
3. *To talk to Mr Renton, the coach, about opportunities for David in athletics*

First family member (*David*) agrees:

1. *To meet Melanie each Tuesday at 5.00 at a place he chooses*
2. *To attend school daily, and remain there after registration*
3. *To ignore people calling him names, but to report bullying to the Year Head*
4. *To say 'Hello' to Ronald each day and not ignore him*

Second family member (*Rosemary*) agrees:

1. *To tell David she is pleased with him each day he attends school*
2. *To put aside __ p. daily towards new clothes/equipment for him*
3. *To read any homework David asks her to and say what she likes about it before she criticises it*

Third family member (*Ronald*) agrees:

1. *To say 'Hello' to David each day*
2. *To speak quietly and calmly if he asks David to do anything, e.g. help clear up*
3. *To thank David if he does what he is asked*
4. *To avoid criticising David's friends*

Form teacher (*Mr Roberts*) agrees:

1. *To spend five minutes each day looking at David's work with him*
2. *To encourage David to follow up his interests and abilities in athletics*

Other points to be noted:

1. *The above agreement is to be reviewed each week*
2. *The agreement can be changed if everyone agrees*

Signed . . . .   Signed . . . .

Signed . . . .   Signed . . . .

Signed . . . .   Date . . . .

MAINTAINING THE IMPROVEMENT

It is known from repeated studies that very substantial help can be given to troubled children, usually by working alongside their parents. A major issue, however, which continues to confront researchers, is how to ensure that improvements are maintained— whether on the part of children, through more regular patterns of sleeping, weight gain and improved diet, in terms of increased confidence in anxious or depressed children, or in calmer and more restrained behaviour of children with conduct disorders. The challenge lies in the fact that many parents are being helped to manage their children in different ways, to notice their strengths rather than their weaknesses, their good behaviour rather than their bad and their successes rather than their failures, but that this teaching and their learning inevitably takes place over a very short period, usually a matter of a few weeks, with perhaps a few booster sessions. This new learning has to compete, as it were, with years of deeply ingrained habits of managing their children and, as we all know from the difficulties we experience in following New Year's Resolutions, the new intentions, the new learning, tend all too easily to fall away.

In my own work I found that while, with boosters, parents were able to maintain gains for up to 12 months, by 18 months after the end of training the gains were beginning to slip. This pattern has been noted in other studies. On the other hand, Kazdin (1995) noted that in his review of the studies, 'gains were often maintained between for 1 and 3 years after treatment', while Long, Forehand, Wierson and Morgan (1994), who followed up a cohort of young people with serious behaviour problems some 14 years after their parents had received training in principles of positive parenting, found them to be indistinguishable from the general population of young people. In other words, the impact of training was to enable their parents to cope better with a very troubled group of youngsters.

Other means of helping parents to maintain their newly learned strategies in managing their children will be the focus of future research studies. Gill (1998) found that enabling parents who had received training to join a support group helped this group to maintain their progress significantly better than parents who had received training but did not have the opportunity of a support group.

CONCLUDING REMARKS

This is an exciting time to be working in the field of attempting to help troubled children—exciting but enormously frustrating. This is because there is at last a body of theory for helping children which has been repeatedly tested and from which many thousands of children, not to speak of their families, are already benefiting. This theory has been shown to be of help to adults, too, who have difficulties in living. It is a frustrating time, however, because so few people have been adequately trained in the theoretical principles and the pace of disseminating knowledge and skill is inevitably extremely slow. Courses have to be planned, validation from professional bodies and universities has to be won, supervisors have to be engaged and students have to be trained. Such processes take years. This book has been written to speed those processes along a little. I hope it will be of benefit to the practitioners who read it, to the families with whom they work and to the children whose distress may thereby be alleviated.

APPENDIX 1 FORM FOR ASSESSMENT OF CHILD BEHAVIOUR DIFFICULTY

(Reproduced with permission of De Montfort University)

CONFIDENTIAL

ASSESSMENT OF CHILD BEHAVIOUR DIFFICULTY

A GENERAL AND MEDICAL DETAILS

1 Name of child .... Boy/Girl ....

2 Age .... Date of birth ....

3 Address ....

.... Telephone no. (if available) ....

4 Family composition

Mother's name .... Date of birth ....

Father's name .... Date of birth ....

Please list all children, including referred child, with ages

1 .... (age) ....   3 .... (age) ....   5 .... (age) ....

2 .... (age) ....   4 .... (age) ....   6 .... (age) ....

5 Difficulties being experienced with the child

1 ....   3 ....

2 ....   4 ....

6 Living circumstances of household (brief information about accommodation, etc.)

....

....

7 Any other information the parents think is relevant ....

8 Were there any medical difficulties at birth or during the first year of life? ...

....

9 Any major illnesses/hospital admissions? ....

10 Have you been worried about his/her development? ....

11 If so, what worried you? ....

12 Is your child allergic to colourings/other substances? ....

13 If you exclude these substances, what happens? ....

14 Is your child having medicine/tablets for the problems? ...   If so, what? ...

15 What seems to be their effect? ....

B *FAMILY CIRCUMSTANCES*

16 What age was the child when the difficulties began? ....

17 Did anything happen around that time that might be linked with the onset of the difficulties?

a) ....

b) Anything else? ....

18 Have there been any events in the family which made things worse? e.g. bereavement, loss of employment, parental separation

a) ....

b) ....

19 What other stresses are you or other household members under?

a) ....

b) ....

20 Why do you think the misbehaviour happens? ....

....

21 In what ways have you tried to deal with the misbehaviour or difficulty?

1 ....   3 ....

2 ....   4 ....

C *SETTINGS IN WHICH THE CHILD MISBEHAVES*

22 People involved: with whom does the misbehaviour happen? ....

Is there anyone with whom it never happens? ....

23 Places involved: where does the misbehaviour happen? ....

24 Times involved: when does the misbehaviour happen? ....

25 Can you think of any reason for the child's misbehaving, such as being afraid or jealous?

....

26 What usually brings the misbehaviour to an end? ....

27 What usually happens immediately after a misbehaviour? ....

28 What are some of your child's good behaviours or things that he or she does that you like?

1 ....   2 ....

29 Which of your child's behaviours would you like to see more of?

1 ....   2 ....

D   CONCERNING BEDTIME/SLEEPING DIFFICULTIES

30 How old was the child when bedtime/sleeping difficulties began? ....

31 Did anything seem to set them off? e.g. illness? ....

32 Where does the child ordinarily sleep? e.g. cot ....

33 Where does the child ordinarily fall asleep? ....

34 Is this usually alone, or is anyone with him or her? ....

35 How have you tried to deal with the difficulty? ....

36 Would you tell me about the child's pattern of sleeping?

   a) What time does he or she wake up in the morning? ....

   b) Does the child have any naps during the day? If so, please tell me how
      many ....

      From .... to .... and   From .... to ....

   c) What time does the child begin to get ready for bed? ....

   d) By what time is the child actually in bed? ....

   e) Does he or she get out to bed after being settled down? If yes, what hap-
      pens? ....

      ....

   f) What time does he or she typically go to sleep? ....

   g) Does he or she wake in the night? .....   If yes, how many times? .....

   h) What happens when he or she wakes? ....

   i) Is anything said to the child when someone goes to him or her? ....

   j) Is the room usually light or dark when the child goes to sleep? ....

37 What is the worst thing about your child's sleeping difficulties? ....

   ....

38 Is there any other information which you think is relevant to these difficulties? ....

   ....

E   CONCERNING EATING DIFFICULTIES

39 How old was the child when the eating difficulties began? ....

40 Did anything seem to set them off? e.g. illness? ....

41 Where does the child ordinarily eat? e.g. at a table ....

42 Is this usually alone, or is anyone with him or her? ....

43 How have you tried to deal with the difficulty? ....

44 Would you tell me about the child's pattern of eating?

    a) What does he or she typically eat at breakfast time? ....

    b) What does he or she typically eat in the middle of the day? ....

    c) What does he or she typically eat in the evening? ....

    d) What is the child happy to eat between main meal times? ....

    e) What are the child's favourite foods? ....

    f) What are his or her favourite drinks? ....

    g) Is there any food that he or she eats a very great deal of? ....

    h) When food is refused, what do you do? ....

    i) What worries you most about the child's eating difficulties? ....

45 What has been the overall impact of the behaviour difficulties on family/ household?

    ....

Thank you for giving me this information.

The assessor should then pass these assessment sheets to the person(s) who has supplied the information and ask that it be checked for accuracy. Invite the informant to sign the assessment, if he or she is willing to do so.

Signed: .... (Assessor)

Professional role: ....

Address: ....

    ....

Telephone number: ....

Signed: .... (Parent/Guardian)

Date: ....

APPENDIX 2　FORM FOR RECORDING 'LIFE EVENTS' FOR THE FAMILY AND CHILD

PARENTING POSITIVELY

Helping parents improve children's behaviour

'Life events' for the family and child

Events in the life of the parents/family   Events/impact in the life of the child

Year:			Child's age
e.g. 19....	Mother had post-natal	Grandma cared for baby for	1–6
	depression	first year of life	months

APPENDIX 3 FORM FOR OBTAINING RATINGS ON THE LIFE EVENTS SCALE

Life Events

This form to be completed by the **client**.

Client's name: . . . .

Worker's name: . . . .

Encircle the number next to any items which have happened to you in the last six months. Add the numbers and insert the sum into the total box on the right.

Life event	Life change value
Death of spouse or partner	100
Divorce	73
Marital separation	65
Jail term	63
Death of close family member	63
Personal injury or illness	53
Marriage	50
Lost job	47
Marital reconciliation	45
Retirement	45
Change in health of family member	44
Pregnancy	40
Sex difficulties	39
Gain of new family member	39
Business readjustment	39

TOTAL ☐

As with all scales, the ratings obtained from this checklist should be treated with caution and used only as clues to possible problems. Cultural issues should also be considered.

Change in financial state	38
Death of close friend	37
Change to different line of work	36
Foreclosure of mortgage	30
Change in responsibilities at work	29
Son or daughter leaving home	29
Trouble with in-laws	29
Outstanding personal achievements	28
Partner begins or stops work	26
Begin or end school	26
Change in living conditions	25
Revision of personal habits	24
Trouble with boss	23
Change in residence	20
Change in school	20
Change in recreation	19
Change in church/temple activities	19
Change in social activities	18
Change in sleeping habits	16
Change in eating habits	15
Vacation	13
Christmas or major religious festival	12
Minor legal violations	11

Adapted with permission from a table by Holmes, T.H. and Rahe, R. (1967). 'Social Readjustment Rating Scale', *Journal of Psychosomatic Research*, 227. Published by Pergamon Press, Oxford.

APPENDIX 4 FORM FOR COMPILING SUMMARY OF INFORMATION RELEVANT TO ASSESSMENT

PARENTING POSITIVELY

Helping parents improve children's behaviour

Summary of information relevant to assessment

Name of child . . . . Date . . . .

Predisposing factors for this child/family

1 . . . .
2 . . . .
3 . . . .

Organic/developmental factors affecting the child

1 . . . .
2 . . . .
3 . . . .

Immediate factors

Behaviour difficulties

1 . . . .
2 . . . .
3 . . . .

A–B–C analysis

Antecedents		*Behaviour*		*Consequences*
1	1	1 . . . .
2	2	2 . . . .
3	3	3 . . . .

APPENDIX 5 FORM FOR NOTING A–B–C SEQUENCES

PARENTING POSITIVELY

Helping parents improve children's behaviour

The A–B–C sequence

The following sheet is blank to give you opportunities of noting the A–B–C sequences for yourself.

	Antecedent (What happened just before the behaviour)	**Behaviour** (The specific behaviour identified)	**Consequences** (What happened just after the behaviour)
1	*Example*		
2			
3			
4			
5			
6			

APPENDIX 6
STRENGTHS AND
DIFFICULTIES
QUESTIONNAIRE

The following questionnaire has been devised by Dr Robert Goodman, and is published with his permission and that of the Association of Child Psychology and Psychiatry and the publishers, Cambridge University Press.

The questionnaire was developed as an alternative to the Rutter questionnaire and involved 403 children drawn from dental and psychiatric clinics. Goodman reports that the

> preliminary findings suggest that the SDQ functions as well as the Rutter questionnaires, while offering the following additional advantages: a focus on strengths as well as difficulties; better coverage of inattention; peer relationships and prosocial behaviour; a shorter format; and a single form suitable for both parents and teachers . . .

Specifically, the questionnaire addresses four areas of difficult behaviour: emotional symptoms, conduct problems, hyperactivity and peer problems, which together give a total difficulties score. It also includes a prosocial behaviour (strengths) score. It is appropriate for children between the ages of 4 and 16, but Dr Goodman has developed a version for children of 3.

For further information, readers are encouraged to write to Dr Goodman at the Department of Child and Adolescent Psychiatry, Institute of Psychiatry, De Crespigny Park, London SE5 8AF. He has prepared the questionnaire in many languages and can send samples of associated materials if contacted.

Goodman, R. (1997). The Strengths and Difficulties Questionnaire: a Research Note, *Journal of Child Psychology and Psychiatry*, 38 (5), 581–586.

*For each item, please mark the box for Not True, Somewhat True or Certainly True. It would help us if you answered all items as best you can even if you are not absolutely certain or the item seems daft! Please give your answers on the basis of the child's behaviour over the last six months or this school year. **NB** For details of how to score the questionnaire, for a scoring screen and other details, readers should contact Dr Robert Goodman.*

Child's Name ....   Male/Female

Date of Birth ....

	Not True	Somewhat True	Certainly True
Considerate of other people's feelings	☐	☐	☐
Restless, overactive, cannot stay still for long	☐	☐	☐
Often complains of headaches, stomach-aches or sickness	☐	☐	☐
Shares readily with other children (treats, toys, pencils etc.)	☐	☐	☐
Often has temper tantrums or hot tempers	☐	☐	☐
Rather solitary, tends to play alone	☐	☐	☐
Generally obedient, usually does what adults request	☐	☐	☐
Many worries, often seems worried	☐	☐	☐
Helpful if someone is hurt, upset or feeling ill	☐	☐	☐
Constantly fidgeting or squirming	☐	☐	☐
Has at least one good friend	☐	☐	☐
Often fights with other children or bullies them	☐	☐	☐
Often unhappy, down-hearted or tearful	☐	☐	☐
Generally liked by other children	☐	☐	☐
Easily distracted, concentration wanders	☐	☐	☐
Nervous or clingy in new situations, easily loses confidence	☐	☐	☐
Kind to younger children	☐	☐	☐
Often lies or cheats	☐	☐	☐
Picked on or bullied by other children	☐	☐	☐
Often volunteers to help others (parents, teachers, other children)	☐	☐	☐
Thinks things out before acting	☐	☐	☐
Steals from home, school or elsewhere	☐	☐	☐
Gets on better with adults than with other children	☐	☐	☐
Many fears, easily scared	☐	☐	☐
Sees tasks through to the end, good attention span	☐	☐	☐

Signature ....   Date ....

Parent/Teacher/Other (please specify:)

Provisional Banding of SDQ Scores

These bands, which are not adjusted for age or gender, have been chosen so that roughly 80% of children in the community are normal, 10% are borderline, and 10% are abnormal.

	Normal	Borderline	Abnormal
Parent completed			
Total Difficulties Score	0–13	14–16	17–40
Emotional Symptoms Score	0–3	4	5–10
Conduct Problems Score	0–2	3	4–10
Hyperactivity Score	0–5	6	7–10
Peer Problems Score	0–2	3	4–10
Prosocial Behaviour Score	6–10	5	0–4
Teacher completed			
Total Difficulties Score	0–11	12–15	16–40
Emotional Symptoms Score	0–4	5	6–10
Conduct Problems Score	0–2	3	4–10
Hyperactivity Score	0–5	6	7–10
Peer Problems Score	0–3	4	5–10
Prosocial Behaviour Score	6–10	5	0–4

APPENDIX 7
FORM FOR CHARTING BEHAVIOURS

CHARTING BEHAVIOURS   Name: . . . . Week beginning: . . . .

Behaviour	Sunday	Monday	Tuesday	Wednesday	Thursday	Friday	Saturday	Total
Positive behaviour. Follows request in one minute.								
Morning								
Afternoon								
Evening								
Negative behaviour. Does not follow request in one minute.								
Morning								
Afternoon								
Evening								

APPENDIX 8
FORM FOR CHARTING A BEHAVIOUR

CHARTING BEHAVIOURS   Name: . . . . Week beginning: . . . .

Specific behaviour

Behaviour	Sunday	Monday	Tuesday	Wednesday	Thursday	Friday	Saturday	Total
Morning								
Afternoon								
Evening								
Morning								
Afternoon								
Evening								

APPENDIX 9 FORM FOR EIGHT-WEEK CHARTING OF POSITIVE AND NEGATIVE BEHAVIOURS

SHOWING THE INCREASE OR DECREASE WEEK BY WEEK

Positive behaviours

Number of instances of beginning to follow a request within one minute

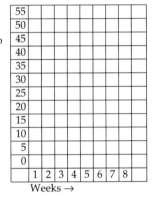

Weeks →

Negative behaviours

Number of instances of not beginning to follow a request within one minute

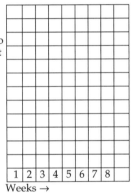

Weeks →

Number of instances of . . . .

Weeks →

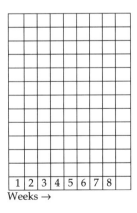

Weeks →

Number of
instances of
. . . .

55							
50							
45							
40							
35							
30							
25							
20							
15							
10							
5							
0							
	1	2	3	4	5	6	7	8

Weeks →

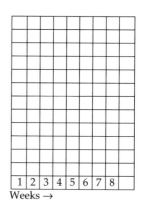

Weeks →

Number of
instances of
. . . .

55							
50							
45							
40							
35							
30							
25							
20							
15							
10							
5							
0							
	1	2	3	4	5	6	7	8

Weeks →

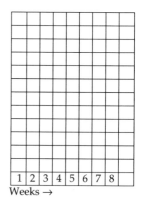

Weeks →

Number of
instances of
. . . .

55							
50							
45							
40							
35							
30							
25							
20							
15							
10							
5							
0							
	1	2	3	4	5	6	7	8

Weeks →

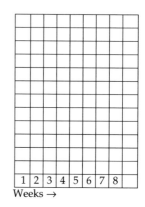

Weeks →

APPENDIX 10   FORM FOR PLANNING WITH PARENTS

PARENTING POSITIVELY

Helping parents improve children's behaviour

Planning with parents

Name of child . . . .   Date of birth . . . .

To help improve patterns of behaviour, we have agreed to focus on the following:

Positive behaviour

1 . . . .

2 . . . .

Negative behaviour

1 . . . .

2 . . . .

Action plan agreed with parent(s)

1 . . . .

2 . . . .

3 . . . .

4 . . . .

This will be reviewed on . . . .

Signed . . . .   Signed . . . .

Date . . . .

APPENDIX 11
PARENTING POSITIVELY: SOME NOTES FOR PARENTS

DE MONTFORT UNIVERSITY

PARENTING POSITIVELY

Helping parents improve children's behaviour

Some Notes for Parents

1. Work out some house or family guidelines: for example, 'All toys must be put away before bedtime'. Everyone helps each other to carry out the guidelines.
2. Find 3 behaviours each day for which you can praise a child. Catch them being good!
3. Reward behaviour you want to encourage, by attending to it and showing how pleased you are with it.
4. Ignore small misbehaviours: whining, pestering, tantrums. Turn your back on the child.
5. Try to be consistent. If you promise to threaten something, you must carry out the promise or threat.
6. Speak directly and firmly to your child when given instructions.
7. Encourage others who care for the child to use these same guidelines.
8. Take a day at a time.
9. You'll have some bad days. Try to commend yourself for what you have already achieved.
10. Try to find someone you can confide in when it all seems to be falling apart. *Don't give up.*

APPENDIX 12   WEEKLY SLEEP CHART

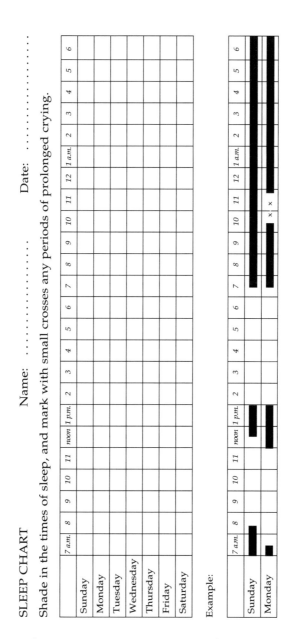

SLEEP CHART   Name: . . . .   Date: . . . .

Shade in the times of sleep, and mark with small crosses any periods of prolonged crying.

	7 a.m.	8	9	10	11	noon	1 p.m.	2	3	4	5	6	7	8	9	10	11	12	1 a.m.	2	3	4	5	6
Sunday																								
Monday																								
Tuesday																								
Wednesday																								
Thursday																								
Friday																								
Saturday																								

Example:

	7 a.m.	8	9	10	11	noon	1 p.m.	2	3	4	5	6	7	8	9	10	11	12	1 a.m.	2	3	4	5	6
Sunday																								
Monday																								

APPENDIX 13
GUIDELINES FOR GOOD PRACTICE OF BEHAVIOURAL AND COGNITIVE PSYCHOTHERAPY

INTRODUCTORY STATEMENT

1. All members of the British Association for Behavioural and Cognitive Psycho-therapies are required to endeavour to adhere to these guidelines.

2. Most BABCP members will already be members of the helping professions and hold appropriate qualifications. They should, therefore, be bound by a code of practice by virtue of their belonging to a profession and so a detailed statement of general ethical/legal principles is not included in these guidelines. It is expected that all members of BABCP approach their work with the aim of resolving prob-lems and promoting the well-being of service users and will endeavour to use their ability and skills to their best advantage without prejudice and with due recognition of the value and dignity of every human being.

3. The term 'worker' and 'service user' are used throughout to designate the person responsible for helping and the person being helped respectively and should be taken to subsume similar relationships, e.g. doctor/patient, therapist/client, teacher/student etc. as appropriate. Similarly 'assessments/interventions' is used to subsume training, treatment, programme etc.

1 ASSESSMENT AND BEHAVIOUR/COGNITIVE CHANGE PROCEDURES

(i) The worker will ensure that any intervention procedures adopted will be based upon evaluation and assessment of the service user and the environment. The worker will also strive to ensure that any assessments/interventions will be in the best interests of the service user, minimising any possible harm and maximising benefits over both the short and long term whilst at the same time balancing these against any possible harmful effects to others.

(ii) Assessments/interventions will always be justified by the available public evidence taking into account all possible alternatives, the degree of demonstrated efficacy, discomfort, intervention time and cost of alternatives.

(iii) Assessments/interventions will be planned and implemented in such a way that effectiveness can be evaluated.

(iv) The aims and goals of assessments/interventions will be discussed and agreed with service users at the outset and may be renegotiated, terminated or a referral made to another worker at the request of either party if the goals are not being met after a reasonable period of time or if they later appear to be inappropriate.

(v) On both ethical and empirical grounds assessments/interventions used will be of demonstrable benefit to the service users both short and long term and will not involve any avoidable loss, deprivation, pain or other source of suffering. It is recognised, however, that circumstances might exist where long term benefits could only be achieved by interventions which involve relatively minor and transient deprivation. Workers will ensure that no such assessments/interventions are used where effective alternatives exist or where long term benefit does not clearly outweigh the short term loss. The design of such assessments/interventions by virtue of the aims would minimise any suffering involved and ensure that dangerous or long term deprivation will not occur. Whenever there is room for doubt about justifying the use of such interventions, workers will always seek advice from an appropriately qualified and experienced colleague who is in a position to give an independent and objective opinion.

2 CONSENT

(i) It is understood that consent to particular assessments/interventions is an ongoing process which places emphasis upon the service user's role in the continual evaluation of the assessments/interventions.

(ii) Where a worker sees a service user only for evaluative or diagnostic procedures, this will be explained clearly to them.

(iii) Upon team agreement regarding the best procedure to implement, the aims, rationale and alternatives of assessments/interventions will be explained to the service user at the start as explicitly and as fully as is consistent with therapeutic effectiveness and the person's best interests. If the assessments/interventions are experimental rather than established and proven, this will be communicated to the service user. If this has been fulfilled, the service user gives consent to the intervention and this is recorded.

(iv) For people unable to give informed voluntary consent, written consent will be obtained from a relative after informing them as described above. If no relative is available, consent will be obtained from an advocate or other responsible professional.

(v) Retroactive consent will only be considered sufficient in emergency situations such that any delay in intervention would lead to permanent and irreversible harm to the person's well being.

(vi) If a service user, when capable of informed consent, or other appropriate person when 2(iv) applies, chooses to withhold consent, the intervention does not proceed. This applies equally to involuntary service users or those referred from the courts.

(vii) Where a service user is within an institution, whether voluntary or otherwise, interventions may take the form of institutional management or specific programmes in which all members take part in these circumstances informed consent may be difficult to achieve but the conditions of 1(iv) are taken as minimum requirement. People are informed of the extent to which they are free to withdraw from any aspect of assessments/interventions. In addition, those responsible for the procedures have the responsibility for collecting objective evidence for their continuing efficacy.

3 QUALIFICATION AND TRAINING

(i) No workers represent themselves as having qualifications or skills they do not possess.

(ii) Workers recognise the boundaries to their competence both from formal training and from work experience and if faced with a situation outside their competence, either refer the person to a colleague who has the required skills or, if taking on the situation themselves, ensure that they receive supervision and training from a competent other.

(iii) Workers expect to continue to develop expertise after formal training has finished and take reasonable steps to keep up-to-date with current research and practice, e.g. reading current research, by attending appropriate courses and receiving regular practice supervision from an appropriately qualified and experienced person.

4   INTERPROFESSIONAL RELATIONSHIPS

(i) Workers in a multi-disciplinary setting keep their colleagues informed of their decisions, consult with them when appropriate and establish clearly the limits of their involvement with a particular service user.

(ii) Where workers have in practice overall responsibility for service users, they recognise aspects where their own professional competence ends and consult other professionals as appropriate.

5   CONFIDENTIALITY

(i) Information acquired by a worker is confidential within their understanding of the best interest of the service user and the law of the land. Written and oral reports of relevant material are made available to other persons directly involved.

(ii) The service user's consent is required where information is passed beyond the normal limits of persons concerned or made available for the purpose of research.

(iii) The service user's consent is required if they are presented to an individual or group for teaching purposes and it is made clear that refusal would have no implication for intervention.

(iv) If an intervention is being published, personal details are restricted to the minimum required for describing the intervention.

(v) If a video tape, film or other recording is made, consent in writing is required specifying whether the recording may be shown to: (a) other professionals; (b) students; (c) the lay public.

6   RESEARCH

(i) If a service user is asked to be tested or interviewed as part of a research project, it is made explicit when the procedures used are not of direct therapeutic benefit to that individual and formal consent is obtained.

(ii) When service users are in a research project where interventions are being compared or a control condition included, if one intervention or condition emerges as the most effective it is subsequently made available to those in the less effective control groups.

7   EXPLOITATION OF SERVICE USERS

(i) Workers have a clear responsibility not to exploit service users in financial, sexual or other ways. Though some interventions entail workers and service users socialising together, a clear distinction between personal and professional relationships is still made.

8   PRIORITIES

(i) Workers will often have to decide areas in which to specialise and this choice is made with due regard to the priorities involved taking into account the known efficacies of interventions available and the overall benefit conferred on service users in general.

9   ADVERTISING

(i) Membership of BABCP does not confer any professional status or qualification. Workers will not refer to their membership of BABCP in advertising or elsewhere to imply any such professional status or qualification.

(ii) Workers accredited by BABCP as Behavioural and/or Cognitive Psychotherapists to meet the criteria for registration with the Behavioural and Cognitive Psychotherapy Section of the United Kingdom Council for Psychotherapy, are free to advertise or otherwise announce that fact.

APPENDIX 14
FORM FOR FRAMING AN AGREEMENT BETWEEN A WORKER AND A CLIENT

A. The agreement

This agreement is drawn up between:

Name: .... Address: .... and

Name: .... worker from (Agency): ....

Address: .... Telephone no: ....

B. What we are trying to do together

Our overall aim is ....

Our particular goals or objectives are:

1. To ....

2. To ....

3. To ....

C. In order to work towards these goals, we have made some agreements:

Agreed by .... (client) Agreed by .... (worker)

1. To .... 1. To ....

   ....

2. To .... 2. To ....

   ....

3. To .... 3. To ....

   ....

D. Other points to be noted

1. The above agreement is to be reviewed and updated every .... days

2. The agreement can be changed if both parties agree to this

3. If the agreement does not work, i.e. if either party does not keep to the agreement, then ....

Signed .... Signed .... Date ....

APPENDIX 15
FORM FOR FRAMING AN AGREEMENT IN ONE-TO-ONE OR FAMILY WORK

This form to be completed by the worker in discussion with the client and the family. It is all-purpose and can be adapted to a wide range of situations.

A. The agreement

This agreement is drawn up between:

1. . . . .   3. . . . .

2. . . . .   4. . . . .

and . . . .   worker from: . . . .

Agency: . . . .

Address: . . . .

. . . .   Telephone no: . . . .

B. What we are trying to do together

We have talked about what we can work towards together, and agree that our goals are to:

1. . . . .

2. . . . .

3. . . . .

4. . . . .

C. To work towards these goals

The worker agrees to:

1. . . . .

2. . . . .

3. . . . .

The following members of the family agree to:

First person (name) ....

1. ....

2. ....

3. ....

Second person (name) ....

1. ....

2. ....

3. ....

Third person (name) ....

1. ....

2. ....

3. ....

Fourth person (name) ....

1. ....

2. ....

3. ....

D. Other points to be noted

The above agreement is to be reviewed every .... weeks.

The above agreement can be changed if everyone agrees.

Signed: ....   Signed: ....

Signed: ....   Signed: ....

Date: ....

REFERENCES

Achenbach, T.M. (1991) *Manual for the Child Behaviour Checklist 4–18 and 1991 Profile.* Burlington, VT: University of Vermont, Department of Psychiatry.

Achenbach, T.M. and Edelbrock, C.S. (1986) *Manual for the Child Behaviour Checklist and Revised Child Behaviour Profile.* Burlington, VT: University of Vermont, Department of Psychiatry.

Allen, D.M. and Tarnowski, K.J. (1989) Depressive characteristics of physically abused children. *Journal of Abnormal Child Psychology,* **17,** 1–11.

American Psychiatric Association (1994) *Diagnostic and Statistical Manual of Mental Disorders,* 4th edn (DSM-IV). Washington, DC: American Psychiatric Association.

Aro, H.M. and Palosaari, U.K. (1992) Parental divorce, adolescence and transition to young adulthood: a follow-up study. *American Journal of Orthopsychiatry,* **62,** 421–429.

Atkinson, R.L., Atkinson, R.C., Smith, E.E., Bem, D.J. and Hilgard, E. (1990) *Introduction to Psychology,* 10th edn. New York: Harcourt, Brace, Jovanovich.

Bakwin, H. (1973) The genetics of bedwetting. In I. Kolvin, R. MacKeith and R.S. Meadow (eds), *Bladder Control and Enuresis.* Clinics in Developmental Medicine, Nos 48/49. London: Heinemann/Spastics International Medical Publications, pp. 73–77.

Bandura, A. (1986) *Social Foundations of Thought and Action. A Social Cognitive Theory.* Englewood Cliffs, NJ: Prentice-Hall.

Bandura, A. and Walters, R.H. (1959) *Adolescent Aggression.* New York: Ronald.

Barkley, R. (1995) *Taking Charge of AD/HD.* New York: Guilford.

Barlow, J. (1997) *Systematic Review of the Effectiveness of Parent-training Programmes in Improving Behaviour Problems in Children Aged 3–10 Years.* University of Oxford: Health Services Reseach Unit, Department of Public Health.

Baumrind, D. (1971) Current patterns of parental authority. *Developmental Psychology Monographs,* **1,** 1–102.

Beck, A. (1976) *Cognitive Therapy and the Emotional Disorders*. New York: International Universities Press.

Bee, H. (1992) *The Developing Child*, 6th edn. London: Harper Collins.

Bellman, M. (1966) Studies on encopresis. *Acta Paediatrica Scandinavica* (suppl), **170**.

Bernstein, G.A. and Garfinkel, B.D. (1986) School phobia: the overlap of affective and anxiety disorders. *Journal of the American Academy of Child Psychiatry*, **25**, 235–241.

Bithoney, W. and Newberger, E.H. (1987) Child and family attributes of failure-to-thrive. *Developmental and Behavioural Paediatrics*, **8**, 32–36.

Bosco, J.J. and Robin, S.S. (1980) Hyperkinesis: prevalence and treatment. In C.K. Whalen and B. Henker (eds), *Hyperactive Children: the Social Ecology of Identification and Treatment*. New York: Academic Press.

Bowlby, J. (1979) *The Making and Breaking of Affectional Bonds*. London: Tavistock.

Brightman, R.P., Baker, B., Clark, D. and Ambrose, S.A. (1982) Effectiveness of alternative parent training formats. *Journal of Behavior Therapy and Experimental Psychiatry*, **13**, 113–117.

British Psychological Society (1996) *Attention Deficit Hyperactivity Disorder (ADHD): A Psychological Response to an Evolving Concept*. Leicester: British Psychological Society.

Brown, G. and Harris, T. (1978) *The Social Origins of Depression*. London: Tavistock.

Burcham, B., Carlson, L. and Milich, R. (1993) Promising school-based practices for students with attention-deficit disorder. *Exceptional Children*, **60**, 174–180.

Bushby, R. (1996) Hyperactive disorder 'not being detected'. *Times Educational Supplement*, **May/June**.

Butler, N.R. and Golding, J. (eds) (1986) *From Birth to Five. A Study of the Health and Behaviour of Britain's Five Year Olds*. London: Pergamon.

Callias, M. (1994) Parent training. In M. Rutter, E. Taylor and L. Hersov (eds), *Child and Adolescent Psychiatry*. Oxford: Blackwell Scientific.

Carter, C.M., Urbanowicz, M., Hemsley, R., Mantilla, L. Strobel, S., Graham, P.J. and Taylor, E. (1993) Effects of a 'few foods' diet in attention deficit disorder. *Archives of Disease in Childhood*, **69**, 564–568.

Clarke, R.V.G. (1977) Psychology and crime. *Bulletin of the British Psychological Society*, **30**, 280–283.

Cohen, N.J., Davine, M., Hordezky, M.A., Lipsett, L. and Isaacson, B.A. (1993) Unsuspected language impairments in psychiatrically disturbed children: prevalence and language and behavioral characteristics. *Journal of the American Academy of Child and Adolescent Psychiatry*, **32**, 595–603.

Colton, M., Drury, C. and Williams, M. (1995) *Children in Need: Family Support Under the Children Act 1989.* Aldershot: Avebury.

Conners, C.K. (1973) Rating scales for use in drug studies with children. *Pharmacology Bulletin,* **9**, 24–29.

Cooley, C.H. (1902) *Human Nature and the Social Order.* New York: Scribner's.

Cooper, C. (1985) 'Good-enough', border-line and 'bad-enough' parenting. In M. Adcock and R. White (eds), *Good-enough Parenting: A Framework for Assessment.* London: British Agencies for Adoption and Fostering.

Cross, M. (1997) Challenging behaviour or challenged comprehension. *Royal College of Speech and Language Therapists Bulletin,* September, 11–12.

Dahl, M. and Kristiansson, B. (1987) Early feeding problems in an affluent society: (iv) impact on growth up to two years of age. *Acta Paediatrica Scandinavica,* **76**, 881–888.

Davie, R., Butler, N. and Goldstein, H. (1972) *From Birth to Seven.* London: Longman.

Department of Health and Social Security (1988) *Present Day Practice in Infant Feeding, Third Report.* DHSS Report on Health and Social Subjects, No. 32. London: HMSO.

Department of Health (Bullock, R., Little, R., Hillham, S. and Mount, K.) (1995) *Child Protection: Messages from Research.* London: HMSO.

Department of Health, Social Services Inspectorate and Department for Education (1995) *A Handbook on Child and Adolescent Mental Health.* London: HMSO.

Department of Health (1998) *Health and Personal Social Services Statistics for England,* 1997 edn. London: HMSO.

Dodge, K.A. (1980) Social cognition and children's aggressive behavior. *Child Development,* **51**, 162–170.

Dodge, K.A. and Frame, C.L. (1982) Social cognitive biases and deficits in aggressive boys. *Child Development,* **53**, 620–635.

Doleys, D.M. (1978) Assessment and treatment of enuresis and encopresis in children. In M. Hersen, R.M. Eisler and P.M. Miller (eds), *Progress in Behavior Modification,* vol. 6, pp. 85–121. New York: Academic Press.

Douglas, J.W. (1973) Early disturbing events and later enuresis. In I. Kolvin, R.C. MacKeith and S.R. Meadows (eds), *Bladder Control and Enuresis.* Clinics in Developmental Medicine, Nos 48/49. London: Heinemann/Spastics International Medical Publications.

Douglas, J. (1989) Training parents to manage their child's sleep problem. In C.E. Schaefer and J.M. Briesmeister (eds), *Handbook of Parent Training. Parents as Co-therapists for Children's Behaviour Problems.* New York: Wiley.

Douglas, J. and Richman, N. (1984) *My Child Won't Sleep*. Harmondsworth: Penguin.

Drillien, C.M. (1964) *The Growth and Development of the Prematurely Born Infant*. Baltimore: Williams and Williams.

Dunning, E., Maguire, J., Murphy, P. and Williams, J.M. (1982) The social roots of football hooliganism. *Leisure Studies*, **1**, 139–156.

Durand, B.M. and Carr, E.G. (1991) Functional communication training to reduce challenging behaviour: maintenance and application in new settings. *Journal of Applied Behavior Analysis*, **24**, 251–254.

Earls, F. (1982) Cultural and national differences in the epidemiology of behaviour problems in pre-school children. *Culture, Medicine and Psychiatry*, **6**, 45–56.

Earls, F. (1994) Oppositional-defiant and conduct disorders. In M. Rutter, E. Taylor and L. Hersov (eds), *Child and Adolescent Psychiatry*, 3rd edn. Oxford: Blackwell Scientific.

Earls, F. and Jung, K.G. (1987) Temperament and home environment characteristics as causal factors in the early development of childhood psychopathology. *Journal of the American Academy of Child and Adolescent Psychiatry*, **26** (4), 491–498.

Egger, J., Carter, C.M., Graham, P.J., Gumley, D. and Soothill, J.F. (1985) Controlled trial of oligoantigenic treatment in the hyperkinetic syndrome. *Lancet*, **9** (March), 540–545.

Eisenberg, L. (1958) School phobia: a study in the communication of anxiety. *American Journal of Psychiatry*, **114**, 712–718.

Emmett, N. (1984) Personal communication.

Emmet, N. (1987) A feedback loop suggested by social learning theory. In C. Sutton (ed.), *A Handbook of Research for the Helping Professions*. London: Routledge and Kegan Paul.

Essen, J. and Peckham, C. (1976) Nocturnal enuresis in childhood. *Developmental Medicine and Child Neurology*, **18**, 577–589.

Falloon, I.R.H., Boyd, J.L. and McGill, C.W. (1984) *Family Care of Schizophrenia*. London: Guilford.

Falloon, I.R.H., Laporta, M., Fadden, G. and Graham-Hole, V. (1993) *Managing Stress in Families: Cognitive and Behavioural Strategies for Enhancing Coping Skills*. London: Routledge.

Farrington, D. (1995a) Intensive health visiting and the prevention of juvenile crime. *Health Visitor*, **68** (3), 100–102.

Farrington, D. (1995b) The development of offending and anti-social behaviour from childhood: key findings from the Cambridge Study in Delinquent Development. *Journal of Child Psychology and Psychiatry*, **360**, 924–964.

Ferber, R. (1986) *Solve Your Child's Sleep Problems*. London: Dorling Kindersley.

Fiore, T.A., Becker, E.A. and Nero, R.C. (1993) *Research Synthesis on Education Interventions for Students with ADD*. NC: Research Triangle Institute.

Fogelman, K. (1983) *Growing Up in Great Britain. Papers from the National Child Development Study*. London: Macmillan.

Forehand, R. and Kotchik, B. (1996) Cultural diversity: a wake-up call for parent training. *Behavior Therapy*, **27**, 187–206.

Forehand, R. and MacDonagh, T.S. (1975) Response contingent time out. An examination of outcome data. *European Journal of Behaviour Analysis and Modification*, **1**, 109–115.

Forsyth, B.W. (1989) Colic and the effect of changing formulas: a double-blind multiple, cross-over study. *Journal of Pediatrics*, **115**, 521–526.

Gabel, S. (1981) *Behavioral Problems in Childhood: A Primary Care Approach*. New York: Grune and Stratton.

Galbraith, L., Hewitt, K.E. and Pritchard, L. (1993) Behavioural treatment for sleep disturbance, *Health Visitor*, **6**, 169–171.

Gardiner, J. (1996) Rise in primary exclusions. *Times Educational Supplement*, 1 November, 1.

Garmezy, N. (1983) Stressors of childhood. In N. Garmezy and M. Rutter (eds), *Stress, Coping and Development in Children*. Stanford, CA: Centre for Advanced Study in the Behavioural Sciences. New York: McGraw Hill.

Gill, A. (1998) Unpublished data.

Goldston, D.B., Turnquist, D.C. and Knutson, J.F. (1989) Presenting problems of sexually abused girls receiving psychiatric services. *Journal of Abnormal Psychology*, **98**, 314–317.

Goodman, R. (1997) The Strengths and Difficulties Questionnaire. *Journal of Child Psychology and Psychiatry*, **38** (5), 581–586.

Goodman, R. and Stevenson, J. (1989) A twin study of hyperactivity. II. The aetiological role of genes, family relationships and perinatal adversity. *Journal of Child Psychology and Psychiatry*, **30** (5), 691–709.

Gordon, S.B. and Davidson N. (1981) Behavioral parent training. In A. Gurman and D. Kniskern (eds), *Handbook of Family Therapy*. New York: Brunner/Mazel.

Goyette, C.H., Conners, C.K. and Ulrich, R.F. (1978) Normative data on revised Conners parent and teacher rating scales. *Journal of Abnormal Child Psychology*, **6**, 221–236.

Graham, H. (1993) *Hardship and Health in Women's Lives*. London: Harvester Wheatsheaf.

Green, C. (1995) *Understanding Attention Deficit Disorder*. London: Vermilion.

Hampton, D. (1996)   Resolving the feeding difficulties associated with non-organic failure to thrive. *Child Care, Health and Development*, **22**, 261–121.

Harrington, R. (1994)   Affective disorders. In M. Rutter, E. Taylor and L. Hersov (eds), *Child and Adolescent Psychiatry*. Oxford: Blackwell Scientific.

Hazel, N. (1980)   *Bridge to Independence*. Oxford: Basil Blackwell.

Herbert, M. (1978)   *Conduct Disorders of Childhood and Adolescence: A Social Learning Perspective*. Chichester: Wiley.

Herbert, M. (1981)   *Behavioural Treatment of Problem Children*. London: Academic Press.

Herbert, M. (1987)   *Behavioural Treatment of Children with Problems*. London: Academic Press.

Herbert, M. (1991)   *Clinical Child Psychology. Social Learning, Development and Behaviour*. Chichester: Wiley.

Herbert, M. (1997)   Personal communication.

Hersov, L. (1977)   Emotional disorders. In M. Rutter and L. Hersov (eds), *Child and Adolescent Psychiatry*. Oxford: Blackwell Scientific.

Hersov, L. (1985)   Emotional disorders. In M. Rutter and L. Hersov (eds), *Child and Adolescent Psychiatry*, 2nd edn. Oxford: Blackwell Scientific.

Hersov, L. (1994)   Faecal soiling. In M. Rutter, E. Taylor and L. Hersov (eds), *Child and Adolescent Psychiatry*. Oxford: Blackwell Scientific.

Hobbs, S.A., Forehand, E. and Murray, R.G. (1978)   Effects of various durations of Time Out on the non-compliant behavior of children. *Behavior Therapy*, **9**, 652–656.

Hollin, C. (1991)   Cognitive behaviour modification with delinquents. In M. Herbert (ed.), *Clinical Child Psychology: Social Learning Development and Behaviour*. Chichester: Wiley.

Holmes, T.H. and Rahe, R.H. (1967)   The social readjustment rating scale. *Journal of Psychosomatic Research*, **11**, 213–218.

Horowitz, M.J., Wilner, N. and Alvarez, W. (1979)   Impact of event scale: a measure of subjective stress. *Psychosomatic Medicine*, **41**, 209–219.

House of Commons Health Committee Fourth Report (1997)   *Child and Adolescent Mental Health Services*. London: HMSO.

Howlin, P. (1998)   Practitioner review: psychological and educational treatments for autism. *Journal of Child Psychology and Psychiatry*, **39** (3) 307–322.

Hudson, B. and McDonald, G. (1986)   *Behavioural Social Work. An Introduction*. Basingstoke: Macmillan.

Illingworth, R.S. and Lister, J. (1964)   The critical or sensitive period, with special reference to certain feeding problems in infants and children. *Journal of Pediatrics*, **65**, 839–849.

Iwaniec, D. (1995)   *The Emotionally Abused and Neglected Child*. Chichester: Wiley.

Iwaniec, D., Herbert, M. and McNeish, A.S. (1985a) Social work with failure-to-thrive children and their families. Part 1: Psychosocial factors. *British Journal of Social Work*, **15**, 243–259.

Iwaniec, D., Herbert, M. and McNeish, A.S. (1985b) Social work with failure-to-thrive children and their families. Part 2: Behavioural social work intervention. *British Journal of Social Work*, **15**, 375–389.

Jenkins, S., Owen, C., Bax, M. and Hart, H. (1984) Continuities of common behaviour problems in pre-school children. *Journal of Child Psychology and Psychiatry*, **25**, 75–89.

Kallarackal, A.M. and Herbert, M. (1976) The adjustment of Indian immigrant children. In *Growing Up: A New Society Social Studies Reader*. London: IPC.

Kazdin, A. (1987) Treatment of antisocial behavior in children: current status and future directions. *Psychological Bulletin*, **102**, 187–203.

Kazdin, A. (1993) Treatment of conduct disorder. Progress and directions in psychotherapy research. *Development and Psychopathology*, **5**, 277–310.

Kazdin, A. (1995) *Conduct Disorders in Childhood and Adolescence*. London: Sage.

Kelly, G.A. (1955) *The Psychology of Personal Constructs*. New York: Norton.

Kendall, P.C. (ed.) (1991) *Child and Adolescent Therapy: Cognitive-Behavioral Procedures*. London: Guilford.

Kerr, S., Jowett, S. and Smith, L. (1997) Education to help prevent sleep problems in infants. *Health Visitor*, **70**, 224–225.

Kolvin, I., Miller, F.J.W., Fleeting, M. and Kolvin, P.A. (1988) Social and parenting factors affecting criminal offence rates (findings from the Newcastle Thousand Family Study, 1947–1980). *British Journal of Psychiatry*, **152**, 80–90.

King, N.J., Hamilton, D.I. and Ollendick, T.J. (1988) *Children's Phobias*. London: Academic Press.

Klackenberg, G. (1987) Incidence of parasomnias in children in a general population. In C. Guilleminault (ed.), *Sleep and Its Disorders*. New York: Raven Press.

Lachenmeyer, J. and Davidovicz, H. (1987) Failure to thrive: a critical review. *Advancement of Clinical Child Psychology*, **10**, 335–358.

Lane, T.W. and Davis, G.E. (1987) Child maltreatment and juvenile delinquency. Does a relationship exist? In J.D. Burchard and S.N. Burchard (eds), *Prevention of Delinquent Behaviour. Primary Prevention of Psychopathology*. Newbury Park, CA: Sage.

Lahey, B.B., Piacentini, J.C., Macburnett, K., Stone, P., Hartdagen, S.E. and Hynd, G.W. (1988) Psychopathology in the parents of children with conduct disorder and hyperactivity. *Journal of the American Academy of Child and Adolescent Psychiatry*, **27**, 163–170.

Lahey, B.B., Russo, M.F., Walker, J.L. and Piacentini, J.C. (1989) Personality characteristics of the mothers of children with disruptive behaviour disorders. *Journal of Consulting and Clinical Psychology*, **57** (4), 512–515.

Lindberg, L., Bohlin, G. and Hagekull, B. (1991) Early feeding problems in a normal population. *International Journal of Eating Disorders*, **10**, 395–405.

Lipsey, M.W. (1992) Juvenile delinquency treatment: a meta-analytic enquiry into the variability of effects. In T.D. Cook, H. Cooper, D.S. Cordray, H. Hartmann, L.V. Hedges, R.J. Light, T.J. Louis and M. Mosteller (eds), *Meta-analysis for Explanation: A Casebook*. New York: Russell Sage Foundation.

Lochman, J.E., White, K. and Wayland, K. (1991) Cognitive-behavioral assessment and treatment with aggressive children. In P. Kendall (ed.), *Child and Adolescent Therapy: Cognitive-behavioral Procedures*. New York: Guilford.

Loeber, R. (1990) Development and risk factors of juvenile antisocial behavior and delinquency. *Clinical Psychology Review*, **10**, 1–41.

Long, P., Forehand, R., Wierson, M. and Morgan, A. (1994) Does parent training with young non-compliant children have long-term effects? *Behaviour Research and Therapy*, **32** (1), 101–107.

Lyon, J. (1996) *The Nature and Identification of Attention Deficit/Hyperactivity Disorder (AD/HD)*. International Psychology Services, 17 High Street, Hurstpierpoint, West Sussex.

Maccoby, E.E. and Martin, J.A. (1983) Socialisation in the context of the family: parent–child interaction. In P.H. Mussen (ed.), *Handbook of Child Psychology*, vol. 4. Chichester: Wiley.

Macht, J. (1990) *Poor Eaters. Helping Children Who Refuse to Eat*. New York: Plenum.

Martin, G. and Pear, J. (1992) *Behavior Modification: What It Is and How to Do It*. Hemel Hempstead: Prentice-Hall.

Maslow, A. (1970) *Motivation and Personality*. New York: Harper and Row.

McGaw, S. (1997) Supporting parents with learning disabilities. Paper given at a meeting of Promoting Parenting Skills, Leicester, 20 November.

McGonaghy, N. (1969) A controlled trial of imipramine, amphetamine, pad and bell conditioning and random awakening in the treatment of nocturnal enuresis. *Medical Journal of Australia*, **2**, 237–239.

MacKeith, R., Meadow, R. and Turner, K. (1973) How children become dry. In I. Kolvin, R.C. MacKeith and S.R. Meadow (eds), *Bladder Control and Enuresis*. Spastics International Medical Publications. Oxford: Heinemann Medical.

Miller, F.J., Court, S.D., Walton, W.S. and Knox, E.G. (1960) *Growing Up in Newcastle upon Tyne*. Oxford: Oxford University Press.

Minde, K. and Minde, R. (1986) *Infant Psychiatry. An Introductory Text.* London: Sage.

Mischel, W. (1973) Towards a cognitive social learning reconceptualization of personality. *Psychological Review*, **80**, 272–283.

Mitchell, S. and Rosa, P. (1981) Boyhood behaviour problems as precursors of criminality: a fifteen-year follow-up study. *Journal of Child Psychology and Psychiatry*, **22**, 19–33.

Moffatt, M.E., Kato, C. and Pless, I.B. (1987) Improvements in self-concept after treatment of nocturnal enuresis: randomized control trial. *Journal of Pediatrics*, **110**, 647–652.

Morgan, R. (1992) *Help for the Bedwetting Child*. London: Cedar.

Nezu, A.M. and Perri, M. (1989) Social problem-solving therapy for unipolar depression: an initial dismantling investigation. *Journal of Consulting and Clinical Psychology*, **57**, 408–413.

Oaklander, V. (1988) *Windows to Our Children*. Highland, NY: Gestalt Journal Press.

O'Dell, S. (1985) Progress in parent training. In M. Hersen, R.M. Eisler and P. Miller (eds), *Progress in Behavior Modification*, vol. 19. New York: Academic Press.

Offord, D.R., Boyle, M.C. and Racine, Y.A. (1991) The epidemiology of antisocial behavior in childhood and adolescence. In D.J. Pepler and K.H. Rubin (eds), *The Development and Treatment of Childhood Aggression*. Hillsdale, NJ: Erlbaum.

Ollendick, T. and King, N. (1991) Fears and phobias of childhood. In M. Herbert (ed.), *Clinical Child Psychology: Social Learning, Development and Behaviour*. Chichester: Wiley.

Olweus, D. (1979) Stability of aggressive reaction patterns in males: a review. *Psychological Bulletin*, **86**, 29–34.

Open University (1980) *Systems Organisation: The Management of Complexity*. T243 Block 1: Introduction to Systems Thinking and Organization. Milton Keynes: Open University Press.

Patterson, G. (1974) Intervention for boys with conduct problems: multiple settings, treatment and criteria. *Journal of Consulting and Clinical Psychology*, **42**, 471–481.

Patterson, G. (1975) *Applications of Social Learning to Family Life*. Champaign, Il: Research Press.

Patterson, G., Dishion, T.J. and Chamberlain, P. (1993) Outcomes and methodological issues relating to treatment of antisocial children. In T.R. Giles (ed.), *Handbook of Effective Psychotherapy*. New York: Plenum.

Patterson, G. and Stoolmiller, M. (1991) Replications of a dual failure model for boys' depressed mood. *Journal of Consulting and Clinical Psychology*, **59**, 481–498.

Pollitt, E., Eichler, A.W. and Chan, C.K. (1975) Psychosocial development and behaviour of mothers of failure-to-thrive children. *American Journal of Orthopsychiatry*, **45**, 525–537.

Porrino, L., Rapoport, J.I., Behar, D., Sceery, W., Ismond, D. and Bunney, W.E. (1983) A naturalistic assessment of the motor activity of hyperactive boys: I. Comparison with normal controls. *Archives of General Psychiatry*, **40**, 681–687.

Puckering, C., Rogers, J., Mills, M., Cox, A.D. and Mattsson-Graf, M. (1994) Process and evaluation of a group intervention for mothers with parenting difficulties. *Child Abuse Review*, **3**, 299–310.

Quine, L. (1996) *Solving Children's Sleep Problems*. Huntingdon, Cambridge: Beckett Carlsson.

Richman, N. (1981) A community survey of characteristics of one to two year-olds with sleep disruptions. *Journal of the American Academy of Child Psychiatry*, **20**, 280–291.

Richman, N. (1985) Disorders in pre-school children. In M. Rutter and L. Hersov (eds), *Child and Adolescent Psychiatry: Modern Approaches*, 2nd edn. Oxford: Blackwell Scientific.

Richman, N., Stevenson, J. and Graham, P. (1982) *Pre-school to School: A Behavioural Study*. London: Academic Press.

Rinn, R.C., Vernon, J.C. and Wise, M.J. (1975) Training parents of behavior-disordered children in groups: a three years' programme evaluation. *Behavior Therapy*, **6**, 378–387.

Roberts, S. (1993) Tackling sleep problems through a clinic-based approach. *Health Visitor*, **66** (5), 173–174.

Robins, L.N. (1966) *Deviant Children Grown Up*. Baltimore, MD: Williams and Wilkins.

Robins, L.N. (1981) Epidemiological approaches to natural history research: antisocial disorders in children. *Journal of Consulting and Clinical Psychology*, **50**, 226–233.

Robins, L.N. and Price, R.K. (1991) Adult disorders predicted by childhood conduct problems: results from the NIMH Epidemiologic Catchment Area project. *Psychiatry*, **54**, 116–132.

Rogers, C.R. (1951) *Client-Centred Therapy*. Boston, MA: Houghton Mifflin.

Rose, S.L., Rose, S.A. and Feldman, J.F. (1989) Stability of behaviour problems in very young children. *Development and Psychopathology*, **1**, 5–19.

Rutter, M. (1988) *Psychiatric Disorder in Parents as a Risk Factor for Children*. Commissioned Review for the American Academy of Child Psychiatry.

Rutter, M. (1978) Family, area and school influences in the genesis of conduct disorders. In L.A. Hersov, M. Berger and D. Shaffer (eds), *Aggression and Anti-social Behaviour in Childhood and Adolescence*. Oxford: Pergamon.

Rutter, M., Cox, A., Tupling, C., Berger, M. and Yule, W. (1975a) Attainment and adjustment in two geographical areas: I. The prevalence of psychiatric disorder. *British Journal of Psychiatry*, **126**, 493–509.

Rutter, M., Yule, B., Quinton, D., Rowlands, O., Yule, W. and Berger, M. (1975b) Attainment and adjustment in two geographical areas. III. Some factors accounting for area differences. *British Journal of Psychiatry*, **126**, 520–523.

Rutter, M., Taylor, E. and Hersov, L. (1994) *Child and Adolescent Psychiatry*, 3rd edn. Oxford: Blackwell Scientific.

Rutter, M. (1986) The developmental psychopathology of depression: issues and perspectives. In M. Rutter, C. Izard, and P. Read (eds), *Depression in Young People: Developmental and Clinical Perspectives*. New York: Guilford.

Rutter, M. (1975) *Helping Troubled Children*. Harmondsworth: Penguin.

Rutter, M. and Cox, A. (1985) Other family influences. In M. Rutter and L. Hersov (eds), *Child and Adolescent Psychiatry: Modern Approaches*, 2nd edn. Oxford: Blackwell Scientific.

Rutter, M. and Sandberg, S. (1992) Psychosocial stressors: concepts, causes and effects. *Journal of European Child and Adolescent Psychiatry*, **1**, 3–13.

Scott, G. and Richards, M.P.M. (1990a) Night waking in infants: effects of providing advice and support for parents. *Journal of Child Psychology and Psychiatry*, **31**, 551–567.

Scragg, R.K., Mitchell, E.A., Stewart, A.W., Ford, R.K., Taylor, B.J., Hassall, I.B., Williams, S.M. and Thompson, J.M. (1996) Infant room-sharing and prone sleep position in sudden infant death syndrome. *Lancet*, **347**, 7–12.

Seligman, M.E. and Peterson, C. (1986) A learned helplessness perspective on childhood depression: theory and research. In M. Rutter, C. Izard and P. Read (eds), *Depression in Young People: Developmental and Clinical Perspectives*. New York: Guilford.

Sears, R.R., Maccoby, E.E. and Levin, H. (1957) *Patterns of Child Rearing*. Evanston, IL: Row Peterson.

Shaffer, D. (1994) Enuresis. In M. Rutter, E. Taylor and L. Hersov (eds), *Child and Adolescent Psychiatry*, 3rd edn. Oxford: Blackwell Scientific.

Sheldon, B. (1980) *The Use of Contracts in Social Work*. Birmingham: British Association of Social Workers.

Skuse, D. (1994) Feeding and Sleeping Disorders. In M. Rutter, L. Hersov and E. Taylor (eds), *Child and Adolescent Psychiatry*, 3rd edn. Oxford: Blackwell Scientific.

Spivack, G., Platt, J.J. and Shure, M. (1976) *The Problem-solving Approach to Adjustment*. San Francisco, CA: Jossey-Bass.

Stewart, M.A., Deblois, C.S. and Cummings, C. (1979) Psychiatric disorder in the parents of hyperactive boys and those with conduct disorder. *Journal of Child Psychology and Psychiatry*, **21**, 283–292.

Sutton, C. (1979) *Psychology for Social Workers and Counsellors*. London: Routledge and Kegan Paul.

Sutton, C. (1992) Training parents to manage difficult children: a comparison of methods. *Behavioural Psychotherapy*, **20**, 115–139.

Sutton, C. (1994) *Social Work, Community Work and Psychology*. Leicester: British Psychological Society.

Sutton, C. (1995) Parent training by telephone: a partial replication. *Behavioural and Cognitive Psychotherapy*, **23**, 1–24.

Sutton, C. (1996) *Positive Parenting. Help for Parents at Home*. Leicester: De Monfort University.

Sutton, C. and Herbert, M. (1992) *Mental Health: A Client Support Resource Pack*. Windsor: National Foundation for Educational Research/ Nelson.

Sykes, D.H., Hoy, E.A., Bill, J., Garth McClure, B., Halliday, H. and Reid, M. (1997) Behavioural adjustment in school of very low birthweight children. *Journal of Child Psychology and Psychiatry*, **38**, 315–325.

Taylor, E. (1994) Syndromes of attention deficit and overactivity. In M. Rutter, E. Taylor and L. Hersov (eds), *Child and Adolescent Psychiatry*, 3rd edn. Oxford: Blackwell Scientific.

Taylor, E., Sandberg, S., Thorley, G. and Giles, S. (1991) *The Epidemiology of Childhood Hyperactivity*. Maudsley Monographs, No. 33. Oxford: Oxford University Press.

Tellegen, A., Lykken, D.T., Bouchard, T.J. Jr, Wilcox, K.J., Segal, N. and Rich, S. (1988) Personality similarity in twins reared apart and together. *Journal of Personality and Social Psychology*, **54**, 1031–1039.

Thomas, A. and Chess, S. (1977) *Temperament and Development*. New York: Brunner/Mazel.

Thoman, E.B. and Whitney, M.P. (1989) Sleep states of infants monitored in the home: individual differences, developmental trends and origins of diurnal cyclicity. *Infant Behaviour and Development*, **12**, 59–75.

Tizard, B., Blatchford, P., Borke, J., Farquhar, C. and Plewis, I. (1988) *Young Children at School in the Inner City*. Hillsdale, NJ: Erlbaum.

Tremblay, R.E., LeBlanc, M. and Schwarzmann, A.E. (1988) The predictive power of first-grade peer and teacher ratings of behaviour: sex differences in antisocial behaviour and personality at adolescence. *Journal of Abnormal Child Psychology*, **16**, 571–583.

Truax, C.F. and Carkhuff, H.R. (1967) *Toward Effective Counselling and Psychotherapy*. Chicago, IL: Aldine.

Turner, K. (1973) Conditioning treatment of nocturnal enuresis. In I. Kolvin, R.C. MacKeith and S.R. Meadow (eds), *Bladder Control and Enuresis*, pp. 195–210. Spastics International Medical Publications. Oxford: Heinemann Medical.

Twito, T.J. and Stewart, M.A. (1982) A half-sibling study of aggressive conduct disorder: prevalence of disorders in parents, brothers and sisters. *Neuropsychobiology*, **8**, 144–150.

Vela-Bueno, A., Bixler, E.O., Dobladez-Blanco, B., Rubo, M.E., Marrison, R.E. and Kales, A. (1985) Prevalence of night terrors and nightmares in elementary school children: a pilot study. *Research Communication in Psychology, Psychiatry and Behaviour*, **10** (3), 177–188.

Wallerstein, J.S. and Kelly, J.B. (1980) *Surviving the Break-up. How Children and Parents Cope with Divorce*. New York: Basic Books.

Warren, D. (1997) Serious failings in the 'Cinderella' service. *Children UK*, **13** (Summer), 4–5.

Watson, J.B. (1930) *Behaviourism*. New York: Norton.

Watson, J.B. and Raynor, R. (1920). Conditioned emotional reactions. *Journal of Experimental Psychology*, **3**, 1–14.

Watson, D.L. and Tharp, R.G. (1981) *Self-directed Behaviour. Self-modification for Personal Adjustment*. Monterey, CA: Brooks-Cole.

Webster-Stratton, C. (1991) Annotation: strategies for helping families with conduct disordered children. *Journal of Child Psychology and Psychiatry*, **32**, 1047–1062.

Webster-Stratton, C. and Herbert, M. (1994) *Troubled Families: Problem Children*. Chichester: Wiley.

Werner, E.E. and Smith, R.S. (1982) *Vulnerable but Invincible: A Study of Resilient Children*. New York: McGraw-Hill.

Weller, R.A., Weller, E.B., Fristad, M.A. and Bowes, J.M. (1991) Depression in recently bereaved prepubertal children. *American Journal of Psychiatry*, **148**, 1536–1540.

West, D.J. and Farrington, D.P. (1973) *Who Becomes Delinquent?* London: Heinemann.

West, D.J. and Farrington, D.P. (1977) *The Delinquent Way of Life*. London: Heinemann.

White, J.L., Moffitt, T.E., Earls, F., Robins, L.N. and Silva, P.A. (1990) How early can we tell? Predictors of child conduct disorder and adolescent delinquency. *Criminology*, **28**, 507–533.

Whiting, J.W. and Child, I.L. (1953) *Child Training and Personality*. Newshaven, CT: Yale University Press.

Widom, C.S. (1989) Does violence beget violence? A critical examination of the literature. *Psychological Bulletin*, **106**, 3–28.

Wilde, E.J., Keinhorst, L.C., Dickstra, R.F. and Walters, W.H.G. (1992) The relationship between adolescent suicidal behaviour and life events in childhood and adolescence. *American Journal of Psychiatry*, **149**, 45–51.

Wilson, H. (1980) Parental supervision: a neglected aspect of delinquency. *British Journal of Criminology*, **20**, 203–235.

Wilson, H. (1987) Parental supervision re-examined. *British Journal of Criminology*, **27**, 275–300.

Woodhead, M. (1995) Disturbing behaviour in young children. In P. Barnes (ed.), *Personal, Social and Emotional Development of Children.* Milton Keynes: Open University.

World Health Organization (1992) *The ICD-10 Classification of Mental and Behavioural Disorders: Clinical Description and Diagnostic Guidelines.* Geneva: World Health Organization.

Wright, P. (1987) Mothers' assessment of hunger in relation to meal size in breast-fed infants. *Journal of Reproductive and Infant Psychology*, **5**, 173–181.

Yule, W., Udwin, O. and Murdoch, K. (1990) The 'Jupiter' sinking: effects on children's fears, depression and anxiety. *Journal of Child Psychology and Psychiatry*, **31**, 1051–1061.

Zaleski, A., Gerrard, J.W. and Shokeir, M.H. (1973) Nocturnal enuresis: the importance of a small bladder capacity. In I. Kolvin, R. MacKeith and S.R. Meadow (eds), *Bladder Control and Enuresis.* Spastics International Medical Publications. Oxford: Heinemann Medical.

Zoccolillo, M., Pickles, A., Quinton, D. and Rutter, M. (1992) The outcome of childhood conduct disorder: implications for defining adult personality disorder and conduct disorder. *Psychological Medicine*, **22**, 971–986.

LIST OF TABLES, BOXES AND FIGURES

CHAPTER 2   SOCIAL LEARNING/COGNITIVE-BEHAVIOURAL THEORY

CHAPTER 3   ENGAGING AND SUPPORTING PARENTS AND FAMILIES

CHAPTER 4   ASSESSMENT

CHAPTER 5   ASPIRE—PLANNING, IMPLEMENTATION, REVIEW AND EVALUATION

CHAPTER 6   HELPING FAMILIES WITH CHILDREN WHO ARE ANXIOUS OR DEPRESSED

CHAPTER 7   HELPING FAMILIES WITH CHILDREN'S SLEEPING PROBLEMS

INDEX

Index compiled by Jean Macqueen